Skis and Skiing

From the Stone Age to the Birth of the Sport

John Weinstock

Copyright © 2017 Agarita Press
Revised and updated edition
Dripping Springs, Texas
ISBN-978-0990766162
Set in Minion Pro

Skis and Skiing From the Stone Age to the Birth of the Sport

Cover design by John Weinstock and Beth Brotherton

Front cover painting: Birkebeinerne by Knud Bergslien
Back cover illustration by Björn Landström:
Hiisi, the demon elk from *Kalevala*

To my wife Beth

Table of Contents

List of Illustrations

Foreword

Preface

Acknowledgements

Introduction	21
1 – Early Evidence I: Literary References	27
2 – Early Evidence II: The Ski in Rock Carvings	37
3 – Early Evidence III: Skis Found in Peat Bogs	43
4 – The Sami and the Evolution of Skiing	55
5 – Circumpolar Myths about Skiing	67
6 – Skiing During the Viking Age	79
7 – The Technological Evolution of the Ski	93
8 – Skiing in Literature I: The Medieval Period	111
Illustrations:	132
9 – Military Use of Skis	187
10 – Skiing in Literature II: 16th, 17th and 18th Centuries	199
11 – Sondre Norheim, Pavva Lásse Tuorda and the Birth of the Sport	217
12 – Skiing in Literature III: 19th Century	233
13 – Skiing Spreads Around the World	257

Appendices:

1 – The Evolution of Man to the Late Stone Age	265
2 – The Reindeer Hunters of Post-Glacial Scandinavia	271
3 – Winter Travel in the North: Snowshoes	279
4 – Literary References to Snowshoes	293
Bibliography	301

Index

List of Illustrations

Introduction
   I.1 Davidson 1937: 49.
   I.2 Davidson 1937: 91.
   I.3 Berg 1950: 38.
   I.4 Catlin 1844: Nr. 15.
   I.5 Rindisbacher 1825: Nr. 41-72/468.

Ch. 1
   1.1 Luther 1962: 8.
   1.2 Luther 1962: 9.
   1.3 Wiklund 1928: 26 (Stephanus Iohannis Stephanius).

Ch. 2
   2.1 Åström 1984: 86.
   2.2 Raudonikas 1938: Planche 4.
   2.3 Raudonikas 1938: Planche 2.
   2.4 Raudonikas 1938: Planche 5.
   2.5 Luther 1926: 504.
   2.6 Raudonikas 1936: Planche 22.
   2.7 Bø 1992: 18.
   2.8 Helskog 1988: 60; Bø 1992: 18.
   2.9 Manker 1952: 139 (from Manker *Die lappische Zaubertrommel*, I & II, Stockholm 1938, 1950).

Ch. 3
   3.1 Berg 1950: 115.
   3.2 Berg 1950: 116.
   3.3 *På skidor* 1935: 37.
   3.4 *På skidor* 1940: 342 (from *Sovjetskaja etnografija*, 1937).
   3.5 Itkonen 1937: 73; Berg 1950: 24.
   3.6 Wiklund 1931: 28. (after K. Moszynski)
   3.7 Zettersten 1939: 402 (from A. Guagninus "*Sarmatiæ Europeæ descriptio*," 1578).
   3.8 *På skidor* 1936: 351 (photograph by Ernst Klein).
   3.9 Wiklund 1928: 13 (illustrations after u. T. Sirelius and Hj. Appelgren-Kivalo).
   3.10 *På skidor* 1937: 75.
   3.11 Berg 1950: 90.
   3.12 Zettersten 1942: 19 (Östersund Museum).

3.13 Vilkuna in Vorren 1995: 67 (sketched by Jyrki Markhausen, 1981).
3.14 Berg 1950: 104.
3.15 Berg 1933: 160.
3.16 Zettersten 1932: 24; Lid 1937: 13; Bø 1966: 14.
3.17 Berg 1950: 155.
3.18 Itkonen 1937: 73
    middle ski from Statens idrotts- och gymnastiknämnds samlingar, Helsinki; Naskali in Vorren 1995: 73 (Finlands Idretts-museum, sketch: Museovirasto).
3.19 Berg 1950: 127.
3.20 Zettersten 1942: 14 (A.-B. Kartografiska Institutet).
3.21 Naskali in Vorren 1995: 72 (sketch: Museovirasto).
3.22 Manker 1957: 169.
3.23 Zettersten 1934: 17.
3.24 Wiklund 1928: 38 (from Carl v. Linné).
3.25 Burov 1985: 393.
3.26 Burov 1985: 394.
3.27 Diagram by JW.
3.28 Berg 1933: 156.

Ch. 4

4.1 Olaus 1972: 596.
4.2 Wiklund 1931: 5 (from title page of Dutch translation of Johannes Schefferus' *Lapponia*, Amsterdam 1682.
4.3 Mehl 1964: 67.
4.4 Vorren 1988: 38.
4.5 Luther 1942: 35.
4.6 Nansen 1890: between 96-97.
4.7 *På skidor* 1938: 380 (from Rothe's German translation of Pehr Högström's Beskrifning öfwer de til Sweriges krona lydande Lapmarker, Stockholm 1747.
4.8 *På skidor* 1938: 381 (as above under 4.7).
4.9 Vorren 1988: 108.
4.10 Savio 1993: Plate 7.
4.11 *På skidor* 1934: 374.
4.12 Bø 1966: 24.

Ch. 5

5.1 *Kalevala* 1988: facing 112.
5.2 Meuli 1975: facing 798.
5.3 Meuli 1975: facing 799.
5.4 Meuli 1975: facing 810.
5.5 Meuli 1975: facing 811.
5.6 Meuli 1975: 798.

5.7 Griaznov 1933: Plate II A.
5.8 Griaznov 1933: Plate II B.
5.9 Meuli 1975: facing 774.

Ch. 6
6.1 Wilson 1980: 30 (British Museum).
6.2 *På skidor* 1929: 8.
6.3 Wilson 1980: 130 (Nationalmuseet, Copenhagen).
6.4 *På skidor* 1929: 14.

Ch. 7
7.1 Wiklund 1931: 28 (artist: Tor Hörlin).
7.2 *På skidor* 1936: 347.
7.3 Manker 1957: 181 (A.-B. Kartografiska Institutet).
7.4 Vaage 1969: 18.
7.5 Bø 1966: 40.
7.6 Bø 1966: 41.
7.7 Vaage 1969: 18.
7.8 Vaage 1969: 18.
7.9 Bø 1968: 57.
7.10 Bø 1968: 57.
7.11 Vaage 1972: 146.
7.12 Vaage 1972: 146.
7.13 Vaage 1972: 147.
7.14 Vaage 1972: 153.
7.15 Tomasson 1928: 21 (Fig. 2).
7.16 Itkonen 1937: 79.
7.17 Berg 1950: 30.
7.18 Wiklund 1928: 47.
7.19 *På skidor* 1931: 408 (Museum für Völkerkunde, Hamburg).

Ch. 8
8.1 Luther 1926: 498.
8.2 *På skidor* 1939: 403 (Adam Olearius Gottorffische Kunstkammer, Schleswig 1674).
8.3 Bø 1966: 25.
8.4 *På skidor* 1931: 406 (Museum Wormianum, Leiden 1655).
8.5 Wiklund 1928: 19 (Knud Leem).
8.6 Wiklund 1928: 30 (Olaus Worm's skis 1655).
8.7 Luther 1942: 43.
8.8 *Kulturhistoriskt Lexikon* 1970: Planche 3.
8.9 Bø 1992: 21.
8.10 *På skidor* 1930: 391 (Balduinus: *De Calceo antiquo*, Amsterdam 1667).

Ch. 9

9.1 Vaage 1979: 4-5.
9.2 Zettersten 1945: 284 (painting by Carl Wahlbom).
9.3 Geete 1948: 241 (L. Loyd's *Scandinavian adventures*, Vol. II, London 1854).
9.4 *På skidor* 1935: 345 (Anders Zorn's painting *The Fugitive*).
9.5 Zettersten 1940: 18 (A. Gæteeris' *Journael der Legatie ghed aien inde Jaren 1615 ende 1616*, 's Gravenhage 1619).
9.6 *På skidor* 1941: 281 (Schwedische Kriegs-Cronick, Mar. 12, 1632).
9.7 *På skidor* 1941: 281 (as above under 9.6).
9.8 Bø 1966: 33.
9.9 Bø 1966: 37.
9.10 Vaage 1979: 81.
9.11 Vaage 1979: 81.
9.12 Vaage 1979: 82.
9.13 Vaage 1979: 82.
9.14 Vaage 1979: 83.
9.15 Vaage 1979: 83.
9.16 Vaage 1979: 38.
9.17 Vaage 1979: 37.

Ch. 10

10.1 Olaus 1972: 595.
10.2 Olaus 1972: 598.
10.3 Olaus 1972: 130.
10.4 *På skidor* 1931: 403 (B. Balduinus, 1667).
10.5 *På skidor* 1931: 404 (C. Titianus "Habiti antichi," 2nd edition, 1598).
10.6 Wiklund 1928: 5. Joh. Rach pinx 1748.
10.7 Vaage 1969: 107.
10.8 Zettersten 1943: 23 (in C. C. Alanus, Kort Berättelse om Kemi lapmarckz tillståndh, författad 1639, Riksarkivet).
10.9 *På skidor* 1932: 332 (etched on stone by Wilh. v. Wright, 1831).
10.10 Luther 1926: 508.

Ch. 11

11.1 Vaage 1969: 273.
11.2 Vaage 1969: 275.
11.3 Vaage 1969: 283.
11.4 Vaage 1969: 281.
11.5 Vaage 1969: 284.
11.6 Vaage 1969: 292.
11.7 *På skidor* 1945: 253.
11.8 Vaage 1979: 238.

11.9 Vaage 79: 243.
11.10 Nordenskiöld 1882: 67.
11.11 Nordenskiöld 1882: 68.
11.12 Vaage 1969: 32.

Ch. 12
12.1 Vaage 1969: 17.
12.2 Vaage 1969: 117.
12.3 Vaage 1969: 16.
12.4 Vaage 1969: 111.
12.5 Vaage 1979: 40.
12.6 Vaage 1969: 89.
12.7 Vaage 1969: 90.
12.8 Vaage 1969: 91.
12.9 Vaage 1969: 87.
12.10 Vaage 1979: 31.
12.11 Bø 1966: 45.
12.12 Vaage 1979: between 48 & 49.
12.13 Vaage 1979: facing 49.
12.14 Egnell 1979: 21.
12.15 Vaage 1979: 130.
12.16 Egnell 1979: 57.
12.17 Egnell 1979: 240.
12.18 Egnell 1979: 137.

Ch. 13
13.1 Vaage 1979: 220.
13.2 Vaage 1979: 27.
13.3 Vaage 1979: 47.
13.4 Vaage 1979: 221.
13.5 *Scientific American*. Supplement No. 1007, April 20, 1895: 16099.
13.6 Vaage 1979: Skimerker fra hele verden.
13.7 Vaage 1979: Skimerker fra hele verden.
13.8 Vaage 1979: Skimerker fra hele verden.

App. 1
A1.1 Map of Fennoscandia.
A1.2 Kühn 1971: Plate VII.

App. 2
A2.1 Vorren 1988: 95.
A2.2 Egnell 1979: 19.

App. 3
    A3.1 Mason 1896: Plate 8.
    A3.2 Mason 1896: Plate 6.
    A3.3 Schefferus 1956: 299.
    A3.4 Clark 1975: 230.
    A3.5 Catlin 1857: 240.
    A3.6 Wiklund 1931: 47 (drawn by Olof Wiklund based on a sketch by S. Sternvall).
    A3.7 Wiklund 1933: 23 (from Hemmets Journal).
    A3.8 Berg 1953: 171 (Dirk Kerst Koopmans, Het Nederlandsch Openluchtmuseum te Arnhem, Bijdragen en mededeelingen, 1941).
    A3.9 Berg 1953: 169.
    A3.10 Berg 1953: 169 (drawn by Erik Olsson).
    A3.11 Mason 1896: Plate 4.
    A3.12 Davidson 1937: 141.
    A3.13 Davidson 1937: 142.
    A3.14 Davidson 1937: 141.
    A3.15 Davidson 1937: 49.
    A3.16 Zettersten 1933: 100.
    A3.17 Davidson 1937: 27.
    A3.18 Davidson 1937: 26.
    A3.19 Davidson 1937: 28.
    A3.20 Davidson 1937: 24.
    A3.21 Davidson 1953: 59.
    A3.22 Davidson 1953: 46.
    A3.23 Davidson 1937: 53.
    A3.24 Davidson 1953: 48.
    A3.25 Davidson 1937: 67.
    A3.26 Davidson 1937: 72.
    A3.27 Davidson 1937: 85.
    A3.28 Davidson 1937: 92.
    A3.29 Davidson 1937: 94.
    A3.30 Davidson 1937: 75.
    A3.31 Davidson 1937: 57.
    A3.32 Gunda 1940: 233 (from Ribnik, Slovenia after V. Kosak; from Cantrabiska mountain area, northern Spain).
    A3.33 Davidson 1937: 71.
    A3.34 Davidson 1937: 91.
    A3.35 Davidson 1937: 75.
    A3.36 Davidson 1937: 72.
    A3.37 Davidson 1937: 150.

App. 4
A4.1 *På skidor* 1938: 388 (photo by John Halldin).
A4.2 *På skidor* 1929: 20.
A4.3 Catlin 1857, Vol. I, No. 109.
A4.4 Catlin 1857, Vol. II, No. 243.
A4.5 Berg 1950: 38.
A.6 Luther 1942: 39.

Foreword

Growing up in Wisconsin I learned how to ski as a youth, and while at the University of Wisconsin there were many weekend trips to the upper peninsula of Michigan to ski at Porcupine Mountain or Marquette. This was downhill or Alpine skiing as practiced on the gentle slopes of the Midwest. Then in 1968-69 on research leave from the University of Texas I spent a delightful year in Norway and was introduced to the sport of cross-country skiing, taking lessons and even participating in some of the races that are so common there during the winter and that attract all sorts of participants. I remember in particular a thirty kilometer race that did not turn out so well for me. There was a staggered start and due to my age and gender I began after most of the competitors were well on their way. Things went quite well to begin with but then I was plagued by leg cramps, perhaps because I skipped the food stations along the course. I fell down in a small gully and had all I could do to get back on my feet and continue. They were just taking down the timing equipment when I struggled to the finish line. But that race gave me a great deal of respect for ordinary Norwegians and their love of skiing. There is an appropriate phrase in Norwegian that "nordmenn er født med ski på beina" or "Norwegians are born with skis on their legs." I was hooked on cross-country skiing from that point on, and I wanted to learn more about how this wonderful sport had arisen.

There was not much available in English on the origins and early history of skiing apart from Olav Bø's *Skiing Traditions in Norway* from 1968. Most of the articles and books in English dealt with the history of skiing in the 20th century. But there was a wealth of material in Swedish and Norwegian, including a now defunct annual journal *På skidor* with a number of important articles from the 1920s to the 1950s. The idea of writing about the history of skiing may have germinated while working with my old friend, former partner and skier Mike Steffen at our joint venture *Sporting Feet* in Boulder, Colorado from 1975 to 1981. I just had to make some of this material available to English-speaking readers included among which were many skiing enthusiasts.

The final piece of the puzzle began to fall in place in 1988 at a Norway Seminar in Edmonton, Alberta where I met Harald Gaski, a Sámi from Tromsø, Norway. The Sámi, the indigenous people of Northern Scandinavia and Northwest Russia, were often mentioned in the articles on the origins of skiing. I realized that to arrive at an accurate picture of skiing's early days I had to find out as much as possible about Sámi history. This was not an easy task in that the Sámi did not write their own history until early in the 20th century. Until then they transmitted culture and history orally from one generation to the next. Hence one has to rely on the writings and reports of missionaries who tried to convert the Sámi to Christianity in the 15th century, and this material is often biased. Eventually, I concluded that the Sámi played a much greater role in the history and prehistory of skiing than they are generally given credit for.

Much of this story took place in the shadowy past. The evidence one must rely on is frequently slim. However, there is enough from which sound inferences may be made. And that is precisely what this book aims to do: present a reasonable scenario of how and when humans began to ski and how skiing evolved into the sport that is so popular today.

Preface

The Social and Political History of Skiing

Today scholarly research on the history of sport has achieved an importance that would have been almost unimaginable forty or fifty years ago. In Europe and North America, as far afield as Australia and New Zealand, entire academic departments are devoted to investigating and documenting the history and sociology of the sports that have become one of the fundamental activities of modern civilization. The global sports economy is now measured in hundreds of billions of dollars annually, while billions of people around the world watch great televised sports spectacles such as the Olympic Games and the Soccer World Championships. In short, the sports revolution of the twentieth century is one of the remarkable cultural phenomena of modern times. In the course of about one hundred years, sports cultures which originated during the last decades of the nineteenth century became part of the social fabric of virtually all modern societies.

Skiing is one of the sports that has become an integral part of our modern cultural landscape. At the same time, skiing is a literally primeval activity that has enabled human beings to survive at the frigid and wind-swept northernmost latitudes of our planet. The winter Olympic Games inaugurated in 1924 thus accorded a kind of official recognition to a physical culture that has developed over thousands of years. This history has been elegantly and expertly reconstructed in John Weinstock's pioneering history of skiing, a richly documented narrative that takes this story up to the middle of the nineteenth century. The fortunate reader who embarks upon the long and fascinating journey recounted in these pages will encounter nothing less than the story of civilization itself. Here are ancient texts and rock carvings that number among the rarest and most dramatic records of our ancient ancestors. Here, too, we find ancient artifacts exhumed from bogs that enable us to read the past. To the history of skiing belong those prehistoric cross-cultural contacts that spread knowledge about skiing across the top of the world. Skiing introduces us as well to the world of Nordic mythology and the Viking civilization that remains one of the most fascinating themes of medieval Europe. In summary, the history of skiing ushers us into a kind of parallel universe in which the timeless story of human development can be read anew in fresh and exciting ways.

Professor Weinstock brings to this project two indispensible advantages that have contributed to the depth and richness of the text. As a lifelong athlete who can look back with pride upon his consecutive careers as a distance runner and cyclist, he can appreciate the exertions required by a physical culture that presumes a capacity for endurance that is beyond the ken of most ordinary mortals. And it is the athlete who understands what it takes to cultivate the skills that produce efficiency of movement across snow or any other surface traversed by humans in pursuit of athletic victory or the spoils of the hunt. Yet even more important to this project has been Professor Weinstock's knowledge of languages, and his mastery of the Scandinavian languages in particular. For it is fair to say that this book could only have been written by a scholar who has devoted a lifetime to Scandinavian studies. More specifically, it is especially fortunate that, many years ago, serendipity brought Professor Weinstock to Norway. For here is the rugged and beautiful terrain that we know as the birthplace of skiing.

The role of skiing in the creation of Norwegian national identity is a compelling story that Professor Weinstock has begun but not completed in this volume. In this sense he leaves us on the threshold of the modern age – the era of emerging nationalism and, in the service of national consciousness, the sports we take for granted as a part of the modern experience. In the course of the transition from the nineteenth to the twentieth century skiing became what one historian has called a Norwegian national ideology. The book you hold in your hand is now the essential introduction to how skiing became nothing less than a badge of citizenship for a proud Nordic people.

John Hoberman, Professor
University of Texas at Austin

Acknowledgements

Since the history – and prehistory – of skiing was played out on the stage of Northern Europe and Central Asia, outside help from individuals and institutions was essential for me to delve into this topic while living and teaching in the state of Texas. I have received assistance and support from many people and would like to express my appreciation to Turid Sverre Nybro and Tove Dahl for their assistance in organizing and translating some of the materials. To Reidar Rødland and Christian Stannow who were always available to track down another book or article in Norway or Sweden respectively. To Nils Bredal who obtained a copy of Oscar Wergeland's 19th century book on military skiing for me. Ollu giitu Harald Gaski and Krister Stoor, and thanks to James Knirk for bringing various materials to my attention. Merja Heiskanen, Curator of the Lahti Ski Museum, not only sent Finnish materials but provided me with translations of important sections. Arnold Dalen received an e-mail inquiry from me and in less than a week two of his articles had crossed the Atlantic. My colleagues Katie Arens and John Hoberman were ready with encouragement or advice when needed.

My gratitude to the many people and institutions granting permission to use the myriad pictures and illustrations without which this book could not succeed. These include Göran Andersson at Friluftsfrämjandets Riksorganisation; Lars Alldén of Universitetsforlaget; the O. Væring Eftf. AS Archive; Professor Grigori Burov of the National University of Tauris at Simferopol; Det Norske Samlaget; Arne Berg; the American Philosophical Society; the *American Journal of Archaeology*; Knut Helskog; the British Museum; Ruth Kuhn; Olof Landström; Verlag Karl Hofmann; Schwabe & Co. AG Verlag; Bayerische Staatsbibliothek; the University of Würzburg Museum; Nauka Publishers; *Scientific American*; Rune Flaten at Skiforeningen; Professor Janne Vilkuna; Eero Naskali; The National Museum of Denmark; Västerbottens Museum.

Any remaining shortcomings or errors are my responsibility.

Introduction

During the twentieth century skiing blossomed into an international sport. It was the stimulus for the creation of a winter Olympic games in 1924 to parallel the modern summer Olympics that began in 1896. At the 19th Winter Olympics in Salt Lake City in 2002 there were seven different disciplines involving skiing: Cross-country skiing, Alpine skiing, Biathlon, Freestyle skiing, Nordic combined, Ski-jumping and even Snowboarding comprising 47 events in all. Skiing as a modern sport spread from Norway in the late nineteenth and early twentieth centuries to other countries where there was snow during some portion of the year and was even taken up by people from countries where there was never snow. Many people had read Fridtjof Nansen's account of his 1888-89 trip on skis over the inland ice of Greenland in his book *Paa ski over Grønland* which appeared in Norwegian in 1890.[1] The book was translated into the major European languages (English included, *The First Crossing of Greenland* in 1890) and helped make skiing a household word.

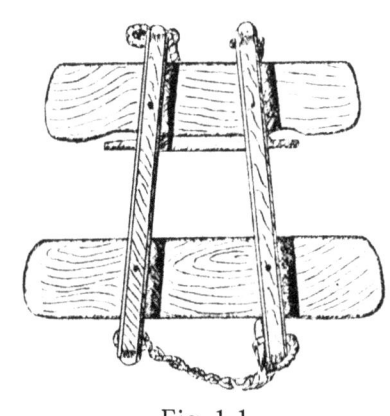

Fig. 1.1

How did Finns, Norwegians and Swedes learn how to ski? How old is skiing and how did the ski evolve? Why wasn't the ski native to North America? These are some of the questions to which few in the English-speaking world know the answers. The roots of skiing go much further back than a century or two. Written sources as far back as 211 BCE mention skis and skiing. There are rock carvings in northwest Russia and northern Norway that depict skiers and they are upwards of four thousand years old. Close to three hundred skis and ski fragments have been found in peat bogs and swamps in Scandinavia and Russia: one

---

[1] Nansen 1890.

of the finds has been carbon-dated to 5,367 years old. Several fragments found at Vis I in North Central Russia have been carbon-dated to ca. 6,700 BCE.[2] And there is comparative linguistic evidence suggesting that skiing is very old. According to Hartvig Birkely several scholars have claimed that the Sámi word *čuoigat*, which means "to ski," is from 6,000 to 8,000 years old.[3]

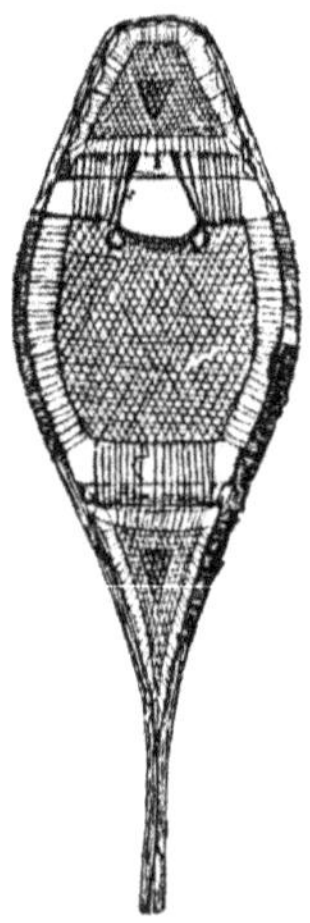

It is the aim of this book to sketch the history and development of the ski and skiing from its birth in the pre-historical Stone Age to the middle of the nineteenth century when all the pieces were in place for the sport to flourish. There exists a wealth of material on the history of skiing, much of which has not previously been available in English or is no longer easily accessible.[4] This book contains a lot of that material as well as ample bibliographical references to more detailed accounts of individual aspects of the story.

Fig. 1.2

When Stone Age people migrated northward in search of prey, they encountered terrain covered with snow during much of the year. Moving about on the snow was difficult without an efficient means of transportation. They had brought with them foot coverings that protected them from the cold and noticed that if they extended the sole of the early boot it would support them on a snow surface. The sole extension became primitive snowshoes, devices that could be attached to moccasins or boots and used, among other things, to pursue animals impeded by the deep snows. One form of snowshoe was made of wood in an oblong shape. It worked quite well although certain types of snow tended to stick to the bottom. A remedy for this was to attach a fur covering to the bottom of the snowshoe with the hairs pointing backward. Stone Age people often transported possessions by dragging them in skins or on a travois, a primitive sledge of netting supported by two long poles the front ends of which were attached to a dog or horse.

Fig. I.3

The earliest forms of clothing, including foot coverings, were made from the hides of herbivorous animals, and a very early form of foot covering was the leg hide of an animal

---

[2] Burov 1985: 392.
[3] Birkely 1994: 12.
[4] Cf. works by Allen 1993, Berg 1950, Bø 1992, Lid 1937 Lunn 1927. All but the first book are out of print.

including the outside fur or hair. Walking around on fur-clad foot coverings with the hairs pointing backwards, Stone Age man would have discovered that he could slide forward with ease, but not backward against the direction of the hairs. When someone familiar with this "gliding principle" put fur on the bottom of a wooden snowshoe he would have noticed that the snowshoe no longer stuck to the snow nor slid backwards. This union of a snowshoe – possibly covered by fur – and the gliding motion produced the ski.

The ski was invented some eight thousand years ago in an area around Lake Baikal and the Altai Mountains in southern Siberia and north of Mongolia. At that time ancestors of speakers of the languages in the Ural-Altaic family were in the area including some forebears of the Sámi (formerly called Lapps in English). These people, following the reindeer, eventually migrated west and north into Scandinavia and brought their skis with them.[5] Then over many centuries they developed and perfected skis for different types of terrain and snow conditions. It was likely the Sámi who taught Norwegians and Swedes how to ski.

Functionally, the snowshoe and the ski differ considerably. A look at the situation in Scandinavia in the recent past where snowshoes and skis have coexisted will shed some light on their different functions. The snowshoe may be considered the property of the common man, of the sedentary farmer. In Norway and Sweden the ladder-type snowshoe (Fig. 1.1) was used close to home, to tread paths to the well, for example, or to facilitate movement from one building to another on a farm.[6] The frame-type was used more for getting about on open ground, for examining trap-lines, or for bringing in hay from the meadow with a sled (Fig. 1.2).[7] Horses frequently needed them, too, as can been seen in Olaus Magnus' *Carta Marina* (Fig. 1.3).[8] Snowshoes were also common in areas where the snow cover was limited to shorter periods of the year since people would not have been able to develop and maintain the skills necessary to use skis. But where speed and distance were essential and where the snow cover was heavy and present for much of the winter, the ski was far superior and soon replaced the snowshoe.

In his 1890 book Fridtjof Nansen had posited central Asia around Lake Baikal (Fig. 4.6) as the area of origin of the ski. Nansen reached this conclusion by looking at a map produced by his friend Andreas M. Hansen of the words for ski in the various languages

---

[5] Dresbeck 1967: 469 sees the ski emerging in northern Scandinavia. Then it would be difficult to account for skis found throughout Eurasia unless one could show that they arose independently in various places.
[6] Davidson 1937: 49.
[7] Berg 1950: 34.
[8] Berg 1950: 38.

spoken by peoples who use skis (cf. Fig. 4.6).[9] Daniel Davidson in a comprehensive study of snowshoes (1937) suggested that wooden snowshoes and primitive bearpaw snowshoes originated in this same area and spread east over the Bering Straits to the Americas and west, eventually reaching Fennoscandia (the Scandinavian peninsula).[10] Davidson's conclusions were based on distributional grounds. Gudmund Hatt pointed out that moccasins and snowshoes go hand in hand and saw their point of origin situated near the northern boundary of Mongolia in the area south of Lake Baikal (for more information on snowshoes see Appendices 3 and 4).[11] In other words, it seems that moccasins, snowshoes and skis evolved in the same Central Asian area. Skis, though, never made it across the Bering Straits. In North America, where there were no skis, snowshoes became so perfected that hunters could attain considerable speed on them. One result throughout the snowy areas of the Northern Hemisphere was the decimation of the wild animal populations, the reindeer and elk in Eurasia, the bison and caribou in North America. The effectiveness of snowshoes and skis in hunting is illustrated by the paintings of George Catlin[12] and Peter Rindisbacher.[13] Catlin, 1796-1872, was an American traveler and artist who spent a great deal of his life living among Indians and painting them and Rindisbacher was a Swiss Indian painter who spent several years among the Indians on the Red River – see figs. I.5-6.[14]

Skis then should be seen as having originated as an accessory to the northern hunter, an accessory that soon became indispensable. They were also superior for long distance communication between villages, and vital for the domestication of the reindeer herds of Eurasia. In fact, skis were so effective that as early as the thirteenth century, laws had to be created to prohibit or limit hunting during the winter. In 1274 in the Norwegian Gulating law it states with reference to elk hunting: "All elks shall be protected within the domain of the property owner from men on skis."[15] The elk cows were pregnant during the winter, and especially easy to overtake on crusty snow which they sank through.

Chapter 1 presents literary evidence for skis and skiing, the earliest being a reference from around 200 BCE to the Dingling people skiing in the Altai region and concluding with

---

[9] Nansen 1890: 94-100, map between 96-97.
[10] Davidson 1937.
[11] Hatt 1916: 247-48.
[12] Catlin 1844.
[13] Rindisbacher 1825.
[14] Catlin 1844: Nr. 15; Rindisbacher 1825: Nr. 41-72/468.
[15] Vaage 1969: 10.

Nordenskiöld's nineteenth century encounter with the Samoyed people. Chapter 2 presents rock carvings from northwestern Russia and northern Norway, some of which have been dated at an age of roughly 4,500 years. There are many rock pictures of skiers including one of a hunting scene. Chapter 3 looks at some of the nearly three hundred skis and ski pairs which have been found in peat bogs, many throughout the area where Sámi forebears dwelt some two thousand years ago, including several finds more than five thousand years old and fragments possibly as old as 6,700 BCE. These ancient skis vary considerably in form and features. Many of them are quite advanced technologically, including the oldest bog skis. This would suggest that skiing is, indeed, even older than the oldest surviving artifacts, for it would have taken many centuries for these sophisticated features to evolve.

Chapter 4 discusses the Sámi and their ancestors and the central role they played in bringing skis along on their migration to Sápmi, their name for the area in Scandinavia and Russia where they live, and in teaching Finns, Norwegians and Swedes how to ski. A look at their history and early life as hunter-gatherers shows how essential skiing was for them in tracking and killing prey such as reindeer. Chapter 5 looks at myths common to circumpolar peoples that speak of the great age of skiing. Tales about heroes as disparate as the Greek Herakles, the Finnish Lemminkäinen and the Algonquian Gluskabe are tied together and it is shown how all derive in part from ancient circumpolar myths. In chapter 6 we look at skiing during the Viking period including the stories of Volund, the master smith, of Ull, the pagan god of skiing, and of Skaði, the goddess of skiing.

Chapter 7 deals with the technological evolution of the ski from a primitive early ski to the relatively advanced device we find at the middle of the nineteenth century. Chapter 8 presents many literary excerpts from the medieval period involving skis and skiing. These examples show that skiing was widespread throughout Scandinavia and skiing as a sport was beginning to develop many centuries ago. Chapter 9 discusses the military use of skis going back more than a thousand years.

Chapter 10 looks at skiing in literature of the 16th through 18th centuries. In Chapter 11 we look at two persons who did much to bring skiing into the public eye during the nineteenth century. Sondre Norheim, a farmer from Telemark, Norway, loved to ski and was very good at it. He performed feats of daredevilry that caught the public's eye. Pavva Lásse Tuorda, a Sámi from Jokkmokk, Sweden, was one of two Sámi on Nordenskiöld's 1883 expedition onto the inner ice fields of Greenland. He and the other Sámi, Anders Rassa, covered 460 km. on skis in 57 hours, a feat that many including Fridtjof Nansen could not believe. The following year Nordenskiöld arranged the first long cross-country race to display the talents of these skiers. Chapter 12 considers references to skiing in 19th century literature. And the last chapter discusses briefly how skiing spread around the world. There are appendices containing sections peripheral to the main focus of the book: on the evolution of man to the late Stone Age, reindeer hunters of post-glacial Scandinavia, snowshoes and literary references to snowshoes.

Let us now turn to the early literary evidence for the ski and its various users. As we shall see, knowledge about skiing extended far beyond the areas where skis were actually used. Please note that many of the figures can be found on 27 pages of illustrations toward the middle of the book. If you find a figure number in a chapter with no figure, it will likely be in the illustration sections.

Early Evidence I: Literary References

In this chapter we list in chronological order a few of the many references to skis and skiing throughout Eurasia over more than two millennia. Interestingly, none of the accounts are by skiers; rather they are by writers who may simply have heard about skiing but never witnessed it.

Han Dynasty

The Hai Nei Jing, the 18th volume of the *Shan Hai Jing*, which is a book on various schools of thought during the West Han period of China (207 to 25 BCE), says:[16]

> "The people of the Dingling Nationality living in the Aletai mountains of Northwest China sped like goats in the valleys and on the flatlands, wearing the 'horns of a goat' – a kind of knee-high fur boot under which is a wooden board with a hoof-shaped front tip."

Liu Qilu and Liu Yueye infer from this that skiing activities existed in the mountain range of Aletai [Altai] "between 211 BCE and 206 BCE, as a popular means for hunting, transportation and war."

Tacitus

Cornelius Tacitus (ca. 55-ca. 117 CE) was a Roman historian whose most celebrated work was the *Germania*[17] which provides the earliest written material on the Germanic tribes. In

---

[16] Goksøyr 1994: 70.
[17] Tacitus 1970: 213, 215.

it the simple German is compared to the morally corrupt Romans. In describing the Fenni (Finns) he is not sure as to whether they are Germans or Sarmatians.[18] He goes on to say:

> The Fenni live in astonishing barbarism and disgusting misery: no arms, no horses, no household; wild plants for their food, skins for their clothing, the ground for their beds; arrows are all their hopes; for want of iron they tip them with sharp bone. This Lapps hunting is the support of the women as well as of the men, for they accompany the men freely and claim a share of the spoils; nor have their infants any shelter against wild beasts and rain, except the covering afforded by a few intertwined branches. To these the young men return: these are the asylum of age; and yet they think it happier so than to groan over field labour, be cumbered with building houses, and be for ever involving their own and their neighbours' fortunes in alternate hopes and fears. Unconcerned towards men, unconcerned towards Heaven, they have achieved a consummation very difficult: they have nothing even to ask for.

There is no mention of skiing, but when this description is compared with the following description of Procopius it will be seen that the Fenni may in fact be the Sámi who were semi-nomadic reindeer hunters at the time. The scant shelter referred to is the Sámi *lavvu*, a transportable, tepee-like structure.

Procopius

The Byzantine historian Procopius of Caesarea (490?-562? CE) accompanied Belisarius on military campaigns and even commanded the imperial navy and served as prefect of Constantinople. Highly educated and a distinguished public servant, he wrote histories that are well respected because they are in many cases first hand accounts of the events described. In his *History of the Wars*, VI. xv. 16-23 he writes:[19]

> But among the barbarians who are settled in Thule, one nation only, who are called the Scrithiphini, live a kind of life akin to that of the beasts. For they neither wear garments of cloth nor do they walk with shoes on their feet, nor do they drink wine nor derive anything edible from the earth. For they neither till the land themselves, nor do their women work it for them, but the women regularly join the men in hunting, which is their only pursuit. For the forests, which are exceedingly large, produce for them a great abundance of wild beasts and other animals, as do also the mountains which rise there. And they feed exclusively upon the flesh of the wild beasts slain by them, and clothe themselves in their skins, and since they have neither flax nor any implement with which to sew, they fasten these skins together by the sinews of the animals, and in this way manage to cover the whole body. And indeed not even their infants are nursed in the Lapps way as among the rest of mankind. For the children of the Scrithiphini do not feed upon the milk of women nor do they touch their mother's breast, but they are nourished upon the marrow of the animals killed in the hunt, and upon this alone. Now as soon as a woman gives birth to a child, she throws it into a skin and straightway hangs it to a tree, and after putting

---

[18] The Sarmatians were closely related to the Scythians and may have spoken Proto-Slavonic.
[19] Procopius 1919: 419, 421.

marrow into its mouth she immediately sets out with her husband for the customary hunt. For they do everything in common and likewise engage in this pursuit together. So much for the daily life of these barbarians.

Skis are not directly mentioned in the above passage, but the name of the people described – the Scrithiphini – consists of two parts: *scrithi* which in Old Icelandic is *skriða* "to ski" and *phini* which is the modern word Finns, i.e., the "skiing Finns." The Scrithiphini are actually the Sámi of northern Scandinavia who had been skiing for centuries before this and whose forebears were responsible for originally bringing the ski to Scandinavia. The accepted name for the Sámi in Norwegian today is *samer*, though occasionally Norwegians have referred to Sámi as "Finns."

Jordanes

Jordanes was a sixth century Gothic historian whose main work – written in Vulgar Latin – was *The History of the Goths*. It is mainly an abridgment of the work of Cassiodorus Senator. Jordanes mentions the Scrithiphini but calls them Screrefennae:[20]

> There are the Screrefennae, who do not seek grain for food but live on the flesh of wild beasts and birds' eggs; for there are such multitudes of young game in the swamps as to provide for the natural increase of their kind and to afford satisfaction to the needs of the people.

As in the descriptions of Tacitus and Procopius it is clear that the people referred to are a hunting group which fits the Sámi well.

Paulus Diaconus

Paul the Deacon (ca. 725-799?) was a Lombard historian who spent some time at the court of Charlemagne. His main work was his *History of the Langobards* covering the two centuries from the middle of the sixth to the middle of the eighth century CE. It is one of the earliest histories of a Germanic nation written by a German. In Book I, Chapter V he has:[21]

> The Scritobini, for thus that nation is called, are neighbors to this place. They are not without snow even in the summer time, and since they do not differ in nature from wild beasts themselves, they feed only upon the raw flesh of wild animals from whose shaggy skins also they fit garments for themselves. They deduce the etymology of their name according to their barbarous language from jumping. For by making use of leaps and bounds they pursue wild beasts very skillfully with a piece of wood bent in the likeness of a bow. Among them there is an animal not very unlike a stag, from whose hide, while

---

[20] Mierow 1960: 56.
[21] Paulus Diaconus 1906-07: 7-8.

it was rough with hairs, I saw a coat fitted in the manner of a tunic down to the knees, such as the aforesaid Scritobini use, as has been related. In these places about the summer solstice, a very bright light is seen for some days, even in the night time, and the days are much longer there than elsewhere, just as, on the other hand, about the winter solstice, although the light of day is present, yet the sun is not seen there and the days are shorter than anywhere else and the nights too are longer, and this is because the further we turn from the sun the nearer the sun itself appears to the earth and the longer the shadows grow.

Again the people referred to are the "skiing Finns," but Paul gives a description of skiing, "leaps and bounds with a piece of wood bent in the likeness of a bow." The animal they hunt that is "not very unlike a stag" is undoubtedly the reindeer. The "bright light" is the midnight sun that shines north of the Arctic circle around the summer solstice.

Huan-jù kî

Writing around 976-984 CE Huan-jù kî has a "description of earth" in which he tells of a people spread out in mountains southeast of the Kirghiz called Pa-si-mi, that is, the Baschmîl who are related to the Turks. It reads as follows:[22]

In hunting they make use of a foot covering called wooden horse. It is similar to a sled, but the head (the forward end) is high (curved upward). The bottom surface is covered with horsehide so that the tips of the hairs run backwards. When the hunter has tied such boards on his feet and runs down a slope, then he overtakes the fleeing deer. If he runs over a plain covered with snow, he sticks a pole into the ground (the snow) and runs like a ship; in this manner he also overtakes the fleeing deer. The same pole serves him as support when slopes are to be climbed.

Fig. 1.1

These "wooden horses" are nothing other than skis. And it is clear that skis provided hunters with a great advantage over the animals in winter snows. In the 4th century BCE Shan-hai-ching described Turkish people of the Ting-Ling as having horse hair and hooves from the knee down, i.e. horse feet or wooden horses, cf. Fig. 1.1.[23] Fig. 1.2 depicts European horse feet from the 13th century on the Hereford map.[24] These "horse feet" may in fact be skis.

Fig. 1.2

---

[22] Schott. 1864: 448.
[23] Luther 1962: 8.
[24] Luther 1962: 9.

T'ang Dynasty

In the Annals of the T'ang Dynasty from T'ang schu covering the period between 618 and 906 CE there are reports of *mu-ma T'u-küe* "wooden horse Turks," a people living east of the Kirghiz on the Yenisei:[25]

> They covered their habitations with birch-bark and owned numerous horses. They are in the habit of running over ice on so-called wooden horses, i.e. on skis, that they put on their feet; moreover, they take curved boughs as shoulder (snow-sticks) supports and push themselves forward very fast.

There are also reports that the Pa-ye-ku (Bayirku) put wooden boards under their feet and pursue deer over the ice. The Liu-kuei tribe, according to Tu Yu (735-812) located "north of the Northern Sea" (presumably Lake Baikal) fasten to their feet wooden boards six inches wide and seven feet long, and hunt game over ice. In northern Korea the word for ski is *sorune* and is written "snow horse" in Chinese characters. In other words, there is quite a bit of evidence for the existence of skiing in eastern Asia.

Alfred the Great

Alfred (849-899 CE) was king of the West Saxons from 871 until his death. He fought long and hard against the Danes, and after capturing London in 886 concluded a treaty with Guthrum that set up the Danelaw north and east of the Ouse, Lea and Thames rivers, an area where Danish law would be in effect. He was responsible for new law codes, which strengthened the monarchy. His greatest achievement came in his reviving Old English literary prose by translating Latin works into Old English, among them Orosius' universal history which contains an account of the Norse explorer Ohtere's voyages. In Bosworth's edition (1858) there is the following passage:[26]

> … to the north, over the wastes, is Cwénland, and to the north-west are the Scride-Finns, and to the west the Northmen. Ohthere told his lord, King Alfred, that he dwelt north-most of all Northmen. He said that he dwelt northward, on the land by the west sea. He said, however, that the land is very long thence to the north; but it is all waste [desert], save that in a few places, here and there, Finns reside, – for hunting in winter, and in summer for fishing in the sea.

Ohthere goes on to tell about his voyage further north and east where he runs into more Finns and then the Biarmians. Cwénland is the area around the Gulf of Bothnia that is

---

[25] Schott 1864: 435f; Laufer 1917: 118.
[26] Alfred, 1858: 38-39.

inhabited by Finns. People of Finnish stock in northern Norway are today called *kvensk* "kvenish," and, since the Scandinavian word for woman is similar to this – e.g., Swedish *kvinna*, some scholars erroneously thought that the Finns were a matriarchal society. Above the Finns are the Scride-Finns, or, as explained earlier, the Sámi.

Adam of Bremen

Adam, the historian and archbishop of Hamburg-Bremen, lived in the eleventh century (dates of birth and death unknown). He reports in 1066 CE that:[27]

> Between Norway and Sweden dwell the Wärmilani and Finns and others; who are now all Christians and belong to the Church at Skara. On the confines of the Swedes and Norwegians toward the north live the Skritefingi, who, they say, outstrip wild beasts at running.

This is yet again a reference to the "skiing Finns," and here Adam mentions only one characteristic of these people, their skiing prowess.

Saxo Grammaticus

Saxo (ca. 1150-ca. 1220 CE) was Denmark's first important historian. His *Gesta Danorum* (Danish History) consisted of sixteen books and covered the period from legendary history down to his own time. In one place he has a description of skiing by the Skrit-Finns as he calls them:

> Within the eastern area of these countries live the Skrit-Finns. In their passion for hunting, these people habitually transport themselves in an unusual manner, having to trace slippery roundabout routes to reach the desired haunts in remote parts of the mountains. No cliff stands too high for them to surmount by some skilfully twisting run. For first they glide out of the deep valleys by the feet of precipices, circling this way and that, frequently swerving in their course from a direct line until by these tortuous paths they achieve the destined summit. They normally use animal skins instead of money to trade with their neighbours.[28]

That this does not much resemble skiing is probably due to the fact that Saxo did not actually witness what he described. Nor, for that matter, does the translator seem to know what is going on. Saxo does better later on:

> Now the Finns are the northernmost of all peoples; indeed they occupy and cultivate a tract of the world which is scarcely habitable. This race use their missiles with an eager

---

[27] Adam 1959: 205-06.
[28] Saxo 1999: 9.

zest; no others are more agile in launching the javelin, while the arrows they shoot are large and broad. They devote themselves to magical skills and are expert hunters. Their homes are impermanent, for they pursue a nomadic existence, pitching their dwelling wherever they have caught game. They travel on curved boards and race on them across the snowfields between mountain ridges.[29]

And later:

> The Finns have always travelled by gliding swiftly on smooth boards and have complete control of their speed as they race along, so that men say they can be there and gone in a flash, just as they please. As soon as they have done damage to their enemy, they shoot away in the same lightning fashion as they flew to the scene. The nimbleness of their bodies and skis combined gives them a practised ease in attacking and retreating.[30]

Here is an early suggestion that skis are used by fighting men.

Fig. 1.3 shows a pair of fur-covered skis in Stephanius' 1644 edition of Saxo.[31]

Raschîd ud-dîn

The Persian Raschîd ud-dîn writing around 1322-25 CE has the following remarkable description of a Mongolian reindeer-hunting people; probably the Yakuts:[32]

> Since there are many mountains and forests in their country and since it snows so much, they hunt in the winter a lot on the snow, and, indeed, in the way that they make wooden boards, which they call *tschana*, get on them, make a rein out of a strap and take a stick in hand. On the snow they then push the stick into the earth, as one propels a boat over water, and then go so fast over steppes and plains, up and downhill, that they overtake "mountain oxen" (reindeer) and other animals. They pull a second *tschana* as a "hand horse" (substitute horse) to the *tschana* on which they are mounted (standing), tied to it. They load the slain prey on it, and even if they load up to two or three thousand "mann" (a weight), they glide with the slightest force, that touches them, easily over the snow … If you haven't seen it, you don't think it possible.

Richard Hakluyt

Hakluyt (ca. 1552-1616 CE) was an English geographer who made many voyages of discovery and published his findings in *The Principal Navigations, Voyages, Traffics, and Discoveries of the English Nation* in three volumes. He reports:[33]

---

[29] Saxo 1999: 153.
[30] Saxo 1999: 287.
[31] Wiklund 1928: 26.
[32] Schott 1864: 448; Luther 1926: 502; Meuli 1975: 787.
[33] David 1981: 52.

> And east-south-east from that castle is a land called Lappia, in which land be two manner of people, that is to say the Lappians and the Scrik Finns, which Scrik Finns are a wild people which neither know God nor yet good order; and these people live in tents made of deers' skins, and they have no certain habitations but continue in herds and companies by one hundred and two hundred. And they are a people of small stature, and are clothed in deers' skins, and drink nothing but water and eat no bread but flesh all raw. And the Lappians be a people adjoining to them and be much like to them in all conditions.

The two groups Hakluyt distinguishes are probably the Sámi who hunt wild reindeer and the Sámi who have some domesticated reindeer.

Herberstein

In his *Description of Moscow and Muscovy* from 1557 CE Sigmund von Herberstein describes skis and bindings:[34]

> The places are usually reached (in the Perm territory around the Kama river) upon *nartyn*, or snow-shoes. It is a piece of wood shaped like a board and a hands-breadth wide; it is about two long elles in length and turned up a little in front; in the middle the sides are turned up and between these rims are holes for binding the feet to it. When the snow grows hard a man may cover a great distance in a day. He holds a very short pike in his hand with which he may guide and assist himself when the way goes downhill or leads to a sharp drop. In these parts they travel much upon these *nartyn*. It is said also that they have great dogs drawing sledges.

Rasmus Rask

Rasmus Rask (1787-1832 CE) was a major linguistic pioneer who helped clarify the relationship of the Indo-European languages. He was the first to give a correct etymology of the term *skridefinn*:[35]

> That Skridefinns means Lapps is clear from the situation. It is also correct, as Porthan notes, that the Icelanders use the term Finns to designate Lapps, and Finmörk for the land of the Lapps (Finmark, Lapland and Russian Lapland). In the oldest times they called the Finns giants, leviathans, behemoths and so on and no doubt mean in later times real Finns (*suomalaiset*), where Finnland, Kvenland, Kyrialaland (Karelia) are mentioned. This word Finns seems to have been the oldest name for the Lapps, before they immigrated into Scandinavia, at least it seems the Fenni of old were rather Lapps than Finns judging from the two groups' patterns of living. Where Scride comes from, which the name is compounded with, has been subject to various conjectures; but it doesn't seem very difficult to figure out. From *scrídan*, or more correctly *scrydan* "to ornament" it cannot derive in that other peoples have been just as well clothed as the Lapps; but the vagabond lifestyle in the snow mountains seems peculiar to them, and

---

[34] Herberstein 1969: 86.
[35] Rask 1834: 351-52.

skríða in Icelandic is just the word used for skiing … And it is most probable that the name which is not taken from their own language comes from Old Norse as the closest bordering nation. Furthermore, the word does not seem to be foreign to the Anglosaxons since Lye cites *Scrídvæn* sella curulis "chariot seat" and *scrídvis* aurigandi peritus "practiced charioteer."

Nordenskiöld

In *The Voyage of the Vega Round Asia and Europe* (1882 CE) by A. E. Nordenskiöld there is a discussion of his encounter with the Samoyed people along with illustrations of skis, sleds, pulks and sleighs. He states:[36]

> Another implement for travelling over snow was offered by a Chukch who drove past the vessel in the beginning of February. It consisted of a pair of immensely wide skates of thin wood, covered with seal-skin, and raised at both sides. I had difficulty in understanding how these broad shapeless articles could be used with advantage until I learned from the accompanying drawing that they may be employed as a sort of sledges.

What Nordenskiöld refers to here are skis of the kind in use among Finno-Ugric peoples long ago.

The next chapter will look at rock carvings that may be as old as 4,500 years.

---

[36] Nordenskiöld 1882: 475.

Early Evidence II: The Ski in Rock Carvings

There is evidence for the use of skis in the distant past that is even older than the literary evidence just surveyed, namely, rock carvings that depict skiers and that go back as far as the Neolithic or even Mesolithic periods of the Stone Age. The oldest rock pictures are located in northwest Russia near the White Sea; the other, possibly younger carvings are in Nordland and Finnmark counties, Norway.

Near the mouth of the White Sea, the Vyg River forms a system of branches between which are a number of islands. The main bed of the river descends fairly steeply here with various rapids and waterfalls. In the area of the lower course of the Vyg – near Vyg-Ostrov – along the rocky banks are found numerous groups of rock carvings. There are two groups on Bessovy Slédki Island[37] that were discovered in 1926, three at Zalavrouga[38] discovered in the 1930s and two others at Iérpine-Ostrov.[39] On the eastern shore of Lake Onega there are additional rock carvings, which archaeologists have known about since 1848.[40] These latter pictures show only one skier.

The carvings are numerous: Zalavrouga has 326 individual pictures, Iérpine-Ostrov 31, and Bessovy Slédki 368. The carvings are of Stone Age human figures in action, some of their material possessions, and the animals that were important for their subsistence, all of them treated in a fairly realistic style. It has been suggested that the carvings are 4,000 to 4,500 years old or from the latter part of the Neolithic Age. All of the carvings known up to the mid-1930s were published in a monumental two volume edition by W. J. Raudonikas:

---

[37] Raudonikas 1938, 59-90.
[38] Raudonikas 1938, 25-52.
[39] Raudonikas 1938, 53-58.
[40] Raudonikas 1936, 82-99.

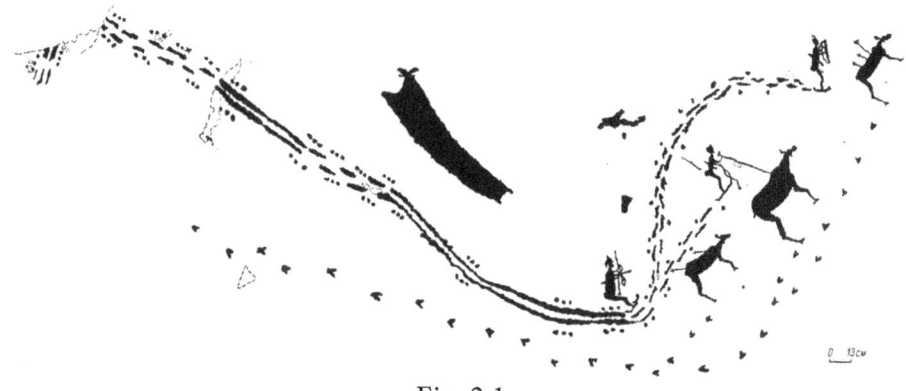

Fig. 2.1

Les Gravures Rupestres des Bords du lac Onéga et de la mer Blanche "The Rock Carvings on the Banks of Lake Onega and the White Sea" (1936). The work is in Russian with a French summary and contains many helpful illustrations and photographs.[41]

Fig. 2.1 is from Zalavrouga but not in the Raudonikas edition. It magnificently depicts an entire hunting scene.[42] One can see the tracks of three hunters on skis as well as the tracks of the three elk they are following. In places it appears that the hunters were walking on their skis, perhaps going uphill, and in other places there are long tracks which may indicate that they were going downhill. The hunters are on equal length skis and are using two poles each as can be seen from the dots on either side of the ski tracks. The poles are actually a bow and a spear. Hartvig Birkely points out that the dots, or pole marks, are placed at the front part of the skis which suggests that the hunters were using the diagonal technique and/or double poling, the normal technique used by cross-country skiers today.[43] When the hunters reached their prey, each one attacked an elk. Two of the elk have arrows in them and one seems to have a spear in it.

Fig. 2.2 – Zalavrouga Skiers

---

[41] Raudonikas 1936, 1938.
[42] Åström 1984, 86.
[43] Birkely 1994, 35-36, 81-82.

Fig. 2.2 is a close-up of three phallic skiers each with a single pole moving to the right.[44]

Fig. 2.3 – Zalavrouga Hunter

Fig. 2.3 shows a hunter on skis in action.[45] The human figure is phallic and has a tail – it was not uncommon for hunters to dress up as animals in order to better commune with nature and facilitate their hunting. The hunter is on skis and has a bow in hand. The line going toward the male reindeer may be a lasso. Birkely mentions the Sámi word *dolgastit* that is the equivalent of the Norwegian word *snørekjøre* meaning "to be pulled on skis by a reindeer."[46] In earlier times a hunter may have caught up with an elk or reindeer in deep snow and gotten a lasso around the animal's neck. If he was unable to tie the other end of the lasso to a tree the hunter may just have hung on and been pulled by the elk until it became tired. This would have been a way to capture an elk or reindeer and tame it so that it could later be used as a decoy animal.

Fig. 2.4 – Zalavrouga Hunter

Fig. 2.4 shows a phallic hunter following a reindeer.[47] The hunter has a tail to help him identify with his prey. This rock picture just as

---

[44] Raudonikas 1938, Planche 4.
[45] Raudonikas 1938, Planche 2.
[46] Birkely 1994, 81.
[47] Raudonikas 1938, Planche 5.

Fig. 2.5

the previous one could be an example of *dolgastit* or being pulled on skis by a reindeer. Note that the hunter has his knee(s) bent; this is precisely what one does when being pulled on skis. Cf. also Fig. 2.5.[48]

Fig. 2.6, from the Lake Onega area, shows a masked hunter holding lunar and solar signs in hand and pursuing a reindeer.[49] The animal mask and tail helped him identify with his prey as in Fig. 2.4. The hunter is probably on skis, though it has also been suggested that he is standing on a serpent. The mask seems to resemble a bear's head.

The first of the Norwegian rock carvings were discovered in 1929 during peat cutting at Rødøy near Tjøtta parish in Helgeland.[50] The Norwegian archaeologist Gutorm Gjessing came to the scene during the summer of 1933 and found part of the rock bared; figures of elk, seals and a boat could be seen depicted. Gjessing continued to cut peat on the other side of the rock and found a smooth surface with carvings, some of which were so sharp that the actual stone blows could be seen. The carvings were done by a hunting society similar to the one that produced the Russian carvings.

The Rødøy skier in Fig. 2.7[51] has on an animal cap that looks something like a rabbit's head; this recalls the hunter depicted in Fig. 2.6 above. He is holding some sort of implement with both hands, probably not a ski pole, rather an ax. His knees are bent in good skiing style, though Birkely suggests this might be another example of *dolgastit* with

Fig. 2.6 – Bessov-Noss Skier

the knees bent to make it easier to be pulled by an elk. Gustaf Hallström suggested that the figure might be rowing a boat;[52] this, however, is unlikely in that the two "skis" are entirely parallel and do not intersect which, if it were a boat, they ought to do at the prow. Furthermore, there is another skier carved just above the large elk but which has largely disinte-

---

[48] Luther 1926: 504.
[49] Raudonikas 1936, Planche 22.
[50] Gjessing 1936: 185.
[51] Bø 1992: 18.
[52] Hallström 1938.

grated. Finally, the elk suggests that it is hunting that is depicted. It should also be pointed out that the pairs of skis are in both cases of equal length. The 5,667 year-old Kalvträsk bog skis that will be examined in the next chapter are also of equal length. These rock carvings are about the same age as the White Sea and Lake Onega carvings or slightly younger. They have been dated at ca. 4,000 years old, in other words the very end of the Stone Age or the beginning of the Bronze Age.

There is also a skier in a rock-carving field in Alta in Finnmark county in Norway (Fig. 2.8).[53] The skier would seem to be in the process of shooting with a bow and arrow with his right arm pulling the bow. He has his skis at an angle to provide good support for shooting. This rock caving has been dated at somewhere between 1000 and 500 BCE.

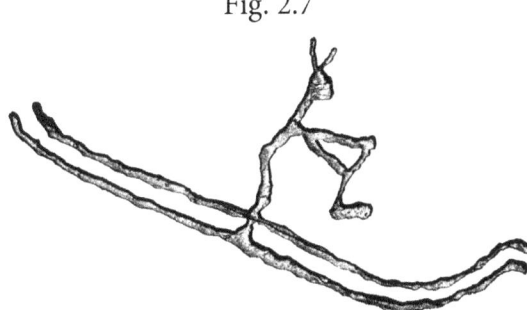

Fig. 2.7

In 1952 Ernst Manker noted that Sámi *noaidi* (shamanic) drums have figures depicted on the skin that resemble the figures on the rock carvings and whose origins may go back even further (Fig. 2.9).[54] The figures are very stylized. In the cases where a pair of skis is depicted they seem to be equal length skis, and only one pole is used. Reindeer are also a common motif on these drum skins. Unfortunately not many of the drums survive: in their attempts to obliterate the Sámi pagan religion and to convert the Sámi to Christianity Finnish, Norwegian and Swedish authorities and Christian missionaries brutally destroyed whatever religious icons they could get hold of. Though the oldest preserved drum skins come from the sixteenth century, there is documentary evidence for the figures from the twelfth century. Playing an important role in the shamanic pagan religion of these early dwellers in the north, such figures probably go back much further.

Fig. 2.9

---

[53] Helskog 1988: 59-60; Bø 1992: 18. Cf. Illustrations 2, lower right.
[54] Manker 1952, 139. There is more information on the *noaidi* in Ch. 4.

The rock carvings demonstrate that at a very early date skis were being used to facilitate the hunt in two widely separated areas in the circumpolar north. The next chapter will look at even older evidence of skiing.

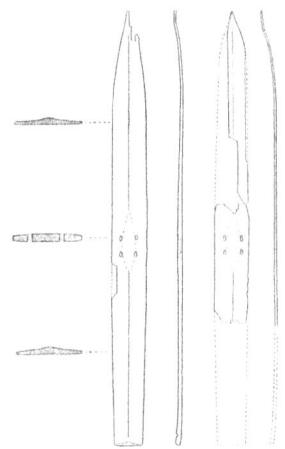

Early Evidence III: Skis Found in Peat Bogs

Skis retrieved from peat bogs and marshes in Finland, Norway, Sweden and Russia provide evidence for skiing that is even older than the rock carvings. Wood normally deteriorates relatively rapidly over time when exposed to air; however, it can be preserved for thousands of years if it is buried in the acidic environment that wet peat or even clay provides. Up to the present, close to 300 skis, ski pairs and fragments of skis have been discovered since the first ski was found in Finland in 1897 and brought to the attention of ethnologists.[55]

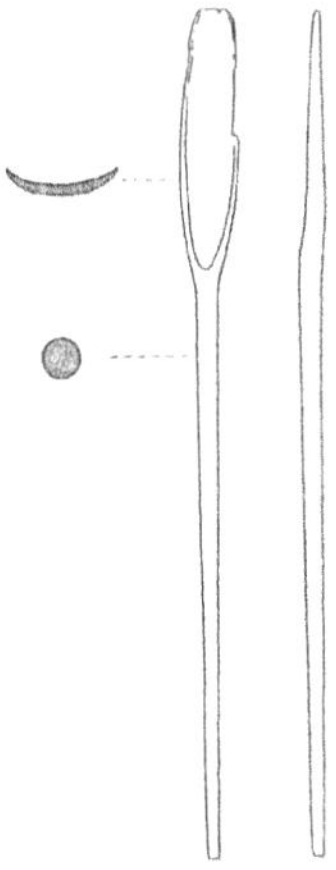

Fig. 3.1

A number of scholars from these countries attempted to date the finds and to classify them as to type. However, it was not until 1933 that pollen analysis methods developed in Sweden were used in an effort to obtain more precise dates as to when the skis had been buried in the bogs. According to this method, geologists arrive at an approximate date for a given find by determining the amount of different kinds of flower dust, pollen, etc. of the coniferous and deciduous trees found in the particular layer where the ski was found. Several decades later a much more precise method of dating organic materials became available,

Fig. 3.2

the so-called ^{14}C method. The carbon isotope ^{14}C is absorbed from the atmosphere by all living organisms and is found in a fixed ratio relative to the ^{12}C isotope. After the organism dies the amount of ^{14}C absorbed is lost with a half-life of 5,568 years.[56] In other words, by

---

[55] Appelgren-Kivalo 1911; Sørensen 1996: 7.

[56] The program CALIB – at http://radiocarbon.pa.qub.ac.uk/calib/index.html – was used to convert ra-

measuring the amount of ^{14}C and calibrating it to a calendar year through a long-lived organism such as the bristlecone pine, one can arrive at a very accurate estimate of age.

Of the forty Swedish finds that Gösta Berg discussed in his 1950 book twenty-one could be dated through pollen analysis.[57] They varied in age from the Hoting ski that was estimated to be 4,500 years old to others which could have been as recent as from our own era. The number of Swedish finds neared 100 by 1995. The Finnish finds (more than 125) include the Riihimäki ski originally thought to date from the final phase of the Stone Age at ca. 1,500 BCE. There were ca. 25 finds in Norway including several grave- and glacier-finds; the oldest Norwegian ski was thought to be the Øvrebø ski, pollen-dated at ca. 2,500 years.[58] These dates, though, have changed considerably, as more precise ^{14}C results have become available. One caution with the ^{14}C method must be kept in mind: though it yields a very accurate estimate of the age of the wood, the skis produced from that wood might be considerably younger.[59] A piece of wood could be made into a ski after lying around for hundreds of years. In this chapter some of the most important bog skis will be surveyed, paying particular attention to how they differ, and then an evolutionary pattern of development will be suggested.

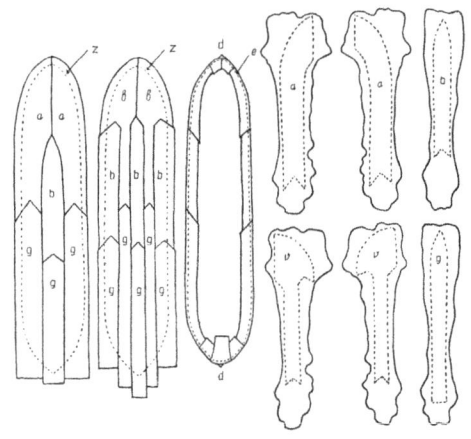

Fig. 3.4

Fig. 3.5

What is most remarkable about these bog skis is the extreme variation in form and features they display. First of all, it must be stressed that many of the ski types existed alongside one another over thousands of years; therefore, any evolutionary typology will be problematic.

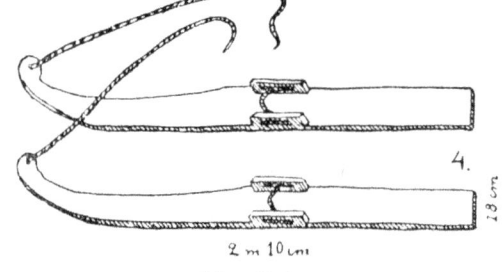

Fig. 3.6

Vorren compared five bog skis found in different parts of Sápmi (Lapland) and varying in age from ca. 250 BCE to 1435 CE. He found a close correlation between the features of

---

fidence level, or 68.3%. "Cal" means "calibrated" rather than "calendar."

[57] Berg 1950. NB: cf. Illustrations 3 for figures not in chapter.

[58] Lid 1937.

[59] Sørensen 1996: 44-47.

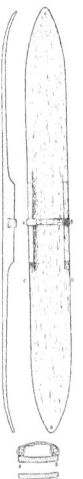

Fig. 3.8

the individual skis and the types of terrain the skis were used in.[60] Secondly, some of the bog finds cannot be classified in that they are fragments; they may lack the footrest on which the classification below is based. Often they are just the front tips of skis. We will see below that the oldest bog skis are actually very advanced in some of their features. Over the years the Swedes Wiklund, Berg and Manker and more recently the Finn Naskali and the Norwegian Sørensen have suggested several typological classifications or refined earlier groupings.[61] The typology presented below is based on Manker's three categories; it varies from Naskali's in that it does not have a separate category for prehistoric skis.[62]

Type A

This type has a low footstep with vertical pairs of holes for the binding strap, a flat bottom and no grooves. Consider first the Kalvträsk find from Västerbotten, Sweden (Fig. 3.1) consisting of a ski, a fragment of another ski, and a pole with one end shaped like a shovel (Fig. 3.2), all made of pine.[63] Pollen analysis yielded an age of just under 4,000 years, but ^{14}C results indicated that the items in this find were much older; they date from cal BCE 3623-3110 and are among the oldest bog skis.[64] The whole ski is flat on the bottom and has a flat foot space on top with four vertical holes going through the ski in pairs. On top of the ski there is a ridge in front of and behind the foot space that made the ski stiffer. There are narrow grooves on the bottom of the ski running lengthwise between the pairs of holes. In this way a thong passing through the holes and grooves functioned both as a toe strap and a heel strap. The ski is cut straight across at the back. There is one other type **A** ski in Scandinavia, the Pattijokki ski from Finland.[65] Parallels to this ski are found today among a number of the Siberian peoples, though many of their skis come to a point in the rear, undoubtedly to facilitate attaching a fur covering on the underside with hairs pointing backward. There

---

[60] Vorren 1998: 19.
[61] Wiklund 1931, 1933; Berg 1950, 1951; Manker 1971; Naskali in Vorren 1995; Sørensen 1993, 1995, 1996.
[62] Vorren 1995: 13.
[63] Berg 1950: 114-20.
[64] Åström 1993.
[65] Naskali in Vorren 1995: 73.

are skis in Slovenia with four vertical holes for the binding. Orel sees this binding type coming from the north with ancient Slavs.⁶⁶ Figs. 3.3 and 3.4⁶⁷ show reindeer skins and how they were sewn together to cover a ski. This provided better glide and allowed the hunter to approach the prey quietly. Furthermore, the Ostyaks and Komi (formerly called Zyrians) have a shovel pole similar to the one found in the bog. K. B. Wiklund called this the Arctic ski type and it is the only Arctic ski among the bog finds.⁶⁸ The Arctic ski is Type **A** in Ernst Manker's typology: low footrest with vertical binding hole pairs, flat bottom and no grooves.

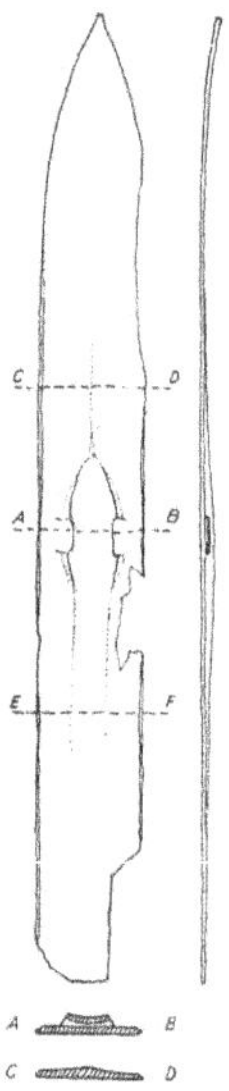

Type B

This type has a lowered footstep – either hollowed out of the ski itself or with lists nailed onto the sides (list = a narrow strip of wood). Each side has a horizontal hole so that a binding strap can pass through the holes and over the foot. The Riihimäki ski, found some 70 km. north of Helsinki, Finland, is younger than the Kalvträsk ski with a ¹⁴C date of cal BCE 3 – CE 257 and of a very different design (Fig. 3.5).⁶⁹ The ski has a flat bottom and is cut straight across at the back. The foot space has been lowered so that a thong could pass through holes in the outside edges or lists to secure the foot. In a later development of this binding method the lists were nailed to the ski rather than being part of the original ski material. This ski is an example of what is called the Southern⁷⁰ ski type, first of all, because in Fennoscandia this sort of ski is found toward the south, and, secondly, because similar skis are found in the Baltic countries, Poland, Russia and possibly Yugoslavia (figs. 3.6-3.9).⁷¹ The Southern ski was more common in areas where it was not so vital to subsistence patterns and where there wasn't as much snow. Note the steering ropes attached to the front of the skis in Fig. 3.6, a common feature of the Southern ski. In Manker's typology the Southern ski is Type **B**: low footrest between side lists with

Fig. 3.9

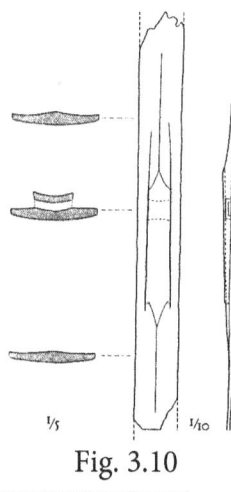

Fig. 3.10

---

⁶⁶ Orel 1956: 87.
⁶⁷ *På skidor* 1935: 37; *På skidor* 1940: 342.
⁶⁸ Wiklund 1931: 5-50; Berg 1933: 143-46; Zettersten 1934: 7-10.
⁶⁹ Itkonen 1937: 72-73; Berg 1950: 24.
⁷⁰ Wiklund 1931; Berg 1933: 149-58; Zettersten 1934, 1938, 1939.
⁷¹ Wiklund 1931: 28; Zettersten 1939: 402; *På skidor* 1936: 351; Wiklund 1928: 13.

horizontal binding holes through them, flat bottom and no grooves.

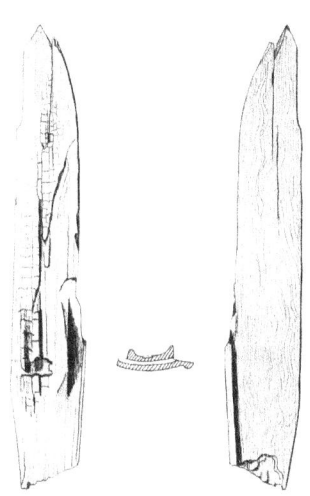

Fig. 3.11

Not many examples of this type are found in the bogs in the south of Scandinavia; the reason for this may be that the kinds of wood found in the south, e.g. birch, were not as resistant to rotting as the coniferous woods further north. However, this type of ski was in use in southern Sweden and western Norway into the present century. It is interesting to note that the Komi, a Finnic people of the northeastern part of European Russia formerly called the Zyrians, use the Arctic ski type with a fur covering for hunting on the tundra where the snow is often crusty. However, in the forest where the snow is loose they use the Southern type with a dugout foot place. The Southern ski may be a forerunner of the Telemark ski, of which more later on. The wide southerly distribution of the ski type suggests that it is very old.

Type C

This type of ski has a raised and indented footstep with a horizontal hole through which a binding strap goes below the foot. The bottom may be without grooves (**C 1**) or with grooves (**C 2**). Type **C 1** is further divided according to whether the bottom of the ski is flat **C1a** or slightly convex **C1b**. Type **C 2** is subdivided according to whether the bottom has a wide groove or side lists (**C 2 a**) or narrow grooves (**C 2 b**).

Type C 1 a: This ski has a flat bottom, no grooves and lacks ornamentation. One example is the Lipen 1 ski from (Fig. 3.10).[72] It has a rounded back end and dates from cal 450 BCE.

Type C 1 b: Gösta Berg termed this ski type the Bothnic ski in 1933.[73] It is relatively short in length and

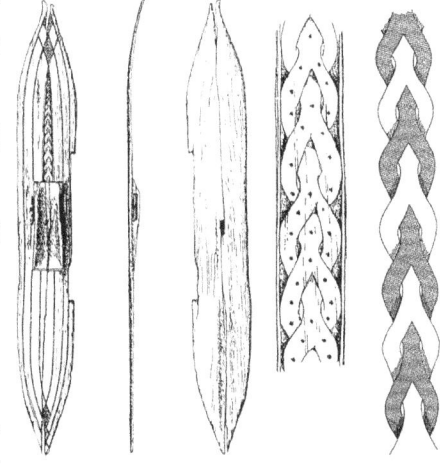

Fig. 3.12

---

[72] *På skidor* 1937: 75; Naskali in Vorren 1995: 74.
[73] Berg 1933: 158-63; Berg 1950: 23, 25.

slightly convex on the underside; it gradually comes to a point at both ends. The footrest is raised and inset from the side edges and it is slightly concave so that footwear such as the moccasin would fit in it. There is a horizontal hole beneath the footrest for the toe strap. Most of the Swedish bog skis are of this type; they date from after cal CE 0, and they are the only Swedish bog skis with a pointed rear end. An example is the Arvträsk ski (Fig. 3.11) from Swedish Lappland which is ca. 1,000 years old or somewhat younger.[74] It was found together with a fragment of a ski that probably made up a pair with it. Another example is the Sörviken ski depicted in Fig. 3.12 – the top surface is at the left.[75] The Bothnic ski type – also represented by bog skis in northern Norway and northern Finland – is found throughout the area where the Sámi have settled, so it is not surprising that the Bothnic ski has been considered a Sámi ski. In fact, the Bothnic ski survived into the 20th century as the South Lapp ski (Fig. 3.27) – so-called by Berg, and it was spread over a large area.[76]

Many of these Bothnic skis are decorated, some with rather intricate braided patterns. A fine example of the decoration is the Kinnula ski from Kinnula Parish in Central Finland dated at cal CE 650 discovered in 1968 (Fig. 3.13).[77] The Badstusund ski (Fig. 3.13) found in Norrbotten has a braided pattern on either end consisting of four pairs of intersecting parallel lines; two of the lines run the entire length of the ski and connect the two braided tips.[78] Its ¹⁴C date is cal CE 750-910. Berg pointed out that this sort of braided pattern is found on other objects of wood and horn that are common in the area around Birka. It was a popular form of ornamentation in central and south Sweden during the Viking period. Wilhelm Holmqvist, a Swedish archaeologist who examined the ornamentation on Swedish skis, dated them at 1000 to 1200 CE.[79] If this is

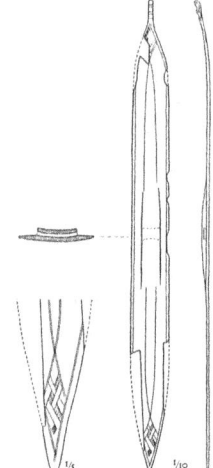

Fig. 3.13

true, then the 650 CE date of the Kinnula ski would suggest either that the wood is older than the ski or that the decoration was added later. The Sámi who traded in skins with the Swedes may well have borrowed the braiding idea from them and went on to develop it to a high degree of perfection. Fig. 3.14 is another example of beautiful ornamentation on

---

[74] Berg 1950: 90-93; Åström 1984: 85.
[75] Zettersten 1942: 19; Berg 1950: 147-50.
[76] Berg 1950: 21-22.
[77] Itkonen 1937: 83; Vilkuna in Vorren 1995: 67-68.
[78] Berg 1950: 103-06.
[79] Holmqvist 1934 : 273.

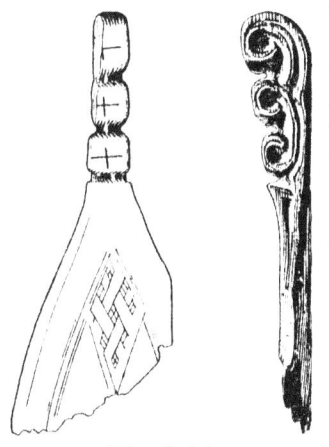

Fig. 3.14

the Klöverfors ski.[80] Berg concludes that the Bothnic ski type represents the final stage of development with most of the impulses coming from the south. Were this correct, it would mean the Bothnic ski did not come with Sámi forebears when they migrated into Fennoscandia which is certainly mistaken.

Type C 2 a: This type is represented by the Furnes ski found in Hedmark, some 65 miles north of Oslo, Norway; it was dated at 150 CE using an earlier ¹⁴C half-life; this date has been revised to cal CE 70-200 (Fig. 3.16).[81] The Furnes ski, constructed of pine, has a raised and indented footrest. The side lists on this wider ski are not at the outside edge of the ski but moved inward so as to provide support on either side of the foot, and there is a horizontal hole running across and through the entire ski below the footrest. This binding arrangement provided much more stability than the Southern type discussed above. Moreover, the Furnes ski has steering rims running lengthwise along the bottom of the ski at the outside edges which helped the ski move in a straight line. They were important for long skis, and the Furnes ski may have been eight feet long. These steering rims may have been the forerunners of grooves.

There is a similar ski – also of pine – found at Färnäs in Dalarna, Sweden and ¹⁴C dated at cal BCE 360 (Fig. 3.17).[82] It has the inset footrest with a horizontal hole across the ski below it. The Viitasaari ski (Fig. 3.18) found in northern Tavastland, Finland is similar to the Furnes and Färnäs skis in its binding arrangement and, in addition, it has a hole at the tip where a rope could be attached and the ski pulled behind a sled.[83] These skis are all representatives of what Gösta Berg called the Scandic type whose main feature is the raised, indented footrest with horizontal binding hole.[84] This is Manker's Type **C4**. They are all quite wide. The Scandic type represented an advance over the Southern and Arctic skis; that is, in areas of heavier snow cover a stronger and more durable binding was needed. Since the ski became wider the footrest was raised and indented to accommodate a horizontal binding hole

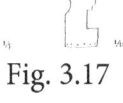

Fig. 3.17

---

[80] Berg 1933: 160.
[81] Zettersten 1932: 24; Bø 1966: 14; Sørensen 1993: 97.
[82] Berg 1950: 153-57.
[83] Itkonen 1937: 73; Naskali in Vorren 1995: 73.
[84] Berg 1933: 146-49

running across the entire width of the ski. The Hoting ski from Ångermanland, Sweden, once thought to be the oldest bog ski yet found at 4,500 years, has now been shown to be no older than 1,500 BCE; it is also a Scandic type ski (Fig. 3.19).[85] Fig. 3.20 shows the areas in Sweden and Norway where Scandic skis have been found (small circles and triangles).[86] **C 2 a** skis generally are not ornamented.[87]

Type C 2 b: This final group of narrow skis – with narrow grooves – includes one of the older bog skis. The Salla ski (Fig. 3.21) from the Särkila area of Finland is ^{14}C dated at cal BCE 3345-3145 and has five parallel grooves on the bottom.[88] Another example is the Liperi 2 ski that is ^{14}C dated to cal CE 280. It is one of the oldest ornamented skis.[89]

Grooves

With regard to the origin of the ski groove on the bottom of the ski that helped the ski steer straight one must first distinguish between grooves that developed naturally and those that were cut into the skis.[90] Natural grooves came about through wear and tear on skis made from certain types of wood, especially fir. If the wood was cut with the rings vertical, the skis would tend to develop natural grooves on the bottom as the softer wood wore away. The latter, man-made type groove seems to have developed out of the older skis with steering rims (**C 2 a**). Steering rims must be very old: they are clearly seen on the Vis I fragment that is more than 8,000 years old – see below. The first stage was a relatively broad, flat-bottomed groove taking up about one third of the ski's width. The oldest example is the Ikaalis ski from southwestern Finland dated at cal CE 290-550. The groove gradually spread northward and eastward, ultimately turning into the narrow groove (**C 2 b**).[91]

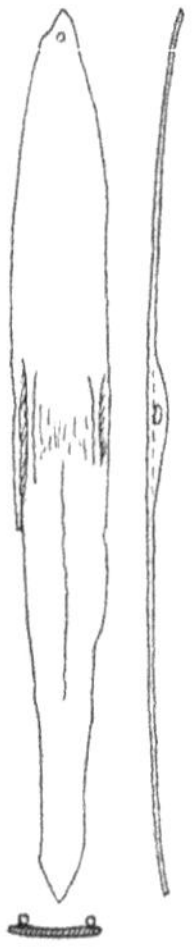

Fig. 3.18

Bindings

Though the classification of bog skis above is based on binding type, very few bog skis have been found with bindings or binding fragments. However, in 1991 a ski was found in Mänttä, Finland with the remains of a bast front binding and leather strap rear binding

---

[85] Berg 1950: 127.
[86] Zettersten 1942: 14.
[87] Berg 1950: 127-31.
[88] Naskali in Vorren 1995: 72.
[89] Naskali in Vorren 1995: 77.
[90] Tomasson 1928: 24.
[91] Valonen 1980: 222; Sørensen 1996: 14 and 11-18 including map.

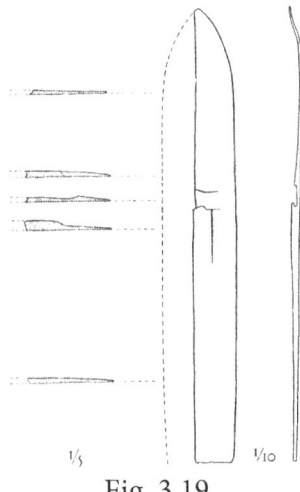
Fig. 3.19

dating from the fifth century CE.[92] This type of binding, the so-called Selbu binding – a withe toe loop plus a leather thong at the rear – was still used at the end of the last century in Norway.[93] From this Vilkuna concludes that a binding developed during the Iron Age stood the test of time and lasted for centuries.

Consider next the Jokkfall ski found in Norrbotten, Sweden (Fig. 3.22).[94] It has been dated to the early Iron Age. The binding arrangement is of particular interest: it has the four vertical holes typical of the Arctic ski, but it also has the Bothnic raised, concave footrest; however, the footrest is not raised enough to accommodate a horizontal hole for the binding thong. Rather, there is a groove running between the two pairs of holes through which the thong could run under the boot. This ski would seem to be a transition form between the Arctic and Bothnic types.

Unequal Length Skis

Finally I mention the Central Nordic ski type which was actually a pair of unequal length skis (Fig. 3.23).[95] There was a long left ski used for gliding and a short right ski – often fur covered – used for pushing in the manner of a scooter. No Central Nordic pairs are among the bog finds, but the Alvdal ski from 90 miles north of Oslo, Norway may have been the right ski of such a pair of unequal length skis. It has a ^{14}C date of cal CE 615-675 and is short and wide with two steering grooves on the underside.[96] There is a raised, inset footrest below which there is a horizontal hole for the leather strap. It would appear that unequal length skis are a combination of two different types: one such as the Jokkfall mentioned above for pushing – possibly skin covered (Fig. 3.24 is a sketch of a fur-covered ski that Carl Linnaeus did on

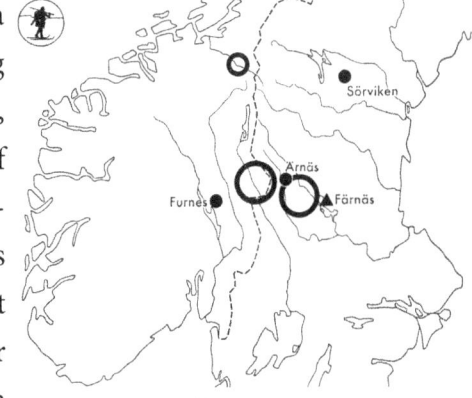
Fig. 3.20

---

[92] Vilkuna 1998: 70-75.
[93] Bø 1968: 41.
[94] Manker 1957: 169.
[95] Berg 1933: 166-68; Zettersten 1934: 10-15, 17; Jirlow 1935: 31-32; Berg 1970.
[96] Vaage 1981: 54.

his 1732 trip around Lapland)⁹⁷ – and a longer one, perhaps an advanced version of the Scandic type for gliding. See Chap. 7 for another theory on the origin of unequal length skis. Though there are medieval references to what may be unequal length skis, there are no positively identified pairs of unequal length skis until the late Middle Ages.⁹⁸ Central Nordic skis were especially good for covering long distances and for hunting in terrain that was not too steep. They became very popular in parts of Sweden and eastern Norway and crowded out the older types of skis.

Early Bog Ski Fragments

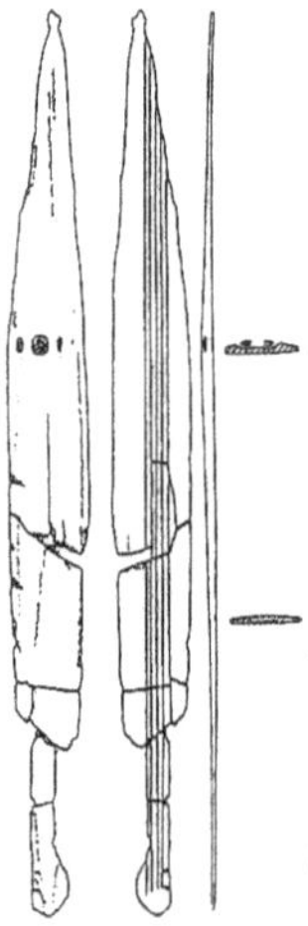

Among the oldest bog skis are the back end of a ski from Drevja in Vefsn, Nordland⁹⁹ with a ¹⁴C date of cal BCE 3343-2939. Sørensen points out that the wood is so knotty and the annual rings so crooked that it could not have been used to glide on; rather it must have been fur-covered. The tips from Vis I in the Vychegda basin near the Vis River, excavated by Grigoriy Burov, have been carbon-dated to between cal BCE 6709-5763. Due to the absence of holes toward the front, the symmetry of the artifacts, and the flat bottom surface Burov interprets them as skis rather than sledge runners.¹⁰⁰ Fig. 3.25, a ski tip that Burov calls the Vis-type, is the older variety from the site and is thus probably more than 8,500 years old. It is made of hardwood. Note the steering rims at the outer edges. The ski fragment in Fig. 3.26 though not as old as the Vis-type is even more remarkable. Burov calls it the Veretye-type. On the lower surface there is a carved projection – an elk's head – pointing backwards. It could have served as a brake to prevent reverse movement over packed snow and to prevent lateral displacement of the ski tip. This somewhat younger fragment, made of softwood, does not have the rims of the Vis-type.¹⁰¹

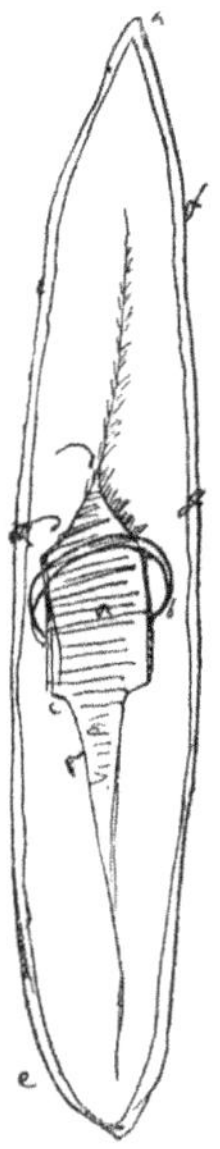

Fig. 3.20

Fig. 3.24

Summing up briefly: Fig. 3.27 gives a chronological sketch of the main ski types and their features. The oldest types are the Southern with the side lists and no grooves and the Arctic with the four vertical binding holes and usually fur covered. The Southern evolves into the somewhat wider Scandic with its inset footrest. The Bothnic ski is primarily an

---

⁹⁷ Wiklund 1928: 38.
⁹⁸ Sørensen 1996: 34.
⁹⁹ Sørensen 1993: 107.
¹⁰⁰ Burov 1985: 393.
¹⁰¹ Burov 1985: 394.

offshoot of the Scandic ski but narrowing at the back like the Arctic ski. The Bothnic ski evolved into the South Lapp ski of this century (Fig. 3.27)[102]. Offshoots of the Arctic and Scandic skis were paired to produce the Central Nordic unequal length skis.

The next chapter will discuss Sámi ancestors who brought skis to Fennoscandia when they migrated from Central Asia and who taught Norwegians and Swedes how to ski.

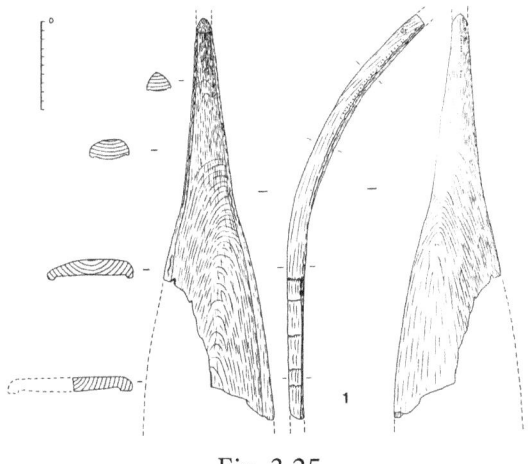

Fig. 3.25

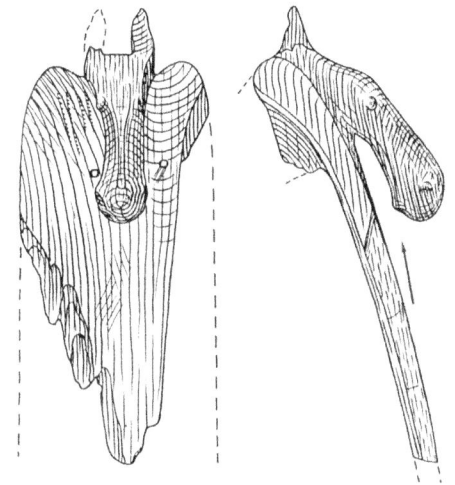

Fig. 3.26

---

[102] Berg 1933: 156; Berg 1950: 20.

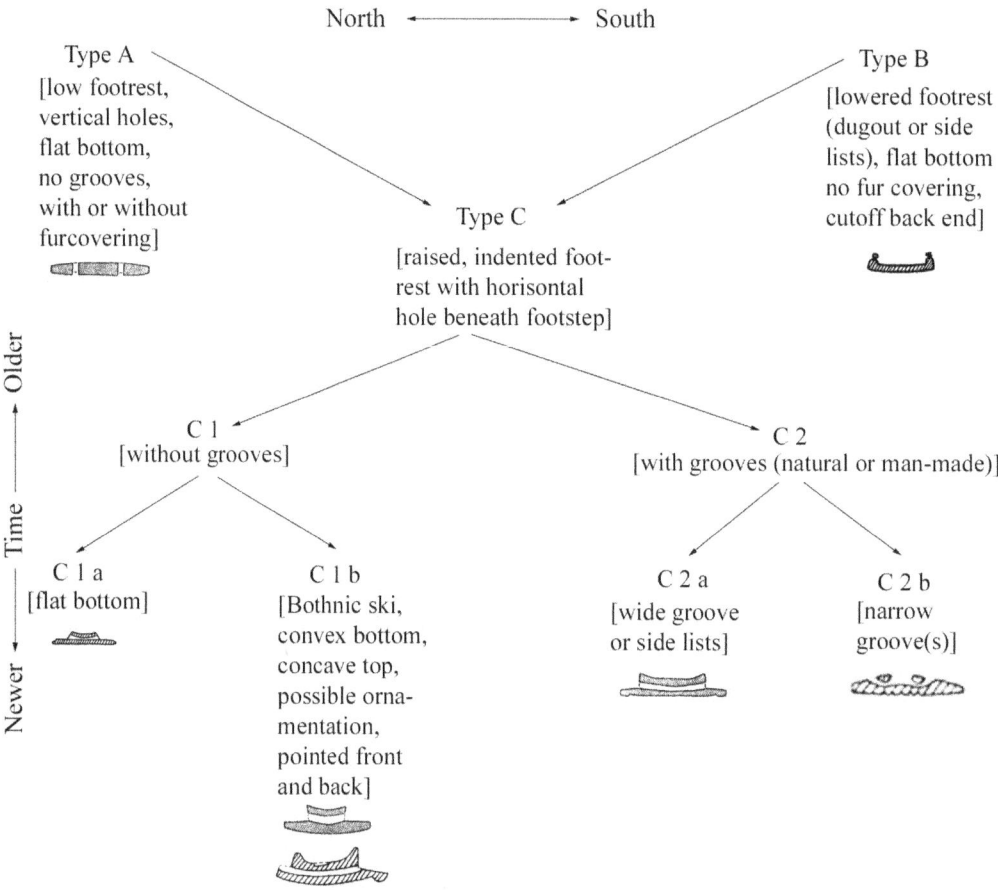

Fig. 3.27

The Sámi and the Evolution of Skiing

The references to skiing and skis presented in Chap. 1 involve a wide range of groups from the Turkic people of eastern Asia northwest to the Sámi of northern Scandinavia. The Sámi were mentioned often, and it has been suggested that Norwegians and Swedes may have picked up skiing from the Sámi. Who are the Sámi, what do we know of their history and what did skiing mean to them? A detailed look at the Sámi will provide clues to the evolution of the ski.

The Sámi are an indigenous people inhabiting northern portions of Norway, Sweden, Finland and Russia. They were once called Lapps[103] and the area they inhabited Lapland, though we now refer to them and their homeland respectively with the names they themselves use, Sámi or Saami and *Sápmi* (or *Sámiid eanan*). The Sámi number around 100,000 today depending on what definition one uses.[104] More than half of the Sámi live in Norway, mostly in Finnmark and Troms counties; some 25,000 are in Sweden, mainly in the districts of Härjedalen and Jämtland; around 9,000 live in northern Finland; and under 2,000 in Russia in the Petsamo and Kola Peninsula areas.

Fig. 4.1 shows a Sámi woman milking a reindeer.[105] Female reindeer are the only members of the deer family with antlers, leading to the joke: "What gender is Rudolph?" The correct answer is female because the male reindeer drop their antlers in late fall during the rut, but the female reindeer still have theirs at Christmas.

---

[103] The word "Lapp" was apparently used first in Russian chronicles – *lop'* – beginning around 1000 CE and is/was most common in Finland and Sweden. Cf. Hansen & Olsen 45-51 for more details on names for the Sámi.

[104] If a person considers him- or herself to be a Sámi and either speaks a Sámi dialect or had a Sámi parent or grandparent who spoke Sámi at home, then he or she is counted as a Sámi.

[105] Olaus 1972: 596.

Sápmi today covers a large area from the White Sea (Russia) in the northeast to Lake Femunden south of Røros in Norway. Along the extensive coastline, which is cut by numerous fjords, there is a relatively moderate climate thanks to the Gulf Stream. Mountains run right down to the seacoast, and forests cover much of the area with deciduous trees such as birch, willow and alder and coniferous trees such as fir in the north and spruce in the south. Forest vegetation consists mainly of heather and reindeer lichen as well as other types of lichen. In the treeless mountain and coastal areas are found heather and grass.

Speculations regarding the origins of the Sámi began in earnest in the seventeenth century when Johannes Schefferus[106] reiterated the widespread assumption that the Sámi had originated as far east as Asia and had migrated through the inner part of the continent to Finland and on into the coastal districts of Fennoscandia. If the Sámi had migrated into Fennoscandia so early – while the glacier covered most of the Scandinavian peninsula – they would have had to follow the ice-free coast.

Fig. 4.2 is on the title page of the Dutch translation of Schefferus' *Lapponia* from 1682.[107]

Some nineteenth century scholars thought the Sámi were descendents of an Arctic race, native to the north, whose ancestors had created the Stone Age tools found at the Komsa sites in Northern Norway. According to this theory they borrowed their language from Finno-Ugric peoples they came in contact with (quite perceptive as it turns out). There are vocabulary items in the language unique to it alone, but this is not conclusive enough by itself. Additional support for this theory was derived from the fact that the Sámi seemed to be of a different racial type than other Finno-Ugrians,[108] though this has been discounted.

Fig. 4.3

Fig. 4.3 shows Ull, the Norse god of skiing, who was no doubt a Sámi.[109]

Nevertheless, to account for the unique Sámi traits K. B. Wiklund – professor of Finno-Ugric languages at the University of Uppsala and one of the most important early contributors to the history of skiing – suggested there must have been a long period of isolation to allow these differ-

---

[106] Schefferus 1673. Cf. Lindkjølen 1994 for a nice discussion of Schefferus.
[107] Wiklund 1931: 5.
[108] Mark 1970.
[109] Mehl 1964: 67.

ences to develop. The Komsa culture artifacts provided evidence that there were people living along the ice-free coasts of the Varanger peninsula as far back as the glacial period more then 12,000 years ago. This was the isolated area Wiklund was looking for, where, according to his theory, the forebears of the Sámi could have differentiated themselves over a long period of time from nearby tribes.[110] He went on to suggest that the Proto-Lapps (Proto-Sámi) borrowed their language from the Tchudes (*Čuđit*), a West Finnic tribe also called the Vepse or Vote. Wiklund guessed that this might have occurred during the Bronze Age around 500 BCE and at a time when the Tchudes and Proto-Lapps were together in the inner parts of Finland and the bordering areas of Russia.[111] Although this theory is no longer viable, Wiklund was clearly on the right track: "his basic hypothesis of a language shift still remains completely plausible."[112] Ante Aikio: "Once Pre-Proto-Saami had become established as a distinct dialect or language spoken in its own speech community, its speakers have been in contact with neighboring groups speaking both genetically related and unrelated languages."[113]

What seems to have happened is the speakers of Proto-Saami brought their Finno-Ugric tongue with them when they migrated into the Scandinavian Peninsula around 300 CE after which they moved north and northeast and merged with the people already in the interior of Scandinavia who spoke what Aikio calls Palaeo-Laplandic. Aikio writes: "we arrive at the surprising conclusion that substrate influence of Palaeo-Laplandic languages was contemporaneous with the adoption of Proto-Scandinavian loanwords. As the Proto-Scandinavian contacts in Scandinavia must be equated with the Early Runic era ca. 200-700 CE, we thus have an absolute dating also for the spread of Saami languages to Lapland and for the disappearance of the unknown Palaeo-Laplandic languages."[114] This, Aikio has demonstrated convincingly: the Sámi languages have acquired hundreds of words for flora and fauna, topographical features and place names from the now disappeared Palaeo-Laplandic languages. The original inhabitants of Scandinavia spoke Palaeo-Laplandic, a language that has disappeared but for the many words and names borrowed from it. So the Sámi today are descendants of both the Palaeo-Laplandic people and the Proto-Sámi and its offshoots. Furthermore, neither the Sámi nor their immediate forebears brought skis to Scandinavia. As can be inferred from above, Palaeo-Laplanders and Proto-Sámi had long used skis, which

---

[110] Wiklund 1948: 6-14.
[111] Wiklund 1948: 23-24.
[112] Aikio 2012: 81.
[113] *Ibid*. 70.
[114] *Ibid*. 87. See also Weinstock 2015: 68-88.

had spread very early on from Central Asia by diffusion.

Fig. 4.4 shows a draft reindeer pulling a Sámi *pulk* "reindeer sled."[115] In Schefferus' *Lapponia*.

Consider the language of the Sámi – *sámegiella* or *sapmelaš* is a member of the Finno-Ugric language group. The Finnic side of this language group includes Sámi, Finnish, Karelian, Estonian, Mordvin, Cheremis, Votyak and Zyrian (Komi). The Ugric languages are Hungarian, Ostyak and Vogul. The Finno-Ugric group together with the Samoyed language makes up the Uralic sub-group of the Ural-Altaic language family. Sámi and Finnish are not mutually intelligible as are, for example, Norwegian and Swedish, but they are quite close because they have the same basic structure and have borrowed many words from one another.[116] Sámi has also borrowed many words from Norwegian and Swedish, some of them so old that they have preserved their Proto-Sámi forms. Pekka Sammallahti published a detailed study of the Sámi language and its history in 1998. He reconstructed a Finno-Saamic protolanguage that did not begin to split until "after the introduction of the Indo-European Battle Axe Culture to the coasts of Finland about 3,200 BCE"[117] One of the enigmas about Sámi origins has always been that Sámi and Samoyed share quite a few vocabulary items and morphological features not found in the other Finno-Ugric languages. Sammallahti wrote that the roughly one hundred stems that Sámi and Samoyed share go back to Proto-Uralic, an earlier stage of the language spoken about 4,500 BCE.[118] This would suggest contact between some Sámi and Samoyed forebears around 4,500 BCE or earlier, after which the Sámi emigrated from their previous home, located in the region of the Urals in central Europe, to follow the reindeer herds north- and westward as the glacier continued to retreat from Fennoscandia.

Fig. 4.10 Schefferus' *Lapponia* from 1682.[119]

Fig. 4.5 is an engraving in the Dutch edition of

---

[115] Vorren 1988: 38.
[116] Sørensen 1996: 53.
[117] Sammallahti 1998: 2.
[118] Sammallahti 1998: 118.
[119] Luther 1942: 35.

We do not know who the people of the Komsa culture were dwelling in the north that far back in time. However, ancient DNA studies show that there were two hunterer-gatherer groups very early: western and eastern.[120] There are somewhat younger artifacts about 4,000 years old found at sites where earth houses or turf huts stood (Sámi *goahti*) – the so-called Fosna culture – along the coast and inland throughout Finland and Sweden, that were used by a Stone Age hunting people.[121] Refuse heaps suggest that these people ate a wide range of animals, fish and birds. The weapons and tools are excellently shaped out of stone, horn and bone. Since the same sort of artifacts are found at dwelling places throughout the area where the Sámi now live, there would seem to be a connection between them. More recent gravesites and dwelling sites contain objects even more typically Sámi.[122] Thus, at the beginning of the Iron Age – ca. 200-100 BCE (there was, by the way, no Bronze Age this far north) – the Palaeo-Laplandic were a hunting and gathering people who had been established in northern Scandinavia for many centuries.

If we look at linguistic evidence first presented in Fridtjof Nansen's *Paa ski over Grønland* the origins of the Sámi become somewhat clearer. Nansen had librarian Andr. M. Hansen investigate the words for *ski* in the languages of Northern Eurasia, the area where skis are likely to have been used for thousands of years. Hansen then produced a map of these words (Fig. 4.6 in Illustrations 5).[123] It turned out that none of the main Indo-European words for ski was original. For example, the word *ski* itself is cognate with Eng. *skid* "a piece of wood or to slide" and Engl. (< Gk.) *Schizophrenia* "split personality." Both of the English words are derived from the I-E root **skhait, skhit* "split" which is to say that the original meaning had nothing to do with skis. Hansen was able to reduce a myriad of names for *ski* to three main families of names, all of which led back to the Lake Baikal area.

Fig. 4.7 shows a Sámi on skis.[124] It appeared in the text of a map of the Åsele Sámi area done by C. W. Cederhielm.

The most important family is the *suks* group. One of the Sámi words for ski is *sâbek* or *sabit*. Finnish has the word *suksi*; Finno-Ugrian peoples between Lake Ladoga and Lithua-

---

[120] Cf. Weinstock forthcoming.
[121] Wiklund (1948: 6-7) theorized that the Proto-Sámi would winter along the ice-free coast of Northern Norway and spend the summer in the Møre and Romsdal area where Fosna culture artifacts were found.
[122] Schanche in Vorren 1994.
[123] Nansen 1890: between 96-97; Wiklund (1926: 2) found the map dilettantish and worthless but did not go into detail.
[124] *På skidor* 1938: 380.

nia have *suhsi, suksi, suks* and *soks*; far to the east the Tungus have the word *suksylta*, the first part of which is related to the above words; and the Golds have *soksolta*. All the words of this first group are original words for ski. The second family is the *solta* group. This appears as the second member of the compounds mentioned above; the Samoyeds have *tolds*, which is related to *solt*. The third family is the *sana*

Fig. 4.12

group found among the Buryats around Lake Baikal. It should be pointed out that there are errors of detail in Hansen's map.[125] Problems notwithstanding, the map strongly suggests that some forebears of Ural-Altaic peoples likely invented the ski in the area of Lake Baikal not far from the Altai Mountains. The Sámi languages belong to the Finno-Ugric branch of Ural-Altaic and, thus, it is most likely that some of their ancestors migrated many millennia ago from Central Asia to their present home bringing skis with them. The migration was undoubtedly a lengthy process induced by the warming of the climate and the movement of reindeer and other prey further north. There were stopping points along the way, some during periods of time before the Proto-Sámi split off from most closely related Finno-Ugric tribes – for example, in the Urals. Once in Fennoscandia they probably came in contact with and were influenced by Neolithic groups living south of them near the Baltic and in southern Scandinavia. Old Sámi myths speak of long migrations before their arrival in their present homeland, a two-part migration from the north and the south. The earliest myth ends at the time when the Sámi began to follow the shamanistic religion.[126]

Fig. 4.8 is an engraving from the 1748 German translation of Pehr Högström's book *Beskrifning öfwer de til Sweriges krona lydande Lapmarker* from 1747.[127]

As is the case with other Arctic groups, the subsistence patterns of the Sámi were based on the animal and plant life found in the area. The forests and mountain plateaus offered a variety of animals, most importantly the reindeer. During earlier periods, other animals may have predominated in the hunters' quarry, but the reindeer was the ideal prey, providing meat for the diet, skins for clothing and tents, sinews for thread and lines, bones

---

[125] Valonen (1980: 104) says that the Sámi term for ski, *savek*, lacks parallels in the other Finno-Ugric languages.
[126] Gaski: 2001.
[127] *På skidor* 1938: 381.

and antlers for tools and weapons, and teeth for ornamentation. However, very few of the peoples living off reindeer hunting could get by without some other means of subsistence. In this respect the sea has always had much to offer: fish, shellfish, whale, walrus, seal and birds. Such sea resources made up much of the diet during the warmer months of those living in coastal areas.

Fig. 4.9 shows a Sámi hunting a bear on skis.[128]

One can almost read Sámi subsistence patterns in their language which has evolved and been honed over thousands of years to describe Arctic nature. The language is rife with words and phrases for the concepts that were essential for exploiting natural resources and for their very survival as hunter/gatherers. Nils Jernsletten points out that there are few names in the Sámi language for small birds in that they were not important for subsistence patterns.[129] On the other hand, sea birds and waterfowl, which were part of the diet, have a more extensive vocabulary. It is not surprising then that the areas of the vocabulary having to do with reindeer, grazing conditions, snow conditions and skiing are extensive. Jernsletten lists 49 words used to distinguish between reindeer by age, sex, hair color and horn type. There are 108 words for different types of snow and ice conditions. "Sami descriptions of landscape can function as maps, in which are incorporated topography, geography and information as to which routes are best to take."[130] Can you imagine trying to translate a passage from Sámi to English that contains a few of these specialized terms?

The Sámi people living in parts of the Fennoscandian area have a long history of living alongside and scattered among other ethnic and national populations in Norway, Sweden, Finland and Russia. As with other ethnic minorities around the world the Sámi have been affected by and assimilated into the larger economic, social and political systems of the modern nations within which their communities lie. Similarities and differences among Sámi communities often cut across political boundaries, reflecting the fact that much of their culture predates historical geopolitical divisions in Scandinavia.[131]

During the greater part of the historical period the Sámi remained hunters and fishers, even as other cultures began to exert pressure on them. The competition between European and Scandinavian economic interests developed into political struggles over borders in which the Sámi often suffered the burden of multiple taxation, zealous missionary activity

---

[128] Vorren 1988: 108.
[129] Jernsletten 1997: 86.
[130] Gaski 1997a: 13. Cf. also Ryd, 2001.
[131] Cf. Niemi 1997: 63-67.

and even the ravages of warfare.[132] In 1326 inland areas where most of the reindeer Sámi lived were defined as joint territories by the nations vying for these areas.

In the 16th century the ancient subsistence patterns of the Sámi, though still intact to a great degree, were being influenced by close contact with neighboring societies. The Sámi had already begun to divide into several distinct groups: 1) Coastal or sea Sámi – fishing plus animal husbandry, berry-picking, and so on; 2) Reindeer herders; 3) Forest Sámi or *dálon* – subsistence agriculture plus fresh-water fishing, berry-picking, small herds of reindeer and hunting. The coastal Sámi suffered most. It is probable that the coastal communities have always been larger than those of the nomadic herders. Today most Sámi are found in coastal areas, especially the Sámi in the west. Their communities were traditionally self-sufficient, but the disappearance of wild game and the taxes imposed on them gradually forced them into a greater dependence on trading with reindeer herders and non-Sámi merchants. They have had to integrate with the surrounding Scandinavian society to a greater extent than other Sámi have.

Fig. 4.10 shows a Sámi reindeer herd at a winter pasture in Finnmark.[133]

By the 16th century the wild reindeer population in Fennoscandia had been heavily depleted by hunting, in part thanks to firearms. Those who had lived primarily from wild reindeer were forced to alter their subsistence patterns. The answer was reindeer nomadism, a relatively recent phenomenon among the Sámi.[134] It has always received more attention from writers on culture even though never more than a minority of Sámi was engaged in it. This is undoubtedly due to the colorful nature of the nomadic lifestyle. Historical knowledge of reindeer nomadism among the Sámi stems from the 16th and 17th centuries. However, as far back as the ninth century Ohthere reports having a herd of 600 reindeer including six prized decoy animals, though the animals may have belonged to the Sámi who paid taxes to Ohthere. Sarauw reported that by the end of the fifth century CE the Chinese received reports of a tame stag pulling a sled and of reindeer being milked.[135] It seems likely that from Ohthere's time on reindeer nomadism developed gradually. There was no need for large-scale reindeer nomadism among the Sámi until the heavy taxes were imposed on them and the wild reindeer began to be depleted. At first a *siida* (cf. below) may have had a few tame reindeer that were used as decoy animals or for transportation. By the 17th century

---

[132] *The Saami* 1993: 22, 31-32.
[133] Vorren 1988: 19.
[134] Laufer 1917; Vajda 1968.
[135] Sarauw 1913; Laufer 1917: 93.

reindeer pastoralism spread, both with regard to the area involved and the number of Sámi living exclusively by it. The spread was primarily from south to north.

Fig. 4.11 is an early picture of a Sámi ski from ca. 1650.[136] It was reprinted in Adam Olearius' "Gottorffische Kunst-Kammer" from 1674.

Most of these nomadic Sámi were found in Norway and Sweden. The migration routes ran basically east west and could be up to 200 miles long, culminating in summer and winter residences on either end. Further south the migratory routes were more circular. The paths taken were dictated largely by the migratory and herding instincts of the mountain reindeer herds, that is, until fences were erected at national borders. The basic unit of the reindeer herders is called the *siida* "group" and consists of a small group of families that migrate together. The leader of the *siida* was usually an older man recognized by the members of the group for his superior personal qualities and wealth in reindeer. Before the Sámi were subjected to forced conversion to Christianity each *siida* had a *noaidi* (shaman), a spiritual leader who acted as an intermediary between humans and supernatural powers. The *noaidi* would beat on a magical drum and *yoik* to get into an ecstatic trance that would aid his/her soul to journey to *Sájvva* (*Saivo*), the nether world, which was the Sámi paradise. The oval-shaped drum had figures painted on it and was also used for divination. It often had small articles attached to it including skis to aid in the trip to *Sájvva*. The *yoik*, a chanted, often repeated brief text originally had a magico-religious nature.[137] Saxo mentioned that they were "addicted to the study of spells."[138] The ancient religion combined aspects of animistic, polytheistic beliefs with ancestor worship and was central to the social life of a hunting people dependent on natural resources for their survival.

The nomadic lifestyle required a material culture that was not overly burdensome. Traditionally, everything that was to be transported during periods of migration was loaded onto sleds pulled by reindeer or put on the backs of the reindeer themselves. Adults were usually on skis for these seasonal movements. Skis had always been essential to Sámi reindeer hunters, but once nomadism was established skis became even more vital. Now the herders had to protect the herds from predators such as wolves, lynxes and bears. During the summer months the herds were corralled and milked, providing not only milk to be stored away but also butter and cheese to carry along on the migrations. In the winter certain animals were slaughtered with some of the meat preserved by drying or smoking.

---

[136] *På skidor* 1934: 374.

[137] Gaski 1997b: 12-15.

[138] Saxo 1999: 153.

The forest Sámi were found mostly in northern Sweden and Finland. They traditionally supported themselves by hunting and trapping of animals and by fishing on lakes and rivers and even by tourism. Reindeer herding played only a small role with the forest Sámi. For them, reindeer were mainly used for transportation, as decoy animals to help capture wild reindeer and for milking. The forest Sámi, like the coastal Sámi, originally moved between dwelling sites at different times of the year but do so no longer. In Finland the encroachment of agriculturalists, who burned the forests to make more farmland available in the seventeenth century and earlier, forced many forest Sámi to move further north or become more dependent on farming. These three divisions of culture – coastal Sámi, reindeer nomads, and forest Sámi – repeat themselves among arctic groups east all the way to the Bering Straits.

Fig. 4.12 shows a Sámi woman on skis.[139] It is in Schefferus' *Lapponia* from 1673.

The clash of Sámi culture with encroaching cultures accelerated during and after the 16th century with a negative impact on the Sámi. Western concepts of nature were alien to the Sámi whose own view of nature was more holistic. In discussing Sámi art, Harald Gaski mentions the following important aesthetic principle: use organic materials, allow the works of art to be exposed to wind and weather and eventually to disappear without a trace.[140] He points out that this parallels the Sámi relationship to the natural environment: the hand of nature will erase all traces of them. This is beautifully expressed in a poem by Paulus Utsi and Inger Huuva Utsi entitled **Our Life**:[141]

> Our life
> is like a ski track
> on the white open plains
> The wind erases it
> before morning dawns

Nation-building by Norway, Sweden, Finland and Russia meant a loss of Sámi territory and self-determination. When coastal fishing stocks shrank in the 16th century many Norwegians moved inland. Kvens – immigrants from Finland, a few of whom had settled in Northern Norway during the Middle Ages – began to come in much greater numbers. In the 18th and 19th century agricultural peasants moved north into traditional Sámi territory. Sámi rights were for the most part respected until the mid-19th century when three developments had a deleterious effect on their society:

---

[139] Bø 1966: 24.
[140] Gaski 1997a: 11.
[141] Utsi in Gaski 1997b: 115.

- The doctrine of "equal rights in the local society" became the norm. Since the Sámi were now outnumbered in their own territory they could simply be outvoted.
- The Norwegian State claimed that it owned all unregistered ground in Finnmark where most of the Sámi lived.
- The policy of Assimilation into the greater society or Norwegianization was emphasized. The children of reindeer-herding Sámi were shipped off to boarding schools where they were not allowed to speak their mother tongue.

There were similar developments in Sweden. Only in recent decades has this situation improved. The Sámi have gained a measure of control over their destiny as a minority culture.

Skis were an extremely important part of Sámi material culture, especially that of the reindeer nomads. Skis were used to follow the reindeer herds and were used to hunt wild reindeer in ancient times. No snowshoes are found among the Sámi. If they existed at one time, they were completely replaced by skis. When Sámi ancestors arrived in Fennoscandia they probably were using skis similar to the Kalvträsk ski that is like the skis found among the Zyrians (Komi), Samoyeds, Chukchee, Lamuts and Ainu (cf. Chap. 3). Then over the succeeding millennia they altered and perfected their skis – perhaps with impulses from the south – so that they became more efficient as accessories to the hunt. This follows from the fact that most of the rock carvings and the over 250 bog skis have been found in areas that were occupied almost exclusively by Sámi forebears 2,000 years ago.

The Sámi then played a vital role in the spread of skis in Scandinavia, perfecting them and teaching others how to use them. In the next chapter we will see evidence of the great age of circumpolar myths including a Sámi creation myth.

Circumpolar Myths about Skiing

Three seemingly unrelated tales from different corners of the world lead to what is undoubtedly the earliest literary evidence for skiing.[142] Consider first of all the *Kalevala*, the Finnish national epic, and Lemminkäinen's chasing down of the demon elk on skis.[143] The *Kalevala* was put together by Elias Lönnroth, a Finnish country doctor of humble origins, from oral folk poetry he and others recorded during the early decades of the nineteenth century. There are epic descriptions of the deeds of mythical heroes, lyric poems, incantations, and more. Lönnroth knew about these songs and was eager to hear them performed. The promised land of the songs was Karelia – mostly part of Russia now, but then in eastern Finland and northwestern Russia, an area with a rich oral folk tradition. Lönnroth's work took him there where he heard the finest singers and recorded their songs. The method of performance was interesting: two singers sat facing each other, knees together and hands clasped. Often the singers were accompanied by someone playing the kantele, a five-string, triangular shaped harp that is related to the Sámi noaide's drum.[144] The singers rocked back and forth, and the one singer would come in toward the end of the other singer's song by repeating the last few lines in different words. In 1835 Lönnroth published the *Old Kalevala* consisting of 32 runes (cantos) and over twelve thousand lines. He was able to weave them into a whole in that every line was trochaic with prominent alliteration. In 1849 the revised and enlarged *New Kalevala* appeared – now 50 runes and 22,795 lines – and immediately became the national epic.

As far as content is concerned the *Kalevala* speaks of the cold and dark mythical land to the north, Pohjola (Sápmi or Lapland), ruled over by an evil old woman Louhi. The he-

---

[142] Meuli 1975: 797-813 is the primary inspiration for this chapter.
[143] *Kalevala* 1988.
[144] DuBois 1998.

roes of Finland to the south go there to try to win the beautiful maidens, to retrieve the sun and moon which Louhi has hidden in a mountain, and to steal the marvelous Sampo, a mill that is the source of happiness and will assure prosperity in the south. The heroes magically put the people of Pohjola to sleep, steel the Sampo and head south. A crane overhears one of them singing and then wakes Louhi. When, in the shape of an eagle, she catches up with the heroes in their boat, a fight ensues and the Sampo breaks apart. The pieces fall into the sea, but the mill continues to grind which is why the sea is so rich. The heroes manage to save a few pieces, which bring modest prosperity to Finland.

The thirteenth rune of the *New Kalevala* contains a dramatic depiction of the young hero Lemminkäinen's attempt to catch the elk Hiisi, demon of the woods, and the ignominious outcome of his effort. The story is important for the history of skiing not only for its literary value but because it provides information on a particular type of ski, viz. unequal length skis.

Lemminkäinen, already married, is interested in getting one of Louhi's maidens. Louhi at first indignantly refuses but then suggests that if Lemminkäinen can ski down the demon elk there might be a chance. He is fully armed and ready for the task but suddenly realizes:

> I've no left ski for swift sliding
> And no right ski for quick heeling.

So he goes out to the Lapplander Kauppi to get some skis. He says to Kauppi:

> Make me now true racing skis,
> Carve out splendid righthand skis
> Swift to race the demon's elk
> From the far-back demon country.

Kauppi warns Lemminkäinen that the chase will be in vain. But Lemminkäinen is not worried:

> "Make a left ski for swift sliding
> And a right ski for quick heeling,
> Swift to catch the demon's elk
> From the far-back demon country."
> Lylikki, the smith of left skis,
> Kauppi, smith of right-hand skis,
> In the autumn made the left ski,
> In the winter carved the right ski;
> Took a day to shape the ski pole
> And the next day carved the snow disks.
> Then the left was fit for pushing

> And the right one for quick heeling.
> Now the ski pole too was ready,
> And the snow disk neatly fitted;
> For the pole an otterskin,
> For the disk a red fox paid.
> Then he greased his skis with butter
> And with reindeer tallow slicked them.
>
> And soon Lemminkäinen is off after the demon elk:
> Lemminkäinen went his way;
> Started pushing with the left ski,
> Quickly kicking with the right one,
> And he boasted as he went:
> "Nothing's under God's own sky,
> Underneath this lid of heaven,
> Not a creature in the forest,
> Not a single four-foot runner,
> None that cannot be surprised,
> None that can't be overtaken
> By the skis of Kaleva's son,
> By the speed of Lemminkäinen."

Of course, at this point in time there isn't even a demon elk, but when the demons hear what Lemminkäinen is up to, they fabricate an elk (Fig. 5.1):[145]

> For the head, a hollow stump,
> For the horns, a fork of sallow;
> Legs of shore-line switches woven,
> Fen-grown saplings for the shanks,
> And a fence rail for a backbone;
> Sinews made of withered grasses,
> Eyes of yellow water lilies
> And the ears of lily pads;
> Made the flesh of rotten wood
> Covered with a skin of spruce bark.

And then the chief evil spirit Hiisi exhorts the goblin reindeer:

> Run now, run you demon's elk!
> Leg it quick, you noble creature
> To the calving grounds of Lapland,
> Where the reindeer drop their young

---

[145] Kalevala 1988.

> On the field of Lapland children.
> Ski this fellow to a sweat;
> Sweat him dry, this Lemminkäinen.
>
> And the chase is on:
> Lemminkäinen, all the while,
> Chasing down the elk of Hiisi,
> Skiing over field and fen
> And across the open clearings.
> From his skis fire was spurting,
> And his ski-stick points were smoking –
> But the elk ran out of sight,
> Out of sight and out of hearing.

The arena of the chase soon becomes larger:

> He skied over hill and hollow
> And the lands beyond the sea,
> Over demon wildernesses,
> Heaths of Kalma, the Grave Spirit,
> And before the mouth of Doom.

Eventually with great effort Lemminkäinen manages to catch the elk:

> Kicking, straining all his muscles,
> He put on a burst of speed:
> With the first kick, out of sight,
> With the second, out of hearing,
> With the third kick, flank to flank;
> Overtook the demon's elk.
>
> But then he begins to brag:
> "Stand there now, you elk of Hiisi;
> Dance, you pretty, prancing reindeer."
> There he stroked the creature's back,
> Smoothing down his handsome hide:
> "There's a soft bed for me here;
> What a smooth pad that, to lie on
> With a sweetheart by my side,
> Sweet young chick just budding out."

Then the elk or reindeer gets angry, breaks the bonds and sets off again. Lemminkäinen who is now fuming with fury takes off again after the elk:

> When he kicked off for the start,
> At the strap the left ski broke,

> Breaking, cracking at the footplate,
> And the right ski at the heel
> As his pole's point popped away.

Soon Lemminkäinen realizes that he will not catch the elk:

> Skiing down the demon's elk
> As did I, unlucky fool!
> I have ruined the best of skis
> And my handsome ski pole too –
> That, the readiest of my spears!

Here is a mythical figure using skis in an attempt to catch a reindeer and covering a huge amount of territory. Note also the unequal length skis, the so-called Central Nordic type, used by Lemminkäinen.

On the other side of the Atlantic in North America among the Algonquian (Wabanaki) Indians, an ancient hunting tribe, is their cultural hero, Gluskabe. The name means something like a man of deceit, which suggests that he possesses trickster characteristics. The myths about Gluskabe come from the Passamaquoddy and Micmac tribes (Kulóskap), from the Malecite tribe (Glúskap), from the Penobscot and Wawenock (Gluskabe), and from the St. Francis Abnaki (Gluskobá).[146] Though these myths were not written down until the nineteenth century, they were part of the oral tradition for millennia. According to the legends, Gluskabe created the earth and taught the Indian tribes. He does not live among them, but each Wabanaki tribe considers its own territory to be the stage where these mythical events took place. Gluskabe is supposed to have arrived from the north in a boat. The hero not only founded the present world order but he transformed the chaos of primordial times into a home that mankind could inhabit. Before his arrival there was only night and darkness; but, he brought the day and light. He slept during the six winter months, then stole summer and defeated the Iceman, thereby tempering winter, and lost an eye in the process (the Norse god Odin gave up one of his eyes in return for a drink from the well of knowledge).[147] He also freed the earth from other monsters and replaced them with animals that could be of use to man. He took these animals and fish and distributed them throughout the world. He tamed dogs and made fire extinguishable and brought the summer north. He was friend and teacher to Indians and taught them how they must live and taught them about supernatural power and how it resided in every living thing.

---

[146] Mechling 1914; Speck 1935; Thompson 1929.

[147] *Poetic Edda: Völuspá*, 1988.

One of his achievements for the benefit of man is of particular interest here: he reduced giant animals to a harmless size. Also, for his various journeys his grandmother, a woodchuck, made a number of travel appurtenances such as a canoe and snowshoes. Here follow some excerpts from some of the tales that Gluskabe is involved in. Before he fixes the rivers and falls he says to his grandmother:

> Now grandmother I am going to travel to search for and transform things so that our descendants will not have such a hard time to exist in the future.[148]

One of his exploits is to chase down and kill the monster moose:

> When Gluskabe started out again in search of other people, he reached a great lake. There the people said "Our village is in great danger from a giant magic moose, for fear of whom we can hardly go hunting. He has killed many of us." "I will search for him," said Gluskabe and destroy him for you. Then he started and reached the yard where the giant moose was and started him running. As he was following the moose suddenly he saw a little bough shelter ahead. Gluskabe followed the moose and on the first day overtook him and killed him.[149]

In another confrontation, Gluskabe's grandmother tells him that many of her descendants have starved to death because of the very hard winter with snow so deep that the treetops were covered. Gluskabe asks where this winter can be found. His grandmother tells him that it's very far away in a place where no one can live and that he would freeze to death if he went there. But Gluskabe says that he would like to try and he asks his grandmother to make snowshoes for him. "Two pairs knotted with caribou, two with deer and two with moose skin."[150] With the aid of the snowshoes, first one pair and then the second and then the last pair, he is able to reach winter. But he is no match for winter and freezes to death and is thrown out by old man winter to lie until spring at which time he wakes up and goes back home. And now Gluskabe comes up with a superior plan, which is to find summer first of all, and, before he departs, his grandmother provides him with seven rolls of rawhide and two pair of snowshoes.

Another tale as told among the Malecite tribe finds the sons of the chief making snowshoes in winter for the moose-hunting season. Glúskap tells his uncle, Turtle, to make snowshoes seven times the span of his hand in length and with fine meshes. Turtle does so and sets out with the others for some moose hunting. He has trouble walking on the snowshoes, falling down every so often and becoming sore. The others want to send Turtle back.

---

[148] Speck 1935: 42.
[149] Speck 1935: 43-44.
[150] Speck 1935: 44.

The narrative continues:

> So they started after the moose and Turtle tried to go too. But he fell down immediately and they passed on their snowshoes right over him. Turtle was way under the snow. He had great difficulty in regaining his feet. Glúskap thought it was time he was doing better. So Turtle started. He jumped over low trees instead of going round them. He passed his brothers-in-law, but they did not recognize him, so fast was he going. They could not even follow his trail, as the steps were too long for them. When they finally overtook him, he had killed and skinned the moose and had cooked dinner for them. They felt very much ashamed when they arrived at the way they had been abusing him.[151]

On the return trip Turtle piled most of the moose on his toboggan. His brothers-in-law said that he couldn't haul so much, but Turtle took a short cut and surprised everyone.

The episode of most concern is the following:

> Once Gluskabe gathered all the different animals about him. He wanted to learn how they would behave toward man. He told them to start and show him what they would do if they should meet a man. All appeared harmless enough just as they were, not strong enough to be dangerous to a man who might be armed. Some of them dug into the ground, others flew about in fear. All behaved according to their ways as we see them now. But then the squirrel, which at that time was as large as a moose is, now rushed up and down trees, dashed across the ground, and used his terrible teeth. And Gluskabe saw at once that he was too agile and ferocious, so he took him in his hands and squeezed him down to his present size, and now the squirrel is one of the most harmless creatures.[152]

Summing up: Gluskabe uses snowshoes rather than the skis that Lemminkäinen used; there were no skis in North American until Norwegian immigrants brought them over in the nineteenth century (or, at least, the knowledge of how to make and use them). Gluskabe chases down a monstrous moose whereas Lemminkäinen chased down an artificial elk. Both of their efforts covered large expanses of area and time. Gluskabe also erased a serious threat to man by reducing the squirrel from a huge beast to its present size. There are a number of similarities between these two myths. The Lemminkäinen portion of the *Kalevala* was, as earlier stated, put together by Elias Lönnroth in the early nineteenth century and the tales of the Algonquian Indians were recorded for the first time in the nineteenth century.

Moving back to the fifth century BCE, the *Odes* of Pindar (522-448) contain a passage of interest. His ode Olympian 3 is as follows:

---

[151] Mechling 1914: 29.
[152] Speck 1935: 49.

> He had set up the holy trial
> In the great Games
> And the feast of the Fourth Year also,
> On Alpheos' holy rocks.
> But in the valley of Kronos' Hill
> The acre of Pelops was not green with beautiful trees:
> Naked of them, the garden seemed to him
> At the mercy of the sun's sharp rays.
> Then did his spirit stir him
> To journey to the land
> Of Ister. There he came
> From Arkadia's ridges and twisting valleys;
> And Lato's daughter, driver of horses,
> Welcomed him, when on the command of Eurystheus
> A doom laid by his father
> Drove him in search of the doe with golden horns,
> Which once Taÿgete offered in her own stead
> Holy to the Orthian Maid.
> In pursuit of it he saw that land
> Behind the blasts of the cold north wind.
> There he stood and marvelled at the trees,
> Sweet desire for them seized him,
> To plant them on the edge of the horses' track
> Where the chariots drive twelve times round.[153]

Reference is made in this ode to one of the Heraclean labors of the dodecathlon in which Heracles reaches the Hyperboreans in his pursuit of the doe with golden horns who is, in fact, the Pleiad, Taÿgete, after she is transformed by Artemis to escape the attentions of Zeus. Heracles' charge is to chase down the Ceryneian hind and to bring it back to Eurystheus alive.

This labor which is in the third or fourth place of the dodecathlon does not sound like a very heroic task compared to, for example, conquering the lion or slaying the hydra. There are various versions of this pursuit of the golden hind. Euripedes says the reindeer was a nuisance to the land, destroying plant life, but a wild pig does much more damage to flora. So this explanation did not work. Others tried to explain the hind as being sacred to the Greek gods so that Heracles had to fight with the gods for the beast, for example, Apollo or Artemis. And this motif is seen on some Greek vases (figs. 5.2-5).[154] Some versions have the hind being killed, others have it brought back alive which would, of course, be a much more

---

[153] Pindar 1947: 77.
[154] Meuli 1975: facing 798; Meuli 1975: facing 799; Meuli 1975: facing 810; Meuli 1975: facing 811.

difficult task. Pindar has Heracles bring the hind back alive. Clearly, the reindeer was not a ferocious beast. The heroic effort involved here is simply equivalent to an early marathon, that is to say, chasing down the hind and killing it. The chase takes roughly a year and covers the areas of Argolis, Arcadia and Elus with the extent gradually widening. These areas are not very far for the Greeks. This was to make the story more understandable to them. But, if the female had horns, it had to have been a reindeer since they are the only members of the deer family with horns. Reindeer have never been found near Greece; therefore, the chase must have gone much further to the north and this fabulous beast must have been a reindeer. Pindar – again the oldest written source – writes that Heracles had to follow the hind from Arcadia's slopes and ravines northward into Istria and past, to the shady source of the Ister and on north beyond the drifts of the cold Boreas, that is, Scythia, in other words to the northern end of the world.

The story of Heracles does not have much in common with the Lemminkäinen and Gluskabe myths already discussed; however, a hero does chase down some sort of reindeer-like animal over a very large area and consumes a large amount of time. Consider now a bronze fibula from the eighth century BCE that shows Heracles killing the Ceryneian hind (Fig. 5.6).[155] A close inspection of this fibula indicates that it is a female because there is a calf sucking from the mother. Furthermore, this female has antlers, and in the deer family, again, only the female reindeer has antlers. In other words, in the very oldest version of this labor of Heracles he is killing a reindeer. There were certainly not any reindeer as far south as Greece during the time of Pindar or the time of the artist who created the bronze fibula. But reports about life further to the north must have reached the Greeks during this period.

Is there any way these three disparate myths can be more closely related? There are myths found among the Finno-Ugric peoples of northern Siberia that provide the link. For the Voguls and the Ostyaks the tale goes as follows:

> At first the elk had six feet with which he ran so fast that no one could catch and kill him. Then mankind asked the son of father heaven to help them. The son made for himself very swiftly moving skis from the wood of the holy tree, chased the elk on them with great speed to the north ocean at the end of the world, and knocked away the third pair of legs. The animal was so large that it covered thirty sandy riverbanks, thirty river courses. Then the hunter spoke to father heaven: "This animal I have killed only with difficulty even though I am an experienced hunter. How then should an ordinary human who is much weaker capture and kill it. As fast and as large as it is, it will on the contrary kill all men however many as there might be. Therefore make it four-footed!" And so it happened. Since then the elk has only four feet and man can hunt it. Its image,

---

[155] Meuli 1975: 798.

though, together with the stumps of the two hacked-off feet is reflected in the ski as the Pleiades, the seven daughters of Atlas, and the snowtracks of the hunter as the Milky Way.[156]

This is again a heroic figure transforming the hostile, primordial world so that it will be inhabitable for ordinary mankind. He reduces in size a very large animal, in this case an elk or a reindeer by removing a pair of legs. The hunt is supposed to have taken place as the god of heaven, Numi-Tarem, created the world. The chase went further and further to the north "where earth and sky meet at their roots;" another version has the chase covering the entire sky before returning to earth, with the animal finally being captured near the Arctic Ocean. The hunter breaks a ski when he lands and continues on one ski. The chase is only successful because a pair of skis is involved. The similarities between the myths looked at are so great that one can postulate a common origin for them. A hunter, chases down some sort of deer-like animal by means of snowshoes or skis, catches the animal and then kills it or reduces it in size so that it won't be such a threat to mankind.[157] This is a genuine circumpolar myth, a myth that is common to all of the indigenous peoples of the circumpolar area.

The Chukchee version of this myth is lengthy and rather confusing, but the following passage contains the main elements of the myth. A man grows lonely for his home country, and his wife tells him to go on a visit:

> She said again, "Here, take it! This is my reindeer with many legs, – a reindeer for flight, for an emergency. Drive it there! If anybody should pursue you, cut off one of its legs, and throw it away. If he should continue to pursue you, cut off another leg; and go on doing so until the reindeer has but four legs left.[158]

And her husband goes on to do just that.

One Sámi creation myth runs as follows:

> The Son of the Sun paying court to the beautiful daughter of a giant. She is enamored of him and asks her father for permission to marry the Son of the Sun. They marry and prepare to return to the Son of the Sun's home. Meanwhile her brothers return from a hunt and are not pleased that she has been married to an outsider. They attempt to catch

---

[156] Kunicke 1940: 43-44; Altheim 1948: 199; Kannisto 1951: 22-28; Altheim 1952: 325-36; Kannisto 1958: 88-90, 192-93, 384-86.

[157] There is a reflection of this myth in Norse mythology when according to Saxo "the hero Starkad, sprung from giants, had many hands. Thor tore four of these off and now his giant's body was contracted and made human." Saxo 1999: 160-61.

[158] Bogoras 1910: 174.

up with their sister on the Son of the Sun's ship. They fail because the giant's daughter is able to increase the strength of the wind three times. The brothers give up and climb a mountain to watch for the Son of the Sun's ship and are turned to stone by the rays of the sun on the following day. The newlyweds marry again, the giant's daughter is transformed into a Sami and she gives birth to the progenitors of the Sami race. Upon their death they are raised to heaven because they were great hunters and because they were the inventors of skis. And they become Orion's belt.[159]

This version of the myth lacks the reduction of a ferocious animal to a more manageable size. It has something similar, though, when the one threat to the newlywed couple is removed, that is, when the brothers of the daughter of the giant are turned to stone.

The impact of this heroic deed was so great that it is reflected in the stars. Among the Finno-Ugric tribes are occasionally seen instead of one hunter a pair of hunters, one with wings and the other going on foot, which is reminiscent of Wayland and his brother Slagfinn (see the next chapter). Sometimes the culture hero is in the shape of an animal. For the Tungus this animal is a bear. And for the Voguls and Ostyaks it can be a wolverine. This also seems to be the case with the Chukchee tribe. Three saddle covers are shown in figs. 5.7[160] and 5.8.[161] A very common motif in Scythian art has a member of the deer family – often an elk – being attacked by another animal, sometimes a cat-like animal, and sometimes an animal with wings. This is clearly a mythical animal and may well be a graphic rendition of the above myth.

Fig. 5.7

The Yakuts refer to the Milky Way as the snowshoe tracks of a hunting hero. And the Golds refer to the Milky Way as the snowshoe tracks of some sort of hero (Fig. 5.9[162] depicts a Gold hunting on skis). In many cases these tribes refer to the Pleiades as either elk, reindeer or deer. On this side of the Atlantic the Eskimos call Ursa Major the heavenly reindeer and the caribou.[163]

Written versions of the tales from the various Finno-Ugric tribes are of relatively recent origins similar to that of the *Kalevala* and the Algonquian Indian tales. However, considering that the Indians of North America came across the Bering Straits some 10,000-25,000

---

[159] Gaski 1997b: 16-19.
[160] Griaznov 1933: Plate II A.
[161] Griaznov 1933: Plate II B.
[162] Meuli 1975: facing 774.
[163] Negelein 1929: 186-87; Harva 1938: 201-03; Werner 1952: 139-41.

years ago and that there are similar myths both in North America and in Eurasia, there must be earlier versions of this myth that are very old. The story of Heracles' labor demonstrates that by taking it back to the eighth century BC.

Fig. 5.8

Skiing During the Viking Age

The Viking era runs from the eighth century when the earliest Viking raids are recorded to 1066 when the Norwegian King Harald the Hardruler lost his life in an attempt to become the ruler of England, bringing to an end Viking expansion overseas. People mostly remember the brutal raids on lands that could be reached by the beautiful Viking ships. Norwegian and Danish Vikings plundered England and Ireland; Swedish Vikings headed east into Russia and eventually reached Constantinople, the heart of the Byzantine empire. But there was much more to this period; many Vikings and their families left Scandinavia permanently and settled abroad in areas such as Iceland, the Faeroe Islands, parts of the British Isles and the Normandy area of France. There is quite a bit of evidence in the literature from this period that the ski and skiing were part of everyday life, not only of the common people but even of kings.

The early Vikings were heathens; they worshiped pagan gods and goddesses such as Odin, Thor, Frey, Tyr, Frigg and Freyja. That these gods were important in the lives of the early Scandinavians can be seen in the fact that four of the English weekday names derive from them: Tuesday < Tyr's Day; Wednesday < Odin's Day; Thursday < Thor's Day; and Friday < Frigg's Day. There was no written literature during much of the Viking period; poetry and tales were handed down orally. At this time, though, Christianity began to exert an influence in the north. Denmark converted in the tenth century, Norway and Iceland in the year 1000, and Sweden in the twelfth century. One of the results of the conversion was that Latin reading and writing became commonplace among clerics and intellectuals. Eventually, the Latin alphabet was used to write down the vernacular languages, and in this fashion much oral literature was preserved.

The case of Iceland is illustrative, especially since the great majority of Viking age literature is in Old Icelandic. Old Icelandic began to be written down in the second quarter of the twelfth century, that is, more than a century after the country had converted to Christianity. Surprisingly, a number of important pagan works were written down and managed to survive in spite of the opposition of the Catholic Church. In fact, most of the evidence for early Germanic religion comes from these Icelandic works. Most important are the *Poetic Edda*,[164] an anonymous collection of poems with mythological, heroic and didactic content, and the *Prose Edda*,[165] a textbook for poets written by the Icelander Snorri Sturluson (1179-1241). Snorri was a great chieftain who served two terms as law speaker at the Alþing (Icelandic Parliament), was involved in a number of bitter disputes, and, who eventually died at the hands of his enemies. The *Prose Edda* is in three parts, a section on Norse mythology, a section on the complicated metaphors whose meanings were beginning to become obscure and a list of the many meters one could write verse in.

Volund

The first ski example is found in the Lay of Volund from the *Poetic Edda*.[166] This is one of the great tales of revenge in early Germanic literature and was very popular throughout the Germanic world. It is mentioned in the Old English *Deor's lament*,[167] and two scenes from the story are depicted on the Franks Casket (Fig. 6.1)[168] that could be as old as the seventh century CE. Volund (Engl. Wayland) is a master smith who has two brothers, Egil, a sharpshooter, and Slagfinn. About the brothers who are the sons of a Finnish king it says: "they skied and hunted game." The brothers who live in the country near a lake meet three beautiful valkyries one day. A *valkyrie* [literally, chooser of the slain] was a battle maiden who assisted Odin by being present at battles and picking out warriors brave enough to go to the Germanic heaven, Valhalla. The brothers fall in love: Volund marries Hervor the Allwise, Egil wins Olrun, and Slagfinn marries Hladgud the Swanwhite; the couples spend eight happy winters together. The valkyries, though, long to return to battle and are gone one day when the brothers come back from their hunting. Egil and Slagfinn take off on skis in search of their brides, while Volund stays at home and practices his craft, hoping Hervor will come back. The evil king Nidud learns about Volund's treasure, has him captured, hamstrings him and forces him to produce treasures for the king's family. Volund gains his revenge by

---

[164] 1988. Tr. Lee Hollander.
[165] 1954. Tr. Jean I. Young.
[166] *Poetic Edda* 1988: 159-67.
[167] *Beowulf*: 98-99.
[168] Wilson 1980: 30.

killing the king's two sons and turning their skulls into bejeweled treasures and by raping his daughter. Volund is referred to as "king of elves" and "leader of elves" in the lay. Elves were divine beings in Norse mythology that resembled ordinary people, were usually small of stature and they were outstanding craftsmen. Elves, in other words, were a reflection of the common people of the period during which the legend arose. Among other things this suggests that hunting in Scandinavia during the winter required the use of skis. Finally, it should be mentioned that a number of translators of this poem have mistranslated the Old Icelandic word *skríða* as "to snowshoe." Snowshoes, which were replaced in Scandinavia by skis very early on, were not used there for hunting.

Ull

More importantly, there were a god and goddess of skiing, Ullr and Skaði respectively (figs. 6.2)[169]. Consider first Ullr since he seems to be a very ancient figure in the Norse pantheon. In the *Prose Edda* Snorri has:

> Ull, Siv's son and Thor's stepson is one [god]. He is such a good archer and ski-runner that no one can rival him. He is beautiful to look at as well and he has all the characteristics of a warrior. It is also good to call on him in duels.[170]

Later on Ullr is mentioned as one of the twelve Æsir who had to be judges. The Lay of Grimnir (possibly from the tenth century) of the *Poetic Edda* is a didactic poem whose purpose is to give instruction in mythology.[171] The evil king Geirroeth tortures Grimnir (Odin in disguise) in an effort to get him to speak. Finally, Geirroeth's young son Agnar gives Grimnir something to drink whereupon he speaks and, among other things, explains where the various gods have their dwellings: "On Ydal's plains Ull hath reared him his hall timbered on high."[172] Ydal means "yew dales" which tallies well with Ullr's role as god of hunting, for the best bows were made out of the wood of the yew tree. Later in the same poem Grimnir says:

> Will Ull befriend him, and all the gods, who first the fire quenches; for open lie to the Æsir all worlds, when kettles are heaved from the hearth.[173]

Although the exact meaning of this stanza is not clear, Grimnir is thanking Agnar for the drink.

---

[169] *På skidor* 1929: 8.

[170] *Prose Edda* 1954: 55.

[171] *Poetic Edda* 1988: 53-64.

[172] *Poetic Edda* 1988: 55.

[173] *Poetic Edda* 1988: 62.

In another *Poetic Edda* lay, the Atlakviða, Gudrun speaks with her husband Atli:

> May it go with thee, Atli, as to Gunnar thou swearest
> with holiest oaths, oft and anon,
> by the southward sun and by Sigtýr's cliff
> by his steed-of-ease and by Ull's temple-ring.[174]

The use of an oath-ring is well attested among the Scandinavians. Dumézil suggests that Ullr represents the majestic aspect of the god, replacing Óðinn as king when the latter is in disgrace (cf. the following on Ollerus). Óðinn is the breaker of troth. Ullr as his opposite is the upholder of good faith, and, thus, an oath sworn on his ring would be the strongest pledge of loyalty.

Ull in Denmark

Saxo Grammaticus (ca. 1150-ca. 1220), Denmark's first important historian, wrote a book in Latin called *Gesta Danorum* in which he discussed Danish history from its legendary origins down to his own time. In it he has a story about Ull whom he calls Ollerus. Odin is sent into exile from the headquarters of the gods (Saxo calls it Byzantium, but he undoubtedly means Asgard where the Norse gods live) for having desecrated his divinity. In his place, the gods elect Ollerus as his successor; in fact, they even call him Odin. After ten years in exile the real Odin clears his tarnished reputation – some say by bribing his fellow gods with gold – and drives Oller (Ollerus) out of Byzantium whereupon he:

> After Oller had been expelled from Byzantium by Odin, he retired to Sweden where, as if in a new world, he strove to restore recognition of his fame, but the Danes killed him. According to one tale he was such a cunning magician that instead of sailing in a ship he was able to cross the seas on a bone which he had engraved with fearful charms, and skimmed the waves that rose before him as swiftly as with oars.[175]

Since Denmark is too low and too far south for there to be any significant skiing, the bone referred to is certainly a pair of ice skates.

Ull Place Names

Ull appears in many place names from Sweden and southeastern Norway, e.g. Ultuna, Ulleråker, Ullånger, Ullvi, etc. and others from the other form of his name, Ullin, as in Ullensvang and Ullensaker. The large number of place names suggests that Ull was an import-

---

[174] *Poetic Edda* 1988: 291.
[175] Saxo 1999.

ant deity in those areas. The second elements in the compound names above (åker = field; vang = meadow; tun = yard surrounded by farm buildings) show that he was worshiped to help the harvest. The place names also seem to be areas where there was plenty of snow during the winter and good hunting conditions, where skis were the primary winter means of transportation and communication, and where the bow and arrow was the principal hunting weapon. Ull does not play a major role in the Norse mythology of the Viking period; he belonged to an older stratum of deities whose star had declined. Away from the snow Ull was more generally a god of hunting. He may once have been a sky god since his name is related to a Gothic word for "glory, splendor." It has even been suggested that he was the chief god at an earlier stage.

Ull and the Shield

There are a number of skaldic kennings (kenning = a metaphorical, compound expression substituting for the name of something) involving Ull. A shield can be referred to as Ull's ship and this by some of the earliest skaldic poets of the tenth century. Skalds were members of the courts of Norwegian kings from the ninth to the fourteenth centuries. Since there was no writing at this time, skalds helped to record the feats of kings, and what they said in their poetry was believable. They could not praise a king for something he did not do; that would have been embarrassing.

Some examples of Ull kennings: Einarr skálaglamm uses *Ullar askr* around 950 CE (Ull's ash, because ships were once built out of ash)[176]; Eyvindr skaldaspillir uses *Ullar kjóll* a few years later (Ull's 'keel' or ship)[177]; Sturla Thórðarson uses *Ullar far* in the thirteenth century (Ull's ship).[178] This kenning has been confusing to many scholars. Though the word for shield occurs frequently in a number of expressions for sun, warrior, sword, valkyrie, and so on, it is not used as an expression for a ship. It may simply be that Ull had a ship called Shield. In Saxo above it was seen that Ull used a bone on which he had written magic runes to cross the sea. And in *Beowulf* Scyld, the eponymous ancestor of the Scyldings, arrives as a little child from the sea, and after his death he departs in the same fashion on a ship laden with treasure. The name Scyld means shield, so that as in the case of Ull a divine figure is associated with a shield.

During the Bronze Age a shield-like disk is associated with the sun, so Ull worship may be very old. A third century scabbard was found in a bog at Torsbjerg on the east Slesvig

---

[176] Kock 1947: I 66.
[177] Kock 1947: I 40.
[178] Kock 1947: II 62.

coast of Denmark that has the following runic inscription: *Owlthuthewar*. This has been interpreted as meaning Ull's man or Ull's servant, and if this interpretation is correct, it is evidence of very early Ull worship and the first literary evidence of a purely Scandinavian god name. One scholar has suggested that it is Ull who appears on the famous Gallehus horn from the fifth century. An archer is depicted three times, once near figures that could be interpreted as Thor and Siv which, if true, would affirm Ull's role as archer supreme and as the son of Siv and stepson of Thor (Fig. 6.3).[179] It has also been suggested that the names Frey and Ull appear on the Sparlösa rune stone.

Skaði

The ski goddess Skaði (Fig. 6.4)[180] is alluded to in an early skaldic poem. Bragi Boddason is the first skaldic poet we have any knowledge of. He lived in southwest Norway possibly as early as the first half of the ninth century. He received a shield from Ragnar – who may be the famous Ragnar of the Hairy Breeches – and wrote a poem about the pictures on the shield which is called *Ragnarsdrápa* or *Ragnar's Poem*. In it the following line appears:

> Hinn es varp á víða
> vinda ǫndurdísar
> of manna sjǫt margra
> mundlaug fǫður augum.[181]

The Old Icelandic original is included here to show how complicated yet beautiful the structure of Skaldic poetry is. Alliteration or initial rhyme is the basic principle. Each pair of half-lines forms an alliterative long line with two or three alliterating syllables. In the first two half-lines above the *v* alliterates in *varp*, *víða*, and *vinda*; in the last two half-lines it is the *m* in *manna*, *margra* and *mundlaug*. The alliteration has three functions: emphasizing emotionally important elements; serving as a mnemonic device; and helping to make structural divisions in the poem. Because Old Icelandic is such a highly inflected language, there is a great deal of syntactic freedom, especially in the poetry. In other words, two words that normally go together in English such as a noun and its modifier might be several lines apart in Old Icelandic. Therefore, it will be useful to rearrange the words syntactically so that they make sense in the English translation:

---

[179] Wilson 1980: 130.
[180] *På skidor* 1929: 14.
[181] Kock 1947: I 3.

Hinn es varp augum	He who threw the eyes
fǫður ǫndurdísar	of the father of the ski goddess
á víða mundlaug vinda	into the wide basin of the winds
of sjǫt margra manna.	over the abode of many men.

An explanation of this puzzling line is found in Snorri's *Edda*.[182] Odin, Loki and Hoenir were out traveling one day and killed an ox for their dinner. The meat would not cook. Then they noticed an eagle in a tree that told them that if they shared the meat it would get done. They agreed whereupon the eagle took most of the ox for itself. Loki became angry, grabbed a large stick and thrust it into the eagle's body. The eagle flew into the air with Loki dangling from one end of the stick and being dragged over the rocks. The eagle would release Loki only if he promised to bring the goddess Idun to the eagle. Idun possessed the golden apples that the gods needed to preserve their youthful appearance. Later on Loki lured Idun out of Asgard so that the giant Thjazi in the shape of an eagle was able to fly away with her to his house in Thrymheim (storm-home). The gods now began to age and suspected that Loki had something to do with it. They tortured him until he agreed to try and bring Idun back. He borrowed Freyja's falcon coat and flew to Giantland. Thjazi was away from home, so Loki was able to change Idun into a nut and fly back with her. When Thjazi discovered that she was missing, he changed into his eagle shape and went after Loki. When the gods saw Loki coming with the nut and with the eagle in pursuit, they readied a bonfire they lit after Loki reached Asgard. The eagle was unable to stop and his feathers caught fire. The gods attacked and killed him. Thjazi's daughter, Skaði, donned her armor and headed for Asgard to avenge her father's killing. The gods offered her compensation. First of all, they would let her select a husband from among a lineup of the gods where she could only see the feet. Secondly, Odin offered to take Thjazi's eyes and throw them up into the sky making stars of them. Now Bragi's meaning becomes clear: Odin who threw Thjazi's (Skaði's father) eyes into the heaven over the earth… And, finally, the gods had to make her laugh which she thought was impossible. However, the mischievous Loki tied a string around his penis and tied the other end to a billy goat's beard. Then the two of them danced and shrieked until Loki fell into Skaði's lap whereupon she laughed.

Skaði and Njord

As for the choice of a husband, Skaði hoped to win Baldr who was generally agreed to be

---

[182] *Prose Edda* 1954:

the fairest of the gods. She selected a beautiful pair of feet and ended up not with Baldr but with Njord who was god of the sea and the father of Frey and Freyja. Snorri tells the story of their marriage: "Skaði wanted to have the homestead her father had had, on some mountains in the place called Thrymheim, but Njord wanted to be near the sea. They came to an agreement that they should be nine nights in Thrymheim and then another nine at Nóatún (Njord's home). When Njord came back to Nóatún from the mountains, however, he said this:[183]

> I am weary of the mountains –
> I was not long there
> only nine nights:
> the howling of wolves
> seemed dreadful to me
> compared to the song of swans.

Then Skaði said this:

> I could not sleep
> in the beds of the sea
> because of the cry of the birds:
> it wakes me
> when from the ocean comes
> each morning: the gull.

Then Skaði went up the mountains and lived in Thrymheim, and she goes about a great deal on skis and with her bow and arrow shoots wild animals. She is called the Ski goddess, or Ski divinity. As it is said:

> Thrymheimr is called the place
> where Thjazi lived,
> he the very powerful giant,
> and now Skaði resides,
> the clear bride of the god,
> at the old site of her father.

This tale of marital problems cannot be older than the transformation of Njord to a male god. In Tacitus, Njord is, in fact, the goddess Nerthus who is worshiped in Denmark. Njord and the other Vanir gods are fertility gods, and they often appear in male-female pairs, e.g. Frey/Freyja; Njord/Nerthus; perhaps even Ull/Ullin. That Skaði was worshiped is shown by the place name Skadevi (Skaði's sacred place) in Uppland, Sweden. Some scholars even derive the name Scandinavia from Skaði's island.

---

[183] *Prose Edda* 1954:

Skaði and Skaldic Metaphors

Another early skaldic poem makes reference to Skaði. Þjóðólfr of Hvinir was a skaldic poet at the court of Harald the Fairhaired (860-933), the king who unified Norway by giving other petty kings the choice of either submitting to his rule or leaving the country. In Þjóðólfr's poem *Haustlǫng* the following verse occurs:[184]

> Þá varð fastr við fóstra
> farmr Sigvinjar arma,
> sás ǫll regin eygja,
> ǫndurgoðs, í bǫndum.
> Límði rǫ við ramman
> reimuð Jǫtunheima,
> enn holls vinar Hœnis
> hendr við stangar enda.

Rearranging the syntactic order of the words leads to:

Þa varð farmr	then became the contents
arma Sigvinjar	of the arms of Sigyn
fastr við	attached to the foster-father
ǫndurgoðs	of the ski god,
sás ǫll regin eygja í bǫndum.	he whom all the gods see in bonds.
Límði rǫ	Stuck the staff
við ramman reimuð	to the strong hunter
Jǫtunheima,	of Jotunheim,
enn hendr	but the hands
holls vinar Hoenis	of the faithful friend of Hoenir
við enda stangar.	[held] onto the end of the pole.

This is another conundrum that Snorri's *Edda* helps explain. Sigyn is Loki's wife, so the "contents of her arms" is Loki. The foster-father of the ski god is Thjazi, the father of Skaði. In other words, Loki became attached to Thjazi (when he thrust a stick into him while he was in the shape of an eagle). And it is Loki whom all the gods see in bonds just before Ragnarǫk. Loki was directly responsible for the death of the god Baldr and is put in bonds by the gods, and:

> Skaði took a poisonous snake and fastened it up over him so that the venom from it should drop on to his face. His wife Sigyn, however, sits by him holding a basin up under the poison drops. When the basin becomes full she goes away to empty it, but in the meantime the venom drips on to his face and then he shudders so violently that the whole earth shakes – you call that an earthquake. There he will lie in bonds until

---

[184] Kock 1947: I 10.

Ragnarǫk.[185]

The strong hunter of Jotunheim is Thjazi, and Hœnir's faithful friend is Loki, so the second part of the stanza says that Loki is hanging onto the stick.

In the tenth century *Háleygjatal*, a poem about the Lade earls, Eyvindr skaldaspillir "spoiler of skalds," so named because he supposedly plagiarized at the court of Hákon the Good (who ruled from 933-61) without improving what he borrowed, has the following:[186]

Þann skaldblœtr
skattfœri gat
ása niðr
við jarnviðju,
þás þau meir
í Manheimum,
skatna vinr
ok Skaði, byggðu.
…
sævar beins,
ok sunu marga
ǫndurdís
við Óðni gat.

Rearranging the syntactic order yields:

gat ása niðr	begat the descendant of the gods,
skattfoeri	worshipped by skalds,
Þann skaldblœtr	this treasure-bringer
við jarnviðju,	with the troll woman of Ironwood,
þás þau skatna vinr ok Skaði,	when they, the friend of treasure and Skaði,
meir í Manheimum byggðu	were living more in the world of men
…	
beins sævar,	of sea-bones,
ok marga sunu	and many sons
ǫndurdís við Óðni.	had the ski goddess with Óðin.

Odin is both the descendent of the gods and the friend of treasure, so he and Skaði have produced a child while living in the world of men. The sea-bones are rocks, and, of course, the ski goddess is Skaði. Perhaps after her ill-fated marriage to Njord, Skaði found happiness with Odin who himself was married to Frigg.

---

[185] *Prose Edda* 1954:
[186] Kock 1947: I

Skaði and Loki

In the *Lokasenna* (The Flyting of Loki) of the *Poetic Edda* Loki is present at a feast with all the gods save Thor. The gods praised Ægir's servants who were bringing everyone ale. Loki did not like to hear the praise and slew one of the servants after which he was kicked out of the banquet. But, with Odin's intercession he returned to the banquet and proceeded to accuse the gods, one by one, of seamy behavior. Here is his exchange with Skaði:[187]

> S: Wanton Loki, you won't much longer feel your tail free: the gods will use your cold son's guts to bind you to a boulder.
>
> L: Perhaps the gods will take Nari's guts and bind me to a boulder, but when it came to killing Thjazi, I was first and foremost.
>
> S: If, when it came to killing Thjazi, you were first and foremost, from my house and holy temples you'll have cold counsel.
>
> L: You spoke more sweetly to Laufey's son when you lay beside me in bed. There's a tale well worth the telling, if we're all to air our faults!

Nari is Loki's son, and Loki himself is the son of Laufey.

The Ski in Ship Metaphors

One Old Icelandic word for ski is *skíð* and it is frequently used in skaldic kennings for ships. The first example is a verse spoken by Skarpheðin in a confrontation with Hallgerð, two of the main characters in *Njálssaga*. The family sagas are works of fiction written by mostly known authors mainly in the thirteenth century but based on events supposed to have taken place in the tenth and eleventh centuries. The saga authors used earlier written works, oral tradition and their knowledge of contemporary thirteenth century Iceland as sources. Skarpheðin's verse would have been created around 995. It goes as follows:[188]

> Auk munu, elda síka,
> orð þín mega, skorða,
> – gjarn seðk úlf ok ǫrnu –
> ekki flessum rekkum.
> Hornkerling ert – Hernar
> hrings víðs freka skíða
> Baldr semr Óðins ǫldu –
> útigangs eða púta.

---

[187] *Poetic Edda* 1988:
[188] *Brennu-Njáls Saga* 1954: 478-79.

Rearranging the syntactic order yields:

Auk, skorða elda síka,	And, support of the fire of trenches,
orð þín munu mega ekki	your words will be able to do nothing
flessum rekkum –	to these men –
seðk gjarn úlf ok ǫrnu.	I feed gladly wolf and eagle.
Ert hornkerling	You are a corner hag
eða útigangs púta.	and an outside whore.
Baldr skíða	Baldr of the skis
víðs hrings Hernar	of the wide ring of Hern
semr freka ǫldu Óðins.	composes harsh waves of Odin.

Support of the fire of trenches is a kenning for woman, i.e. gold, the fire of trenches, is supported by a woman on her arm (rings). Baldr of the skis of the wide ring of Hern is a kenning for Skarpheðin himself and works as follows: Baldr = lord; ring of Hern = sea; skis of the wide sea = ships; lord of ships = I, or Skarpheðin. The waves of Odin are poetry. Thus, the entire verse means: And, woman, your words will have no effect on these men – I will gladly satiate the wolf and eagle [by providing them with carrion]. You are a corner hag and a street whore. I compose harsh poetry.

Another verse from *Njálssaga* is spoken by Steinunn Refsdóttir to the priest Thangbrand as she tries to convert him to paganism around 999:[189]

Þórr brá Þvinnils dyri
Þangbrands ór stað lǫngu,
hristi búss ok beysti
barðs ok laust við jǫrðu.
Munat skíð of sæ síðan
sundfœrt Atals grundar,
hregg þvít hart tók leggja
hónum kent í spǫnu.

Rearranging the word order results in:

Þórr brá	Thor caused
lǫngu dyri Þvinnils Þangbrands	Thangbrand's long animal of Thvinnill
ór stað,	to move from its moorings,
hristi ok beysti búss barðs	shook and shattered the wood of the prow
ok laust við jǫrðu.	and struck it against the ground.
Skíð Atals grundar	The ski of Atall's green fields
munat sundfœrt of sæ síðan,	will no longer be able to swim in the sea,
þvít hart hregg –	for a hard storm –
kent hónum	attributed to him –
tók leggja í spǫnu.	began to break [it] into pieces.

[189] Kock 1947: II 71.

The animal of Thvinnill (a sea-king) is a ship; the wood of the prow is also a ship; and the green fields of Atall (another sea-king) are the sea, so that the ski of the sea is a ship. The meaning is then: Thor caused Thangbrand's long ship to move from its moorings, shook and shattered the ship, and struck it aground. The ship will no longer be seaworthy, for a hard storm – attributed to him (Thor) – began to break it to pieces.

One further example uses another Old Icelandic word for ski in a kenning for ship, viz. ǫndur. Here Gunnlaug Serpent Tongue who lived from ca. 984-1011 says the following:[190]

> Rœkik lítt, þótt leiki
> – létt veðr es nú – þéttan
> austanvindr at ǫndri
> andness viku þessa.
> Meir séumk hitt, an hæru
> hoddstríðandi bíðit,
> orð, at eigi verðak
> jafnrǫskr talið Hrafni.

Rearranging the word order leads to:

Rœkik lítt –	I care little –
es létt veðr nú –	it is nice weather now –
þótt austanvindr leiki þéttan	though the east wind plays continually
at ǫndri andness þessa viku.	with the ski of the headland this week.
Meir séumk hitt orð	I fear more the comment
at eigi verðak	that I will not be
jafnrǫskr talið Hrafni	counted equally bold as Hrafn
an hoddstríðandi	than that the harmer of treasure
bíðit hæru.	will not attain gray hair.

Ski of the headland refers to a ski that slides around the headland or a ship. The treasure destroyer is Gunnlaug himself; he destroys the treasure by giving it away. Thus, the whole verse means: I don't mind that the east wind is continually playing with the ship this week. I fear more the comment that I am not counted as bold as Hrafn than that I don't attain gray hair. Since he lost his life when he was in his twenties, Gunnlaug did not have to worry about gray hair! Many more examples of kennings for ships using the words for ski could be cited. These examples imply that skis were in widespread use during the Viking period.

Legendary Origin of Norway

The *Flateyjarbók*, which is mostly a compilation of kings' sagas, was assembled by the Ice-

---
[190] Quirk 1957: 25.

landic clergymen Jón Þórðarson and Magnús Þórhallsson in 1390. It contains a legendary version of how Norway was settled and the origin of the kings' families whether in Norway or elsewhere. The author mentions such eminent families as the Budlungs, Bragnings, Odlings, Volsungs and Niflungs which are familiar from the legendary era before the Viking period. It says that Jokul (glacier) was the father of Snær (snow), and that Snær's children were Thorri (the fourth winter month), Faunn (snow), Drifa (snowdrift) and Mioll (fresh, powder snow):

> Thorri was an excellent king. He ruled over Gotland, Kvenland and Finland. He performed a sacrifice to the Kvens so that snow would come and that there would be good skiing conditions. That is their harvest. This sacrifice was to be performed in the middle of winter, and from then on it was called Thorri's month. King Thorri had three children. His sons were Norr and Gorr and Goi his daughter... Norr had a great battle to the west of the Keel (range of mountains running north-south between Norway and Sweden) and killed there the kings named Vee, Vei, Hunding and Heming, and he conquered all the land to the sea.[191]

In other words, Thorri ruled over an area that would correspond to Sweden, Finland and northern Norway. His son Norr conquers the land to the west that becomes Norr-way (north-way, Norway). This story is, of course, no more and no less than a legend.

---

[191] *Flateyjarbók* 1860: 21-22.

The Technological Evolution of the Ski

The evolution of the ski – and other skiing equipment – from its creation in the late Stone Age to the middle of the nineteenth century when the sport of skiing was alive and expanding in Scandinavia and already on its way to conquering the world, is a fascinating story. As has been suggested earlier, the ski came into existence when the gliding motion was added to a pair of solid wooden snowshoes. These snowshoes may have had a fur covering to facilitate gliding forward and to prevent backsliding when going up an incline.

The most likely area of origin is in central Asia near Lake Baikal. This conclusion was arrived at on distributional grounds: when the various traits or improvements of snowshoes and skis are mapped, some traits appear exclusively in the center of the map. These traits are assumed to be of relatively recent origin in that they have not had time to spread more widely. Other traits – perhaps more primitive – are seen almost exclusively at the periphery; this would suggest that they are older in that they have had much longer to spread from the area of origin. One assumes, first of all, that primitive snowshoes were created out of expediency in areas where people had to get about during those times of the year when there was significant snow cover. The circumpolar forest belt or taiga was one such area. Eventually three main types of snowshoes evolved: 1) bearpaw, with outside frame and some kind of filling in the middle; 2) ladder, with parallel boards intersecting other parallel boards at a right angle; and 3) solid wooden snowshoes. It would have been impossible to glide on the first two types. The solid wooden snowshoe was probably round to begin with but gradually became more oblong, longer and narrower. This would have made it easier to attach the leg skin of a reindeer to the bottom.

Soon Stone Age hunters in central Asia were gliding or "skiing" on these devices. And since they were vastly superior to what preceded them in terms of facilitating winter hunting, they began to spread both east toward the Bering Straits and on across, west toward northwest Europe and south to northern Japan and Korea. The map seen earlier (Fig. A3.36) shows that solid wooden snowshoes are found at the periphery in, for example, Norway and northeastern North America. There was no skiing in North America until Norwegian immigrants brought knowledge about skis with them in the nineteenth century. In other words, the solid wooden snowshoe that crossed the Bering Straits was not a ski but a snowshoe used as other snowshoes to walk on the snow.

How old are skis? There is no archaeological record of old snowshoes, but physical evidence of skis goes back more than 8,700 years as seen in Chap. 3. In the case of the Salla ski, which is one of the older ones, there are features that are relatively advanced technologically. It has a raised, indented footstep with horizontal binding hole beneath, a much more durable binding than other early types. And it had five parallel, possibly natural grooves on the bottom that helped the ski steer straight. The earliest skis must go back even further with a ^{14}C date of cal BCE 6828-6589 for what may be the oldest find yet. It is not known exactly when, but the ski was probably invented in the late Stone Age, perhaps as much as ten thousand years ago.

Southern and Arctic Ski Types

On the basis of primitive features the Southern and Arctic skis (Types **B** and **A** respectively) are probably earliest. The Southern, of which the Riihimäki bog ski is an example, is characterized by a lowered footrest (Chap. 3, figs. 3.5-9). Horizontal holes went through the side edges to accommodate a leather strap for the binding. This was, to begin with, exclusively a toe binding. Instead of a lowered footrest, side edges came to be attached to the ski with nails; many more recent specimens show this. The Southern ski was usually cut off at the back, was flat on top and bottom, had no grooves and did not have a fur covering. There were often holes through the tips to which steering ropes could be attached (Fig. 7.1).[192] K. B. Wiklund suggested that the inspiration for the lowered footrest originally came from the dugout canoe, but there is no way to affirm this hypothesis.[193]

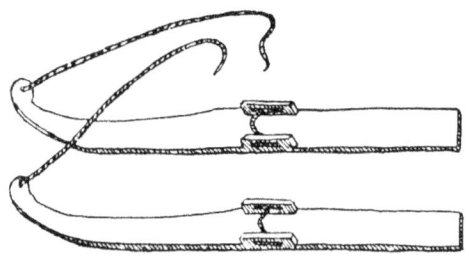

Fig. 7.1

The Arctic ski, found among circumpolar peoples from northern Scandinavia to the Pacific, had as its main feature the four vertical holes through the ski for the binding straps

---

[192] Wiklund 1931: 28.
[193] Wiklund 1933.

(Chap. 3, figs. 3.1-4). In this way the strap bound the toe and heel, a more secure binding. Though the earliest example of an Arctic ski, the Kalvträsk ski, was cut off at the back, all other examples are pointed front and rear so that the bottom could more easily be fur-covered. Another difference between Southern and Arctic ski types was one of function: the areas in which the Arctic skis were used had heavy snow cover during much of the year; areas where the Southern skis predominated generally did not have so much snow to contend with. The Arctic ski was hence wider than the Southern (Fig. 7.2).[194] It is, of course, conceivable that the Arctic ski evolved from a Southern type because a better binding was needed for the heavier snow cover. But the vertical binding arrangement made a fur covering almost mandatory; otherwise the binding straps on the bottom of the ski would have impeded the glide. The fur-covered bottom would have been more efficient in heavy snow as well.

Scandic Ski Type

With the help of bog skis it is possible to trace the further evolution of ski types. The first improved ski is the Scandic type (Type **C 2 a**), which combines the width of the Arctic variety with an improvement on the Southern variety's binding. The Southern lowered footrest was replaced by a raised and indented footrest with a horizontal hole running crosswise through the entire ski. This provided an inherently stronger binding. The Scandic ski (Chap. 3, figs. 3.16-21) became wider like the Arctic variety, and there are steering rims on the bottom of the ski running along the edges. These were the no doubt forerunners of the grooves that help a ski run straight. The long ski in some pairs of Norwegian unequal-length skis had a steering groove, and there are Norwegian dialect words for groove, for example [e:l], that, according to some scholars, were borrowed into Sámi and Finnish around the beginning of the Christian era. That theory has been subsequently rejected.[195] Grooves will be discussed below.

Central Nordic Ski Type

This type actually refers to a pair of skis of different lengths, a long left ski with grooves used for gliding, and a short right ski – usually fur-covered – used for pushing (Ch. 3, Fig. 3.24). They were found in the central Nordic mountain plateau region of Norway, Sweden

---

[194] *På skidor* 1936: 347.
[195] Dalen 1997: 5, 9.

and Finland where the slopes were not too steep and in the reindeer forests of northern Sápmi.[196] If one pictures a scooter or a coaster wagon where the left foot or knee is in the vehicle gliding along while the right foot pushes against the ground to keep it going, one can see how unequal length skis work. This ski type seems to have originally been a combination of the Scandic and Arctic types (Types **C 2 a** and **A**), the former becoming the long left ski and the latter becoming the fur-covered, short right ski (or the pattern could be reversed if a person's left leg were stronger).[197] There was even a special name for the short right ski, *ǫndurr* in Old Icelandic and *andur* in Norwegian dialect; this word has already been encountered in Skaldic verse. There are several possible etymologies for the word, but most likely it is related to the prefix *and-* which means "facing" as in Norwegian *andlet* "face."[198] The word was borrowed into Finnish as *antura* meaning "sole." The word refers to the hairs on the fur covering which "faced" or pointed backward so that the ski could glide forward but which provided friction against the snow when pushing. In the beginning, the difference in length was considerable with the long ski up to nine feet in length, but they gradually became more equal in length. This is the ski type that became the standard among the military as will be seen in Chap. 9.

Wiklund claimed that unequal length skis were unknown outside of Scandinavia and that they were, in fact, an original Norwegian-Swedish invention.[199] One of the problems with this theory is that one would have to assume that the short, fur-covered ski was invented independently in two separate areas, which is highly unlikely. Tomasson offered a different theory as to how unequal length skis came about.[200] The Sámi discovered that a natural groove was produced in the heartwood, *tjur*, of a special kind of fir tree. See below under Making Skis for details. This led to a heavy left ski, *kuovte*, for spring work in the reindeer forests – 9 to 13 pounds. It was then important to have a much lighter right ski, *pietsek* or *träuka*, to go along with the *kuovte*. It could be fur-covered or not, could even be made of *tjur*, as long as it was shorter and lighter than the *kuovte*. In other words, Tomasson saw unequal length skis and grooves as evolving naturally together with the discovery of *tjur*.[201]

---

[196] Dalen 1997: 4.
[197] Jirlow 1935: 44.
[198] Dalen 1997: 7.
[199] Tomasson 1928a: 15.
[200] Tomasson 1928b: 23-24.
[201] Tomasson 1928b: 23-24.

Bothnic Ski Type

The Bothnic ski (Type **C 1 b**), known exclusively from bog finds, is a descendant of the Scandic and Arctic ski types. It is relatively somewhat shorter than the Scandic, narrows at front and back ends, and is convex on the bottom (Chap. 3, Figs. 3.11-12). It has the raised and indented footrest of the Scandic type to accommodate the leather binding strap. It was concave on top at the footrest so as to fit a moccasin-type shoe. Bothnic skis could be ornamented as some of the examples in chapter 7 illustrate (Chap. 3, figs. 3.13-15)). None of the Bothnic-type bog skis are older than 0 CE and all were found in the areas of Sámi settlement in northern Norway, Swedish Norrland and northern Finland. The map in Fig. 7.3 shows where Bothnic skis were found.[202] The Bothnic ski evolved into the South Lapp ski found in areas of Sámi settlement into the present century (Chap. 3, Fig. 3.28). It was lancet-shaped, had a concave bottom, and had the raised, indented footrest that was also concave to fit the moccasin.

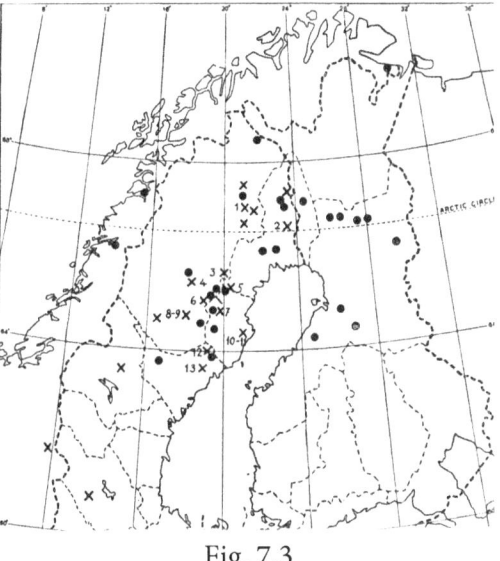

Fig. 7.3

Equal Length Skis and Withe Bindings

In areas of western and southwestern Norway with steeper, hillier terrain equal length skis became the norm. These skis seem to have evolved out of the Scandic type and tended to be much narrower. They did have the horizontal hole running across the entire ski, but the hole was larger so that another type of binding could be used. Most of the skis looked at so far made use of leather straps for bindings. Leather was readily available and quite durable if taken care of, but it tended to stretch. The other binding was made of osiers or withes. An osier is any variety of willow (or birch) tree whose pliable twigs are used for basketry, furniture, etc. The withe was, in other words, a flexible, slender osier twig that was used to bind something, in this case the ski boot to the ski. According to Vaage the Anumark bog ski from Västerbotten, Sweden that dates from cal BCE 970 shows traces of withes.[203] He concludes that the withe binding is just as old as the leather binding. The withe had the

---

[202] Manker 1957: 181.
[203] Vaage 1969: 230.

advantage of being a much stiffer binding which in turn allowed some degree of control of the ski. The main disadvantage was that they were not very durable and could break at any time. The skier had to carry along a supply of withes so as not to get stuck without a binding. Woodcutters and trappers who had to get into and out of their skis quickly used withes up to the present century. Sometimes there were two withe loops in front with the back one bent down to go between sole and heel (Fig. 7.4).[204] Withe bindings worked especially well with softer boots or moccasins.

Some equal length skis have been found with nail holes at the tip. These holes were not necessarily for steering ropes; rather, when these skis were being made they were nailed together so that the skis could be made the same size.[205] These skis were usually made of hardwood, which provided more tension or camber at the center. No ski was more useless than one that turned up at the front and back so that all the weight was on the middle of the ski. The heartwood of pine was a good choice, especially that from a bent pine tree – which provided a natural curve at the front – or from the side of the tree facing north.[206] Such skis were very durable and kept their shape, but they were also brittle. This meant that they had to be thicker at the middle and often had a ridge running from the footrest to the front and back of the ski. The ridge meant that the ski was thicker at the footrest, normally the weakest point, and it helped prevent warping. Equal length skis were the type used in Telemark in Norway, from where they spread toward the end of the nineteenth century to all areas of the world where there is now skiing.

Bindings

Two distinct types of bindings have been mentioned so far, leather straps or thongs and withes. These two types could be used together in various combinations. Some skis had only a leather toe strap; others had leather thongs attached to the toe strap and

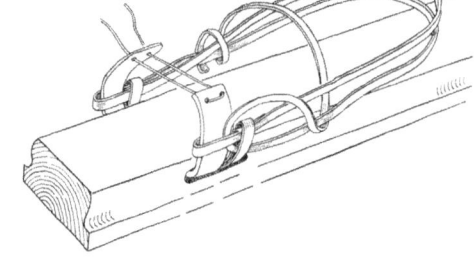

Fig. 7.6

running around the back of the boot or moccasin to provide a binding for the heel (Fig. 7.5).[207] Instead of a leather toe strap withes could be used in front with leather thongs as a heel-band (Fig. 7.6).[208] Pastor Smith of Trysil wrote in 1784 that "the skis of east and north-

---

[204] Vaage 1969: 18.
[205] Bø 1968: 59; Berg 1993: 55.
[206] Vaage 1972: 150-55.
[207] Bø 1966: 40.
[208] Bø 1966: 41.

east Norway are fastened to the feet with thongs after the toes or front of the foot have been thrust into a little arch made of withes above the center of the skis."[209] Bø says that military and civilian uses of skis were probably influencing each other at this time. Pastor Smith knew that bindings were different to the west where only a toe binding was used: "so that the skis can be slipped off in a moment, if one so desires." Normally, skiers used a thin layer of birch bark under the foot, though sometimes a metal plate of copper or brass was under the foot.

It was the ordinary withe binding around the toe that Sondre Norheim (Chap. 11) was given credit for having perfected in the nineteenth century and which made the modern sport of Alpine skiing possible. The earlier bindings did not keep the foot firmly enough attached to the ski to allow for sharp turns while going downhill. The bindings on modern skis keep the ski boots firmly fixed to the skis so that the skis respond immediately to movements of the lower legs. That was not generally the case prior to the nineteenth century. What Sondre did was to attach a withe heel band to the withe toe band already in use (Fig. 7.7).[210] Considering that the withe toe binding is very old it is likely that Sondre did not come up with the idea himself. What he clearly did is to take an idea and perfect it and then demonstrate its superiority in competitions before large numbers of spectators. This fixed the boot quite firmly to the ski and allowed sharp turns for the first time. It worked well for downhill skiing and jumping but was too stiff for cross-country skiing. This was a relatively simple improvement over previous bindings, and it is surprising that no one came up with the idea earlier considering how frustrated skiers must have become at having their skis come off in the middle of a jump or while skiing downhill.

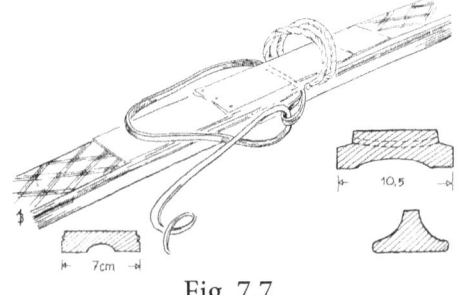
Fig. 7.7

Withes were preferably gathered and twisted during the summer when they were more plentiful and tougher than when they were prepared during the winter. Bø reports that they could even be purchased in certain areas.

Telemark Skis

Another important feature of Telemark skis which Sondre Norheim was usually given credit

---

[209] Bø 1966: 40.
[210] Vaage 1969: 18.

for was their distinctive shape, widest at the front, narrowing toward the middle, and wider at the rear but not as wide as at the front. It should be noted, though, that Sondre may have gotten the idea for this shape from Sámi he was acquainted with and who lived in the area. Again Sondre took a good idea, brought it to perfection with the materials available to him at the time, and popularized it before the masses. Typically, farmers made their own skis in the old days, and Sondre had a reputation as a good ski maker. Bø gives the measurements of a pair of skis Sondre made in 1870 for Mathias Rye Florentz, the tax collector in Kviteseid: 3.3 inches wide at the front, 2.7 inches at the middle, and 3 inches at the rear.[211] Skis of this shape won a gold medal at a ski-making exhibition in 1879; and the first commercially manufactured skis used these measurements as well. Fig. 7.8 shows a pair of skis that belonged to Sondre and that are now in the Ski Museum at Holmenkollen outside Oslo, Norway.[212] Thus, Sondre's model became the pattern for most ski types produced for a long time, and still for the slalom and downhill skis of today. There were two types of skis in general use in Telemark in Sondre's day and earlier: longer "mountain skis" and the so-called "lowlanders' skis" which were shorter and wider, narrowing a bit toward the tips. The mountain skis were widest at the front, narrowed toward the middle and again widened a bit toward the rear. This latter type was the one Sondre based his design on.[213]

Until skiing began to spread from Telemark and surrounding areas to the capital and beyond, the best ski makers in a given area set the standards for the skis made and used there. So there were numerous variations in the many districts; some ski makers experimented with various innovations, most of which have not survived, such as making the right and left skis slightly different from one another.

Curved Front Ends

There were two methods of providing a curve at the front of the ski: the ski could be cut from material that had a natural curve to it or the tips could be bent during manufacture. Bent pine trees of the wood from the north-facing side of a pine tree worked well in the former case. There seem to have been two ways to provide a curved tip for a ski made of originally flat material. The two skis of a pair were put together bottom to bottom, the front

---

[211] Bø 1966: 55.
[212] Vaage 1969: 18.
[213] Bø 1968: 57.

ends were treated with tar and heated, and then the front ends were forced apart and held apart by a clamp until they dried (Fig. 7.10).²¹⁴ This process was repeated until the desired curvature had been attained. The other method involved drilling a small hole in the ski back of the tip, tarring and heating as above, and then pulling the tip back and up and fixing it with a withe band as can be seen in Fig. 7.11.²¹⁵

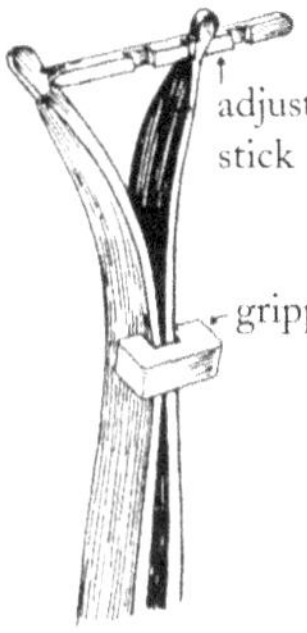

Fig. 7.10

Tips came in many shapes from a fairly sharply upturned tip to a long, flowing curve. The former variety tended to push the snow in front of it and did not work so well in wooded terrain where the skier frequently had to pass over branches and other low-lying obstacles. The long curved tip, though it meant that the bearing surface was somewhat less, worked better in looser snow and in wooded areas. Telemark skis usually had this latter variety tip with a slight downward bend at the very front so that the ski resembled a serpent with upturned head. This downward tip was not functional except when the skis were pulled after the skier with ropes attached to the tips. Some ski tips had knobs at the very front end, e.g. on Middle Age Finnish skis with grooves.²¹⁶

Making Skis

Until relatively recently skis were normally made by the person using them. The word *ski maker* first occurred in 1749 in connection with a military ski unit. Most soldiers brought their own skis from home, and that meant there were as many different kinds of skis as soldiers. Since communication between small villages was poor, every village developed its own type of skis, and every farmer made his own skis using available material. The most common wood types used were pine, spruce, birch and oak. Ash began to be used more in the 1880's. The art of making skis passed from father to son. When city dwellers took up skiing in the nineteenth century, it provided an opportunity for farmers to earn some extra money making skis during the winter. There are ads for skis going back as far as 1820.²¹⁷

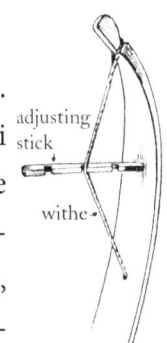

Fig. 7.11

---

²¹⁴ Bø 1968: 57.
²¹⁵ Bø 1968: 57.
²¹⁶ Sørensen 1996: 18, 53.
²¹⁷ Berg 1959: 43-51.

Ski makers were experts on wood. They knew about the consistency of deciduous vs. coniferous woods; they knew about edge wood vs. flat wood; outer layers vs. heartwood.[218] There were two ways to cut wood, either with the annual rings vertical (Fig. 7.12) or with the rings horizontal (Fig. 7.13).[219] The rings of coniferous woods form alternate hard and soft layers. If such wood is cut with the rings horizontal, skis made from the material would tend to get wavy on the bottom with wear. However, if the rings were vertical, then the skis would tend to develop natural grooves on the bottom through wear, and this helped steering. If the raw material was deciduous wood, wood closer to the surface was better: it was harder, and if one used the outer surface as the bottom, a natural bow would develop. Also, the outer layers of wood were looser than the inner ones; the former tended to buckle and shrink on drying. How did they cut the log? Fig. 7.14 shows various possibilities for a coniferous log. The best skis would come from the 6-7 section with no part of the annual rings of the surface and with the bottom surfaces facing each other at 4. They would then consist of heartwood exclusively and would thus be very durable.[220]

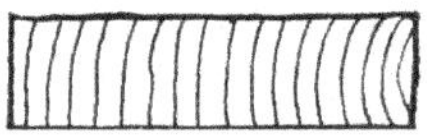

Fig. 7.12

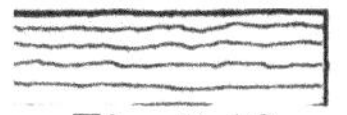

Fig. 7.13

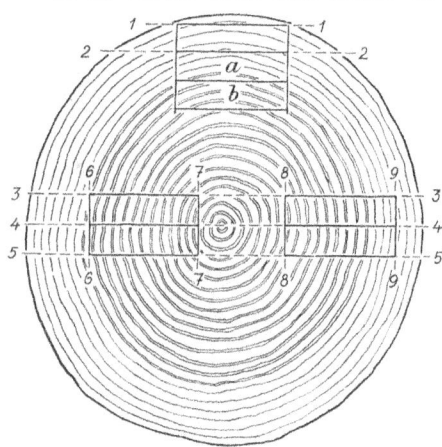

Fig. 7.14

Even better were skis made of Sámi *bye* or *bije*, Swed. *tjur* or Norw. *tenar* (burl, or the heartwood area in fir or spruce – fir was preferable).[221] In other words, skis made from the heartwood of coniferous raw material were best. With normal growth, wood formed in the summer is harder than that formed in the spring. Not so with burl wood: the side nearer the water has more of the summer type growth. But other than for skis such wood was virtually useless; nails wouldn't sit in it. If the tree grew at an angle from the vertical and eventually straightened up toward the sun through geotropism, this so-called burl wood was excellent material for skis for it was very hard and elastic (Fig. 7.15) – note that there is almost no difference in color between the wood formed in the early spring and that formed later in the summer.[222] A Sámi with a trained eye could spot such a tree and

---

[218] Vaage 1972.
[219] Vaage 1972: 146.
[220] Vaage 1972: 147.
[221] Tomasson 1928b: 23-24; Vaage 1972: 150-55.
[222] Vaage 1972: 153.

know immediately that it contained heartwood without probing it with an axe.²²³ The one proviso was that the tree had to slant toward the morning or noonday sun. Such trees were very rare. Then he would investigate the convex side of the tree (cf. Fig. 7.15) by cutting into it with an axe to make sure that the heartwood was thick enough for a ski. If it was an especially fine sample, the heartwood would almost separate from the rest of the wood by itself and the heartwood would have a natural groove, round, broad and deep. Fig. 16 shows such a piece of raw heartwood before the ski

Fig. 7.15

maker turned it into a ski and the cross section of the ski produced.²²⁴ Tomasson wrote that the Sámi considered Swedes and Norwegians to be dilettantes in choosing and using *tjur*.²²⁵ The ski made from *tjur* became the left ski of a pair of unequal length skis and it was likely to be rather heavy – from 9 to 13 pounds. Such skis were essential for work in the reindeer forest during the spring.²²⁶ According to Sigrid Drake's treatise on the Västerbotten Lapps from the first half of the 19th century settlers in the north of Sweden bought skis from the Lapps in that they were better at selecting wood containing the best *tjur*. Norwegians even got their skis in Sweden.²²⁷

Early on this natural groove was a detriment: one could not use the heartwood surface for the bottom of the ski in that the other wood had loosened, taking away the foot space. Then it was noticed that putting the heartwood side of the material near a fire caused the resin to come out and the material could be straightened in the same way as a ski tip was curved. The ski maker then used a plane to get the final form for this left ski, which was called *kuovte* in Sámi.

---

²²³ Tomasson 1928b: 23.
²²⁴ Tomasson 1928b: 21.
²²⁵ Tomasson 1928b: 24.
²²⁶ Tomasson 1928b: 23.
²²⁷ Tomasson 1928b: 24.

There were two other desirable types of wood for skis. *Gåsefuru* was a fir that was attacked by a mushroom so that only the outer shell remained. Even better was *lågfuru*, a windfallen tree found in a bog with high iron content.[228] In this case, only the heartwood resisted the rot. Drying was very important: the wood preferably had to lie for at least one to three years in a cow barn. When the demand for skis rose and wood that had not been sufficiently dried was used, the result was "crooked skis:" they were not straight and the people who bought them got gypped. Trees were usually cut in the fall when there was least sap.

Grooves

Grooves on the bottom of skis helped them steer straight. This was not so important for skiing in soft, loose powder snow but was essential for skiing on harder, crusty snow. As we saw in Chap. 3, grooves are very old. The Salla ski ^{14}C dated Fig. 7.16 to cal 3,245 BCE ± 100 had five narrow, parallel grooves running the length of the ski and covering the middle third of the bottom. Since there were no grooves on the rest of the ski bottom, it would seem as if they had been man-made. Wiklund argued that grooves were found mainly in Scandinavia in earlier times.[229] He also claimed that the Sámi and Finns borrowed both the idea for the groove and the name for grooves from the Scandinavians. His main argument was linguistic, viz. that the Proto-Sámi word for groove must have been **oalas*, which in turn had been borrowed from Proto-Nordic **alaz* before 700 CE in the Torne Sámi area. There was no evidence that **alaz* had the meaning ski groove. Norwegian *ål* and Icelandic *áll* < **alaz* mean "deep channel" as in a river. Torkel Tomasson looked at the earliest historical document from that area, which was Johannes Tornæus' "Berättelse om Lapmarckerna och Deras Tillstånd" from 1672.[230] Tornæus described in detail how the material for the left ski (the long, gliding ski of a pair of unequal length skis) was chosen from hard spruce and then a ski was made that on the bottom was "smooth like glass." There is no mention whatsoever of a groove. Tomasson rejects Wiklund's hypothesis adding that not until 60 years later was there written evidence of grooves in Sámi skis apart from the broad, deep groove mentioned above under Making Skis. That was in 1732 when Linné described grooves on skis in the Jokkmokk area.

---

[228] Vaage 1972: 156.
[229] Tomasson 1928a: 21.
[230] Tomasson 1928b: 21-22.

Among the bog skis in Finland, Norway and Sweden are quite a few with various kinds of rims and grooves. There are those with a concave or rounded bottom and those with a wide, rectangular groove on the bottom. One can consider both of these types as having steering rims at the outside edges of the bottom; in other words, the ski maker carved out the center part of the bottom of the ski with a knife or he chose the material in such a way that the concave bottom occurred naturally (cf. above).[231] Itkonen suggested two possible schemes for development of the narrow groove from the wide groove – cf. Fig. 7.17.[232] The steering rims, or wide groove as it were, then gradually evolved into the narrow groove or two narrow grooves, both of which were fairly common.

The Southern ski type had no grooves. Telemark skis, a distant descendant of the Southern type, usually had a flat bottom surface with no groove, certainly a drawback.[233] In fact, it was not until late in the last century that grooves came into general use. However, if the right kind of wood were used, grooves would develop naturally. For example, when the material was pine or holly, when it had been sawn with the annual rings vertical (Fig. 7.11),[234] and when the skis had been used a bit, the softer, winter growth wore away in between the harder, summer growth leaving something akin to grooves on the bottom.

Fig. 7.17

There are a number of Norwegian dialect words for groove such as [eːl], [eːle], [elje] and [eːl], all of which Dalen derives from Old Norse *il* (*iljar*), a feminine noun meaning "sole of the foot."[235] Note that they do not seem to be related to *ål* mentioned above. In the Sámi languages the most common words for groove are *oales, oalle, oales, ulla*, which are not related to ON *áll* either. Finnish has the related word *olas*, probably borrowed from the Sámi. It is most likely that the groove developed from skis that had a natural concavity on the bottom as mentioned above, though it is conceivable that it could have developed from side lists as seen on some Southern type skis.

---

[231] Tomasson 1928b: 23; Dalen 1997: 9.
[232] Itkonen 1937: 79.
[233] Dalen 1997: 9, especially the map.
[234] Vaage 1972: 146.
[235] Dalen 1997: 9.

Ski Poles

The ski pole was an essential part of the skier's equipment. Not only skiers but hikers, for example, often use a pole to help themselves negotiate difficult terrain. In the chapter on bog skis it was mentioned that a pole was part of the Kalvträsk find. It had a round shaft with a scoop at the end (Chap. 3, Fig. 3.2). This type of pole with a scoop at one end is also found among the Sámi, and it frequently has a spear fitted to the other end turning it into a weapon. The scoop was used to dig into snow when looking for reindeer moss and to get melted snow to drink. The use of a single stick or pole with snowshoes and skis was the norm until well into the nineteenth century. Curiously, there is no record of staff or pole use among Indians of eastern North America; moreover, there were some Russian and Estonian skiers who, instead of using poles, mainly walked on their skis which often had steering ropes attached to the tips (Fig. 7.17).[236] Throughout the rest of the circumpolar area, though, the pole was universally used.

There is some evidence for the early use of a pair of poles, and that is in the *Kalevala* (cf. Chap. 5) where Lemminkäinen seems to have two poles. The W. F. Kirby translation has: "And he fixed the poles on one day, Fixed the rings upon another."[237] And a bit later: "Poles he bought with skins of otter, And the rings with ruddy foxskin." The Eino Friberg translation has for the same lines: "Took a day to shape the ski pole And the next day carved the snow disks." And: "For the pole an otter skin, For the disk a red fox paid." Rings and disks are what today are called baskets. The second translation is inconsistent in that it speaks of disks in the plural the first time and disk in the singular the second time. The material in the *Kalevala* comes from as far back as the thirteenth century, but some believe the version of the ski tale with two poles is no older than the nineteenth century.[238] Another problem with the Lemminkäinen episode is that he uses unequal length skis that were normally used with only one pole. It may have been the peasants of northern Finland who began to use two poles on level ground where the ability to move forward depended more on arm strength. Berg suggested that unequal length skis developed and spread together with the use of a spear and a bow (later on a rifle) and that the spear and bow eventually turned into two poles.[239] From Finland the usage spread to Sweden and the rest of Scandinavia later in

---

[236] Berg 1950: 30.
[237] *Kalevala* 1985.
[238] Zettersten 1943: 19.
[239] Berg 1944: 93-94.

the nineteenth century.[240] Norwegian competitive skiers then led the way in the 1880's in the use of two poles. Late nineteenth century cross-country ski races in Finland consisted of the skiers going around a triangular course on a flat, frozen lake using mostly their arms and poles. The single ski pole was made of hardwood or slow-growing pine and was generally longer than the skier was tall.

In 1639 the Finnish cleric C. C. Alanns wrote: "the 'hand bow' is especially useful, for the Lapp can have it in his hand like a stick when he skis, and under the end of the hand bow a little wooden ring is used as wide as a pot lid."[241] There is even an old picture of a skier with a long pole in the left hand and a bow in the right hand. J. G. Scheller who was in Lappland early in the eighteenth century wrote: "In both hands were poles which down below were provided with a little wheel so that the poles did not push through the snow."[242]

Ski poles as they are known today have disks or baskets above the tips that help keep the stick from sinking into the snow. These baskets can be made of wood, metal or bone with leather thongs often used to attach the basket to the pole. In northern Sweden the basket is made of withes and kept in place by leather thongs. This is also the sort of pole the Gilyaks and Chukchees use far to the east in the most northern reaches of Asia.

Ski Wax

Waxing skis is a relatively recent phenomenon. As late as the 1870's and 1880's ski races had to be canceled or postponed if the conditions were not right.[243] Soft, wet snow might have prevented a ski jumper from even making it to the takeoff. However, skiers have been putting substances on skis for a long time. The earliest written report from 1673 mentions the use of pitch. In 1733 skis "smeared with tar and put against a wall in the sun … such a ski will become as hard as bone. Also in 1733 Holberg wrote that skis were, "sometimes brushed with tar." In 1761: "when the weather is bad so that the snow sticks, a man should have fat along, otherwise he won't get far." Clearly, it was common knowledge for several centuries that under certain conditions some sort of impregnation – tar, resin, vegetable fat, animal fat, tallow, and so on – could help prevent snow and ice from sticking to the ski. For skiing uphill only the fur covering with the hairs pointing backward was known. The icing

---

[240] Berg 1950: 53.
[241] Zettersten 1943: 21.
[242] Zettersten 1943: 20.
[243] Vaage 1969: 165.

problem was worst with new, "fat" skis. Though not much new happened during the nineteenth century it was known that fir that had lain in a peat bog or wood cured in fertilizer had less tendency to stick.

Curiously, the California "gold diggers," many of which earned their living as loggers, experimented with wax fairly early in their ski races. Those who were really good at it were known as "dopers." One formula for wax was the following: 2 oz. of sperm, ¼ oz. pitch, ⅛ oz. camphor, 1 T balsam fir, 1 T oil of spruce.[244] This presumably made the skis faster. Toward the end of the nineteenth century people began to experiment with wax in Norway. In 1884 a paper reported that a mixture of wax and tallow was used on skis. There was even a report of a large cheese atop the Huseby ski jump for the competitors; it was just right to put on the skis! The first ad for ski wax came in 1888, and the winner at Holmenkollen in 1892 used "virgin" wax on his skis, the same kind that women waxed their thread with.

Children's Skis

"Norwegians are born with skis on their feet" goes the saying, although it is probably not very old.[245] By the 19th century it was mostly children in rural areas of Norway who knew how to ski. Sámi children, especially in reindeer herding families, learned to ski at a young age. In the larger towns and cities children didn't take to skiing until the sport began to take off. Figs. 7.18-19 show some unusual children's skis found in Sweden and called *kässjor*.[246] They have handles in the form of arches to help the children stay upright.

Skiing Terminology

Fridtjof Nansen published a map in *Paa ski over Grønland* that he worked out with the help of the librarian Andr. M. Hansen on which are plotted all the names for ski they could find in the languages of the peoples of Eurasia who use skis (Fig. 4.6). On the basis of the etymological relationships found, Nansen suggested that the area of origin for the ski lay near the Altai Mountains and Lake Baikal. He thought that Finno-Ugric people introduced the ski to the Germanic inhabitants of Fennoscandia. In spite of some problems with it this theory seems to have stood the test of time; no better suggestions have been forthcoming. This hypothesis undoubtedly came as a shock to some Norwegians who assumed that the birth of skiing must have taken place on Norwegian territory.

---

[244] Vaage 1969: 166.
[245] Vaage 1979: 70-77.
[246] Wiklund 1928: 47; *På skidor* 1931: 408.

The Norwegian word *ski,* which long ago was adopted into the languages of people who participate in the sport of skiing, comes from Old Norse *skíð* neuter noun (cf. Germ. *das Scheit* "log"); there is also a feminine form *skíða* "splint, stick." Germ. *Der Schi* is masculine by analogy to *der Schuh* "shoe." The Germanic form comes from the Indo-European root **skhait, skhit* "split" which can be seen in Gk. *schizophrenia* and *schism,* Lat. *scindo* "cut," Eng. *rescind, shed* and Germ. *der Scheitel* "part in hair." The Eng. noun *skid* "a piece of wood" and later "a timber or log used in sets to form a slideway" becomes the verb *skid* "to slide." The basic idea of splitting wood leads back to Stone Age times. The hunters split the trunk of a tree not with a saw but with a stone ax which was to the advantage of the ski, because split wood follows the grain and is more durable than sawn wood (cf. shakes vs. shingles). The other Scandinavian word for ski is *andur* that was discussed in the section on Central Nordic skis above.

The other international ski term is *slalom* which is a compound from *sla(d)* "sloping" plus *låm* "a track in the snow." In other words, *slalom* meant a ski track down a slope, quite different from today's meaning of a run with many turns down a very uneven hill. The first occurrence in print came in 1879 in an article about Telemark skiers' technique. The terms *hoppelåm* and *slalåm* are discussed: about *slalåm* it says there is no real jump, but it has its own difficulties which demand as much proficiency as *hoppelåm* (a course with jumps). The terms Telemark turn and Christiania turn refer to turns done on the outer ski and inner ski respectively. Christiania was the name of Oslo from 1624 to 1925.

There are actually many other words for "ski track" from other parts of Norway such as *ei meidd(e)* from southeastern Norway presumably from "to make a track." Then there is the family *(ann)dår, (ann)dørgje* from various areas in Norway and Sweden that derives from the verb *draga* "to pull" – "track left by something being pulled."[247] This family is quite old and its occurrence in isolated areas suggests that it is a relict term replaced in some areas by newer form such as *spor, renne* and *ekkje.* Cf. Dalen's map for further details.[248] Apart from *ski* the only other word to spread beyond the borders of Scandinavia is *slalom* and that is no doubt due to the Telemarkers achievements in cities such as Oslo in the 19th century.

---

[247] Dalen 1997: 16.
[248] Dalen 1997: 17.

Skiing in Literature I: The Medieval Period

The large number of references to skiing and skis in various kinds of literature over the past one thousand years show that skiing was widespread, at least in most of Scandinavia. The references are not exclusively Scandinavian: a number of people from other parts of the world took an interest in Scandinavia and its unusual culture. All of this began when the Vikings made a somewhat dubious reputation for themselves beyond Scandinavia's borders. Skiing became an object of wonder for many that had not seen it practiced before. In this chapter we consider the fascinating literary references to skiing from the Middle Ages found in the Icelandic family sagas, the sagas of Norwegian kings and early folk tales.

Egilssaga

According to *Egilssaga* King Håkon the Good sent two groups of twelve men each to Värmland (now part of Sweden) to collect taxes from Earl Arnvid. They were attacked and killed. Then he sent a third group to force one Thorstein to get the taxes. The great Icelandic hero and skaldic poet Egill Skallagrimsson offered to go in his stead. Egill and his comrades set off with the king's men in bad winter weather with much snow. At a fork in the road Egill has the king's men go one way while he and three others take the other route:[249]

> But this has to be reported of the king's men, that the moment they and Egill were out of each other's sight they took the skis they had with them, put them on, and then took the road back as hard as ever they could. They kept going night and day, turning for the Uplands and from there north past Dofrafjall, and made no stay before they fell in with King Hákon and told him of their journey.

This would have occurred abound 950. The saga also contains reports of skiing in the northernmost part of the country, but among Norwegians rather than Sámi.

---

[249] *Egil's Saga* 1960: 187.

Skiing and Education

In 960 skiing was discussed as a sport belonging to the upbringing of every well-born warrior. Both kings and chieftains practiced it. In 1030 King Harald the Hardruler composed a verse about the eight sports he mastered, one of which was skiing. He had learned this sport while he was living in Ringerike as a child.

In 1040 Ragnvald Jarl, the Earl of the Orkneys, imitated and outdid King Harald by mentioning the nine arts he mastered in a skaldic verse. Here is that verse in Old Icelandic:[250]

Tafl emk ǫrr at efla, -	I'm quick at playing board games,
- íþróttir kannk níu –	I master nine skills
tynik trauðla rúnum,	I scarcely forget runes,
tíð es bók ok smíðir.	I often write and make things.
Skríða kannk á skíðum,	I know how to ski
skytk ok rœk, svát nytir.	I shoot and row, decently enough.
Hvárttveggia kannk hyggja:	I understand both of these things:
harpslótt ok bragþóttu.	harp playing and poetry.

Fig. 8.1

Böksta Rune Stone

A skier carrying a bow with arrow ready to shoot and a man on horseback hunting an elk, with falcons and hounds, are depicted on a rune stone at Böksta, Uppland, Sweden from ca. 1050 (Fig. 8.1).[251] The runic alphabet was the possession of a select few Norsemen for over a thousand years from ca. 100 CE until well past the Viking era. Runic inscriptions were cut on wood, metal and stone and were perforce brief. Time and human carelessness have not treated the Böksta stone well: in the seventeenth century it was broken into five or six pieces of which one disappeared. A fire in front of the inscription spoiled part of it. Nevertheless, what remains is rather unique among runic inscriptions in the north. The inscription reads: "Ingemund and Jogärd, husband and wife,

---

[250] *Orkneyinga Saga* 1965: 130.
[251] Luther 1926: 498.

had this stone raised in memory of their son Est. Ärnfast and his brothers raised it after their brother."

The King's Mirror

Speculum Regale or *Konungs skuggsjá* (The King's Mirror) from around 1250 is a didactic work on courtly manners and proper conduct written in Old Norwegian in the form of a dialogue. Its purpose was to provide instruction for princes. Under the heading Popular Doubt as to the Genuineness of Marvels it states:[252]

> For it must be possible to tame wild beasts and other animals, though they be fierce and difficult to manage. But it would seem a greater marvel to hear about men who are able to tame trees and boards, so that by fastening boards seven or eight ells long under his feet, a man, who is no fleeter than other men when he is barefooted or shod merely with shoes, is made able to pass the bird on the wing, or the fleetest greyhound that runs in the race, or the reindeer which leaps twice as fast as the hart. For there is a large number of men who run so well on skis that they can strike down nine reindeer with a spear, or even more, in a single run. Now such things must seem incredible, unlikely, and marvelous in all those lands where men do not know with what skill and cleverness it is possible to train the board to such great fleetness that on the mountainside nothing of all that walks the earth can escape the swift movements of the man who is shod with such boards. But as soon as he removes the boards from his feet, he is no more agile than any other man. In other places, where men are not trained to such arts, it would be difficult to find a man, no matter how swift, who would not lose all his fleetness if such pieces of wood as we have talked about were bound to his feet. We, however, have sure information and, when snow lies in winter, have opportunity to see men in plenty who are expert in this art.

The author used the word boards for skis either because he was not familiar with the prevailing ski vocabulary of that time or, more likely, because he knew that his readers might not know the technical terms. Moreover, it is clear that one does not just put skis on and suddenly become proficient; it takes practice. Or, as the adage goes: Norwegians are born with skis on.

Skiing in Norwegian Kings' Sagas

Snorri Sturluson has already been mentioned as the author of the *Prose Edda*. Snorri spent time abroad on two different occasions at the court of the Norwegian king and with other important people of Norway and Sweden. He took the wrong side in a dispute between

---

[252] Larson 1917: 103-04.

King Hákon and Duke Skúli, and after Hákon had killed Skúli, he had his agents kill Snorri as a traitor.[253] But Snorri, his political machinations notwithstanding, was a marvelous writer. His other great work is the monumental *Heimskringla*, a history of Norwegian kings from their legendary origin through the reign of King Magnús Erlingsson.

King Óláf Tryggvason who brought Christianity to Norway and her colonies is referred to as someone who skied better than other men (ca. 995).[254]

About Einar Thambarskelfir (ca. 1000) Snorri writes: "It is said that Einar was a man of enormous strength and the best archer that ever lived in Norway; and his hard shooting excelled that of all other men. With a blunt-headed arrow he could shoot through a raw ox hide suspended from a beam. He was a most skilled runner on skis, a great athlete, and most courageous."[255]

"There was a man called Finn the Little, of Uppland origin, though some say he was Finnish. He was of unusually small stature, but extraordinarily fleet so that no horse could overtake him. He was also a fast runner on skis and an excellent shot (ca. 1018)."[256] Most likely Finn was a Sámi.

Fig. 8.2 shows a Sámi ski (7) and a boat-shaped reindeer sleigh (6) as well as a ski pole.[257]

Earl Emund, the lawspeaker in West Gautland, tells the following story to King Óláf the Holy:[258]

> The news from us Gautar is of but little importance. But this we consider news that Atli the Fool from Vermaland this winter went up into the forest on his skis and with his bow. Him we consider a great hunter. In the mountains he gathered so many squirrel pelts that he had filled his ski sled with as many as he could drag after him, and then he returned from the woods. Then he saw a squirrel up in a tree. He shot at it but missed it. Then he grew furious. He abandoned the sled and ran after the squirrel. But the squirrel always jumped to where the woods were thickest, sometimes it went among the roots of the trees, sometimes up into the branches, and then it would sail between the branches to another tree. And when Atli shot at it, the arrow would fly too high or too low; but he never lost sight of the squirrel. He became so intent on this chase that he hunted the squirrel all day long, but never did bag it. And when it began to grow dark he threw

---

[253] When Håkon was a baby he was saved from Skúli by two skiers. Cf. the section on the Birchlegs in the next chapter.
[254] Vaage 1969: 8.
[255] Snorri 1977: 259.
[256] Snorri 1977: 323.
[257] *På skidor* 1939: 403.
[258] Snorri 1977: 344.

himself down on the snow, as he was accustomed to, and lay there during the night. Then there came a snowstorm. Next day Atli went to look for his ski sled. But he never found it again and so returned home empty-handed.

Atli may have been a better skier than hunter.

Arnljót Gellini

Arnljót Gellini from Jamtaland in what is now Sweden surely was one of the most extraordinary skiers of his era, judging from the one exploit described in the *Saga of St. Olaf*. According to the story, King Óláf had an Icelander at his court (ca. 1026) by the name of Thórodd Snorrason whom he would not allow to travel freely because of some difficulties in Iceland. Thórodd, looking for a way to escape, volunteered to go to Jamtaland (Sweden) and try to collect taxes. He was taken prisoner by the Jamtalanders but managed to escape with a companion:[259]

> Thórodd and his companion traveled for a long time in the desert woods and one evening came to a small farm. They went in, and found a man and a woman sitting by the fire. The man gave his name as Thórir and said the woman sitting there was his wife. He also told them that he had settled there because he had to flee the village on account of a killing. Thórodd and his companion were well entertained, and they all ate by the fire. Afterwards a place for their bedding was made for them on the dais, and they lay down to sleep. The fire in the fireplace had not died down yet. Then Thórodd saw a man come in out of another house. He had never seen so large a man. That man wore a scarlet cloak with a gold lace border and was of a most stately appearance. Thórodd heard him reproach their hosts for taking in guests when they scarcely had enough to eat themselves. The woman of the house answered, "Don't be angry, brother, this has rarely happened before. Rather do you give them some help, because you are better able to do so then we." Thórodd heard that large man called Arnljót Gellini, and gathered that the woman of the house was his sister. Thórodd had heard Arnljót mentioned and that he was a wicked highwayman and evildoer. Thórodd and his companion slept during the night, for they were tired from walking. But when two thirds of the night had passed, Arnljót came to them and told them to get up and make ready for the journey. So Thórodd and his companion got up quickly and dressed. They were given a breakfast. Then Thórir provided them both with skis. Arnljót made ready to go with them. He mounted his skis, which were both broad and long. But no sooner had he stuck down his ski pole (*skíðageisl*) but he was far ahead of them. Then he stopped for them and said they would get nowhere that way, and told them to get on his skis [behind him]. So they

---

[259] Snorri 1977: 426-27.

did. Thórodd stood close to him holding onto Arnljót's belt, and his companion held onto him. Thereupon Arnljót ran as fast as though he were unencumbered.

Fig. 8.3 shows a pair of skis in Ole Worm's catalogue. Worm (1588-1654) was a Danish doctor, archaeologist and antiquarian and one of the most learned men of his time. He had a pair of skis in his museum collection. The picture is from the catalogue that his son published in Leiden in 1655.[260]

The Saga of Magnús Barelegs

In this saga, which is found in *Heimskringla*, the Sámi are said to have sold skis (ca. 1050).[261] Among those in the know the Sámi had the reputation of making the finest skis.

Heming Ballads

The greatest skier of the Viking era, though, was Heming Aslaksson. According to the *Saga of King Harald the Hardruler* Harald forced Heming to ski off a cliff.[262] This would have been around 1050 CE. There is a short story about Heming found in the *Flateyjarbók* from 1390, a compilation mainly of sagas about Norwegian kings. The Icelandic historian Thormóðr Torfæus (1636-1719) says in his *Historia rerum Norvegicarum* (Norwegian history to 1387) that ballads about Heming were present in the oral tradition.[263] The Danish scholar Peter Erasmus Müller (1776-1834) has a version of the Heming legend in his Saga Library.[264] But, it is the oral tradition that is most important here. The nineteenth century folk tale collectors, Peder Christian Asbjørnsen and Jørgen Moe, recorded versions of the Heming ballad in Telemark (30 stanzas), Ullensvang (14 stanzas; recall that Ullensvang means Ull's meadow, an appropriate place for these events to have occurred), and Sørum (15 stanzas). The hymnist Magnus Brostrup Landstad (1802-80) collected material on Heming ballads, and Ludvig Mathias Lindeman (1812-87), who is known for his collections of Norwegian folk melodies, wrote the music to Sophus Bugge's version of a Heming ballad.

Fig. 8.4 shows part of the cover plate of Ole Worm's "Museum Wormianum" published in Leiden in 1655.[265]

---

[260] Bø 1966: 25.
[261] Vaage 1969: 8.
[262] Snorri 1977:
[263] Vaage 1969: 108.
[264] Müller 1820: 356-68.
[265] *På skidor* 1931: 406.

Heming and King Harald

There are, in fact, two main Norwegian legends about Heming, his confrontation with the Norwegian King Harald the Hardruler and his episode with a giantess and subsequent rescue of a maiden in distress. The ballad of Heming and King Harald is also found in the Faeroe Islands, and there was a Heming short story in the Icelandic manuscripts *Hauksbók* and *Flateyjarbók*. According to the first tale, King Harald hears about the exploits of the young Heming and, since Harald considers himself superior to anyone else in a number of skills, he sets out to test the boy. He comes to Hálogaland in northern Norway where he stays with the rich farmer Aslak at Torgøya. Harald asks to see the boy, but Aslak says that his son is dimwitted and has been sent away from home. The Icelandic sources say that Heming is being fostered by some *finnefolk* (Sámi, no doubt) far to the north. Harald returns the following year and threatens Aslak with death if the boy is not back at home within two months. Aslak then has to send a boat with twelve men north to Framnes. From there it is four days' journey on foot to the mountain valley where Heming is being reared. They tell him that if he doesn't go to his father then his father will be killed by King Harald. Heming tells the men that they can leave, and then he will go alone down to the coast. When after four days of hiking they come back to the ship and get ready to depart, they see Heming come skiing down toward them. The stretch that had taken them four days Heming had managed to cover in a few hours; he had left his foster parents that very morning.

Fig. 8.5 shows two Sámi skiing downhill with one of them picking up his cap.[266]

After they get back to Torgøy, individual two-man competitions between the king and Heming come about. The king had said that as far as skiing was concerned he didn't think anyone could outdo him. In shooting Heming proves to be better than the king who then becomes embittered, so he demands an extra text of Heming's skill with bow and arrow. Heming is supposed to shoot a hazelnut from the head of his brother Bjarne. He refuses, but his brother is not worried about being a target, especially since the king has threatened to kill Heming if he doesn't comply with the order. And Heming shoots so confidently that the arrow lifts the nut from Bjarne's head without hurting him. The day after there is a swimming race between the king and Heming after Heming has first said: "Beak to beak the eagles are going to fight." The king grabs Heming and ducks him under the water while the waves wash high over them. Only after it becomes dark does the king reach the shore alone, and everyone believes that Heming has drowned. There is complete silence at the drinking

---

[266] Wiklund 1928: 19.

table afterwards, but when the candles are lit and the king has sat down on the throne Heming suddenly walks in and hands the king a knife which the king had had in his belt. This shows to all present that in the struggle under the water Heming could have killed the king.

Fig. 8.6 shows a close-up of the Ole Worm ski from 1655.[267]

The next day the king demands that Heming follow him to the mainland. They land at a steep mountain, and the king demands that Heming ski down the mountain without falling. In spite of many objections the king forces Heming to use his skis on a path that twists down the mountainside. To everyone's surprise Heming stays on his skis. Then the king demands that Heming ski down the mountain to a bluff that is so narrow that there isn't even room for a horse on it. Heming for his part says that the king could just as well kill him, and the king replies that this will happen if he doesn't obey. His father Aslak offers his entire fortune for Heming's life, but the king answers curtly that he doesn't care about Aslak's things. Heming doesn't want anyone else to plead his case and goes to a man by the name of Odd Ofeigson who gives him a linen scarf of St. Stephen which is supposed to have the property that it saves the one who carries it from all mortal danger. The king then goes up on the bluff dressed in his red cloak, sticks his spear into the ground, and is supported at his back by his kinsman Thorgerson who in turn is supported by another, and so on by other men. Heming puts on his skis and begins to ski down the mountain peak so that everyone is astonished, and he doesn't lose his skis on the first few jumps. When he approaches the bluff, he jumps, lets his skis fall from his feet, and lands on the edge of the bluff where the king stands, and grabs him by the cloak, but the king gets free in such a way that Heming plunges down the mountain. "Here you see the difference," said the king, "between someone who is going to live and someone who is going to die." But Heming isn't dead! The wind takes hold of the St. Stephen scarf so that it gets caught on the tip of a cliff. Soon Heming sees a bright light approach. It is King Olaf the Holy who takes hold of Heming and says that he doesn't want King Harald to be responsible for his death.

Fig. 8.7 shows a Sámi hunting with a cat.[268]

This is an absolutely captivating story in a number of respects. First of all, Heming's two trips down the mountain may be the first demonstration of both slalom and ski jumping. Secondly, Heming's name is related to *ham* "shape" and *hamskifte* "to change shape." According to ancient belief certain people were able to change their shapes, shed their skin,

---

[267] Wiklund 1928: 30.
[268] Luther 1942: 43.

and take on a different appearance; they could turn into animals for example. One thinks of the berserks of Old Icelandic literature. Berserk means "bear cloak" and suggests that certain warriors donned bear cloaks or wolf skins, which increased their strength through the animal spirit or at least their mental resolve, and became wild, "went berserk." As far as Heming is concerned it probably meant that he assumed a new "shape" when he went hunting in the winter and had to move more quickly (on skis) to catch game. There are, in fact, legends about Heming in northern Norway that he possessed *kvikski* "living skis" which moved by themselves on level ground and uphill; these magic skis gave him his supernatural speed.

The Heming legend is a conflation of three separate legends. The ski tale is probably Norwegian in origin. The bow-shooting episode is very old; it exists in England around 800 CE and was known in Norway during the Viking period. It is also in *Þiðriks saga* from the thirteenth century. It wandered east to Finland and south through Germany to Switzerland where William Tell is the hero. The swimming competition may come from *Laxdoela saga* where the Icelander Kjartan Óláfsson swims against the Norwegian King Olav Tryggvason in the river Nid at Nideros (now Trondheim). Curiously, there was no skiing in Switzerland at the time the William Tell story was told. Skiing did not reach the Alps until brought there by Norwegian students a century or so ago. Saxo Grammaticus' *Gesta danorum*, written around 1200 CE, has a remarkable version of the story according to which the hero Toke (the crazy one) skis down Kullen in Skåne, which is now part of Sweden.[269] There are not even many hills in Skåne. Here is the complete Heming ballad:

> I
> Harald sits on the broad bench
> looks over all his men:
> "I don't know my equal,
> he is yet to be born!"
> – young Heming could really ski.
>
> Harald sits on the broad bench
> looks over all his retainers:
> "I don't know of my equal
> in this world!"

---

[269] Bø 1968: 22.

To this answered the little boy,
who was so quick-tongued:
"I know of a huge giant
who squeezes water from steel.

Then there is Heming's horse
when you meet him on the road:
His eyes are like those of a snake,
and fire gushes from his nostrils."

It was king Harald,
from his nostrils snorts:
"If I live one day after this night,
I want to try him!"

II

Then they raised their silk sail
so high on the gilded mast,
they did not lower the sail
until they saw Aslak's land.

Aslak stands in the loft
looking out in the distance:
"I see so many of those war ships
coming in to land."

Sit at home now, my son,
and stick to your mead;
I'll go down to the shore
and look at the gilded ships.

It was King Harald,
who first jumped ashore there:
"Listen, you man on the turf,
say your rightful name!"

"You ask me and I answer you,
if you think it's important:
Aslak the farmer is my name,
and Heming my youngest son."

It was young Heming,
he didn't think it normal:

he saddles up his nice horse
and rides down to the shore.

"God help you, my son,
why aren't you sitting at home?
Better to be shy than overly bold,
it is good to preserve your health."

"Listen here, my good father,
don't worry about it:
I am no longer a child,
I rode out on my horse."

"I can hear, Heming,
that you want to fight with me,
meet me tomorrow in the play field,
when the sun reddens on the hill!"

III

It was early in the morning,
the sun was reddening on the hilltop,
eager was young Heming
to find king Harald.

They had a go at it on the play field,
the sun was reddening on the hilltop,
they could not hit each other,
the arrows met at the tips.

They had a go at it on the play field,
fought in different ways;
Fifteen shots one right after the other –
all of them hit the tips.

"I can see, young Heming,
that you are a brave boy,
you shall shoot a walnut
off your brother's head!"

"If I am to shoot a walnut
off my brother's head,
then the king shall stand beside him
and see how the shells fall."

My dear brother, you don't have
to stand blue and pale,
but instead under the walnut
stand both erect and brave.

It was young Heming,
he has surely shot before;
one half of the nut fell down,
the other remained still.

Harald spoke to Heming:
"You are experienced with the bow.
But what did you want to do with that arrow
which you hid from the quiver?"

"If I had shot my brother
if that evil had happened,
then this shiny arrow would have
gone through you, Harald!"

   IV
"Listen, my clever man,
to what I say to you:
you are going to break Heming swimming,
you shall do it for me!"

It was young Heming,
who was good at swimming:
Tired and exhausted the king's man
stepped back onto the green shore.

Harald spoke to Heming,
he was ill of temper:
"You and I shall go out on the ocean,
to try each other in the blue waves!"

They set out from shore
as fast as they could swim;
the king pulled his silver-adorned knife,
intending to stab him to the bottom.

Heming took the knife from him
and threw it out over the fjord:
"this could have been my death –
but you acted a little too late."

        V

"I can see on you, Heming,
that you won't give up:
you will ski down that mountain
which men call Snara!"

"If I am to ski down that mountain
which men call Snara,
then you, king, shall stand at its foot
and see how well I can go."

Heming skied down Snara mountain,
his skis ran back and forth,
reminding everyone who watched
of a star falling from the sky.

Heming skied Snara Mountain,
his skis crackled on the crusted snow,
grabbed the king's shoulder bone,
ripped his garments.

Heming skied Snara mountain
his skis crackled in the snow,
grabbed the king's shoulder bone
so his nose scraped the ground.

It was young Heming,
he turns around again:
"If you think you haven't had enough,
then I can always do more!"

Heming gets onto his oak skis
runs north over the hills:
everyone asks and no one knows
where the boy has his home.

Heming gets on his oak skis
runs north over the hills,
everyone asks, no one knows,

where the boy is destined to die.
– young Heming could really ski.

Fig. 8.8 is a skier depicted on a wall in the Österunda Church in Uppland, Sweden from the middle of the 15th century.[270]

Heming and Gyrvi

The subject of the second Heming ballad is not found elsewhere in earlier Norse literature.[271] Here he becomes a fairy tale hero who saves a maiden from the trolls, a rather common motif. According to the ballads as well as the *Fornaldarsögur* (pre-Viking period material), the giant is on a journey to the far north when he saves the maiden. In the first ballad about Heming, *Hemings-tåtten* (*tått* = anecdote), it is said that he grew up in the home of a couple of *finnefolk* (people of Sámi or Finnish extraction) in a valley far north and that he hunted during the day and didn't come home until late at night. Then he meets a giantess (female troll) up there in the mountains. He promises the troll marriage, but while she is away preparing the wedding, he finds the king's daughter and runs away with her. The troll pursues them, but at sunrise she turns to stone. The material appears in the Icelandic historian Thórmoðr Torfaeus' *Historia rerum Norvegicarum* in 1711; it is one of the best-known Norwegian ballads. Jørgen Moe took it down from Blind-Anne in Hardanger, and there are many written versions from East and West Telemark, Valdres and Romerike. It probably came to Norway from Sweden where it was composed in the seventeenth century. Here is a portion of it:

> Heming put his bow on his back
> And the quiver at his side,
> Then got ready to go to the mountains,
> He knew of a bear lair.
> – Young Heming could really ski.
>
> Heming went round the mountain,
> On skis he made his way,
> He shot fifteen white bears
> Before the day was done.
>
> He covered both hill and dale,

---

[270] *Kulturhistoriskt Lexikon* 1970: Planche 3.
[271] Liestøl 1967: 145-49, 286-87.

How light he flew on his skis.
Then suddenly in the mountain
He saw a bright flame.

Inside sat the old troll
Poking in the fire with her nose.
"What kind of little boy is it
Who comes so late at night?"

"I am no little boy nor
Do I wish to be called so,
I have come here to the mountain
In search of a good marriage.

In the mountain I want to play,
In the mountain I want to live,
In the mountain I want to place
My whole destiny and my faith."

"If you have come to the mountain
To stay for the rest of your days,
Then I will travel through the land
And invite our wedding guests."

Goatskin boots on her feet
Were 15 ells long,
The sun was 4 ells wide,
They were even a little tight.

They led the horse out of the stable,
It measured 18 ells below the knees,
The troll woman jumped into the saddle,
And her shanks dangled on the ground.

She invited near and invited far,
She asked all her friends;
Invited even the old Grenjehetta,
Who lived at the world's end.

Heming ambled around the mountain,
He thought she took a long time.
Then he found a bunch of keys,
Hanging on a silver nail.

Then he unlocked the first door,
And then unlocked the second;
He unlocked the third door:
There sat an imprisoned maiden.

"God bless you, Heming,
And God bless that you came;
God bless your dear mother,
who brought you into the world!"

He gathered together so much gold,
What fifteen horses could carry,
Then he got the proud maiden out,
Wanted to hurry out of the mountain.

Down the high mountains he skied
And down the slopes below,
Followed by the cross-eyed troll
With eleven of her relatives.

The troll woman shouted at Heming,
They heard her from fifteen miles:
"I didn't think you'd leave so soon,
I didn't think to doubt your word.

Listen, young Heming, listen
To what I have to tell:
If you put down the young girl,
You can keep the gold."

The troll woman yelled at Heming,
It echoed over hill and dale;
As soon as the maiden heard her,
She fell off her skis in a faint.

Heming took some white snow
and rubbed it on her breast:
"Hear me, my proud maiden,
you will stand firm on my skis!"

It was brave young Heming,
Who turned his eyes to the east:
"There rises the prettiest maiden,
she will comfort you best."

The troll woman turned to the east.
The sun shone in her eyes;
Then she turned to flint stone
Standing there on the hill.

"Stay there as a milestone,
Amid fallen stump and stone,
Then you can't do any man
Any kind of harm!"

The king stood in his high loft,
Looking into the distance:
"Either Heming is scared or angry,
While the sun shines on his skis."

- - - - - -

"If you have found my daughter today,
Then she shall be your bride,
You shall enjoy great honor here
and later inherit my kingdom."

It had been fully fifteen years
Since the king did rejoice,
Since his daughter was stolen away.
She slept under silk covers.
 – Young Heming could really ski.

Fig. 8.9 is the painter Gerhard Munthe's depiction of Heming (also called Hermod) skiing away from the troll woman with the maiden on the back of his skis.[272]

Grim's Skis

Erik Lindgren, a perpetual curate – permanent assistant minister – in Jämtland, composed the following poem based on the legend about Grim. Though the poem was written in the 1940's, the legend was part of the oral tradition for a long time. The basic legend can be found in Johan Lindström-Saxon's *Saga, sägen och sång i Jamtbygd*. Skot, Sjul and Rut are giants; the *andor* is the fur-covered, right ski used for pushing.[273]

---

[272] Bø 1992: 21.
[273] Lindgren 1946: 278-80.

There was a terrifying giant named Grim.
He lived near the Handöla river.
At least five fathoms measured
Grim's skis – that went by themselves!
Gold glittered on the pole. There was
no finer spear nor grip.
But the skis, the one as the other,
were made of good Swedish iron.

There was skiing of some sort
 – dry crust or thirteen days' thaw:
Grim always went to a Yule feast
to the giant Frö on Frö's island.
The mountain birch thicket was in bloom
and burned, like forest bast,
and dry fields were torched in the tracks
behind the skis' sparks.

For Grim went like a madman.
And Skot at Ot
often got a lurch
at Ott mountain's worst uphill.
And in over the Norwegian side
stood Sjul at Suul
and thought the skis were singing
Merry Christmas, Merry Christmas.
And in the pull of the bark sack
Rut at Skut tumbled
 – though Grim was at Rannås hill
and the trip was already over.

And Grim brought joy to the lads of Frö.
They made games in a hurry.
Destroyed the church tower
with wrathful giant casts.
Until Frö got rickety in his legs.
Evening drew near.
Grim threw the last stone.
That stone was the Hafra boulder.
And then it was time to go.
Soon he was at home.
His were the most amazing
self-running pair of skis.

But when he got old and tired
and settled down to rest,
he stuck them in Bunnerstöten
so deep that the binding broke.
And without a pole and incapable
Grim languished and looked like a wreak.
And became a hill dweller in Snåsa hill.
Then Grim went to his grave.
Oh Grim, at a bluemoon hour
on a sparkling midwinter evening
I have seen your skis glimmer
far in among Jämtland's mountains.
Now loan to the men of the ski tracks,
who run around ridge and around stream,
your giant will as an andor
– and the skis that go by themselves!

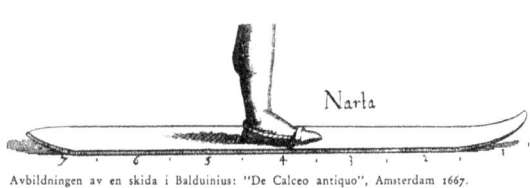

Fig. 8.10

The Saga of the Sons of Magnús

In this saga the kings Sigurð Jersusalemfarer and Eystein brag about their exploits and talents (ca. 1120). The dialogue at one spot is:[274]

> King Sigurð replied, "Do you remember how it was with our swimming, and that I could duck you whenever I wanted to?"
>
> King Eystein said, "I could swim as far as you could, nor was I worse at diving. Also, I was so good at skating that I did not know anyone who could vie with me; but you were not better at that than a cow."
>
> King Sigurð said, "A more chieftainly sport, and a more useful one, it seems to me, is to shoot well with bow and arrow. And I believe you would not be able to stretch my bow even though you used both feet [to stretch it]."
>
> King Eystein answered, "I am not as strong at the bow as you are; but there is less difference between our marksmanship. And I am better at the use of skis than you, and that has also been considered a worthwhile accomplishment."

---

[274] Snorri 1977: 703.

Legal Protection of Animals

The Gulating (Gula Assembly) Law was compiled by King Magnús Lagabøter (Lawmender) in the *Landsloven* (Law of the Land) around 1274. Concerning moose hunting it reads: "All moose shall be protected everywhere within the domain of the property owner from men on skis."[275] The female moose were pregnant during the winter and were easy prey to hunters on skis who could overtake them on crusted snow that the animals sank into.

In the *Diplomatarium Norvegicum* from 1520 it appears that skis were used so diligently during hunting that royal privileges were sought in order to spare wildlife from the skiers' pursuits.[276]

In a letter to King Frederik I of Denmark-Norway from the people of Jämtland in 1530, it says: "Furthermore, we inform your Highness that it is written in our Law book, that moose should be left in peace by all the men who run on skis all over Jämtland. But there are some men who are in the habit of going to your Highness' bailiffs and asking them for permission to hunt animals on skis, and that harms the entire region. Therefore we ask the government officials there in the region to grant you permission to ski after moose in the winter time."[277]

Fig. 8.10 shows a ski in Balduinius' *De Calceo antiquo* from Amsterdam in 1667.[278]

The Saga of Grettir the Strong

Grettir was Iceland's most famous outlaw. The saga about him was written around 1325. As an outlaw he was banned from normal social contact with other people. If he defied this ban, anyone could legally kill him. Nevertheless, Grettir went to a district assembly to participate in the fun and games. He went under disguise calling himself Gest. The man who organizing the wrestling – an enemy of Grettir – didn't recognize him and wanted him to join in. Gest said that he would wrestle if he was given safe conduct at the assembly and until he got back home. A man named Hafr then eloquently proclaimed a truce. Part of the formula reads:[279]

> He shall be branded a truce-breaker who violates this pledge or destroys this peace –
> to be banished and driven away from God and good men, from heaven and all holy

---

[275] Vaage 1969: 10.
[276] Vaage 1969: 10.
[277] Vaage 1969: 10-11.
[278] *På skidor* 1930: 391.
[279] *Grettis Saga* 1936: 232-33.

men; he shall be deemed unfit to live among men, and, like a wolf, shall be an outlaw everywhere – wherever Christians go to church or heathens hold sacrifices, wherever fire burns, the earth grows, a speaking child calls his mother and a mother bears a son, wherever people kindle fires, where a ship sails, shields glitter, the sun shines, snow drifts, a Lapp goes on skis, a fir tree grows, where a falcon flies on a long summer's day with a fair breeze blowing under both wings, where the heavens turn, where lands are lived in, where the wind washes water down to the sea, where men sow seed – in all those places the truce breaker shall be barred from churches and Christians, from heathens, from houses and holes, from every place except Hell alone.

In other words, the truce breaker would be barred everywhere. It is interesting that the area where the Lapp goes on skis is included. There does not seem to have been any skiing in Iceland at this time. However, since it was part of the upbringing of Icelandic young men to travel abroad – to Norway – to gain some experience, people would have known about skis. Needless to say, Grettir surpassed everyone in wrestling, and the organizers were irate at having been bamboozled by Grettir.

Fig. 9.1

Illustrations 1

Knud Bergslien: Birkebeinerne (The Birchlegs)

This painting is Bergslien's depiction of the two Birchlegs on their way with the prince (the later King Håkon Håkonsson) from Lillehammer to Østerdalen in 1206. The Birchlegs were a group of poor insurgents in the Norwegian Civil Wars of the 12th and 13th centuries. Their opponents, the Baglers, were adherents of the clerical party. The Birchlegs joined the pretender to the throne Eystein Møyla in 1174. At the battle of Re near Tønsberg in 1177 the Birchlegs were defeated and Eystein was killed. The Birchlegs fled to Värmland in Sweden. There they met Sverre Sigurdsson who had grown up in the Faroe Islands and they took him as their leader. He was a capable warrior and led them to many victories. King Sverre died in 1202 and his son Håkon Sverresson became king. But he died suddenly in January of 1204. Right after his death his son Håkon Håkonsson was born in Østfold. The Baglers tried to get hold of the young heir apparent, but just before Christmas in 1205 some of the Birchlegs moved north with the child to Inge at Nidaros. At Christmastime they went on to Lillehammer and hid until January of 1206. In a storm with cold weather and snow Thorstein Skevla and Skjervald Skrukka went over the mountains with prince Håkon in their arms. Håkon became king in 1217 and ruled for 46 years. The event is certainly historical, and the names of the two Birchlegs are mentioned in *Håkon Håkonssons saga*.

The painting was done in 1869 in the typical national romantic style. The skis and the clothing of the skiers are surely the flight of Bergslien's fancy. Bergslien lived from 1827 to 1908.

Illustrations 2

Upper: Fig. i.4
George Catlin: Prairie Indians using snowshoes on a buffalo hunt, 1844.

Center: Fig. i.5
Peter Rindisbacher: Prairie Indians using snowshoes on a buffalo hunt, 1825.

Lower left: Fig. 1.3
A pair of fur-covered skis in Stephanius' 1644 edition of Saxo.

Lower right: Fig. 2.8
Rock carving of a skier at Alta in Finnmark county, Norway.

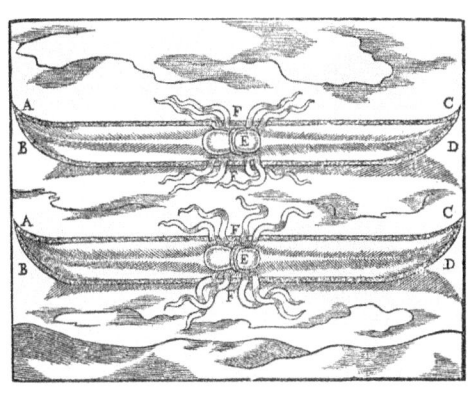

Illustrations 3

Upper left: Fig. 3.3
Reindeer hide to cover a ski.

Upper right: Fig. 3.7
Southern ski type.

Center left: Fig. 3.16
Furnes ski.

Center right: Fig. 3.22
Jokkfall ski.

Lower left: Fig. 3.27
South Lapp ski.

Bottom: Fig. 3.23
Central Nordic ski type.

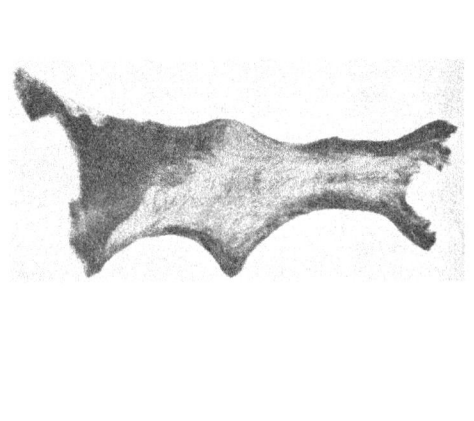

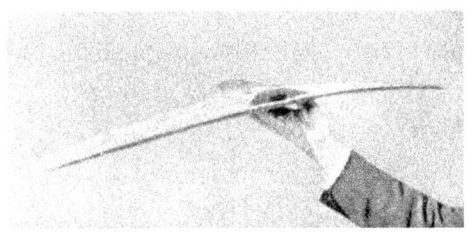
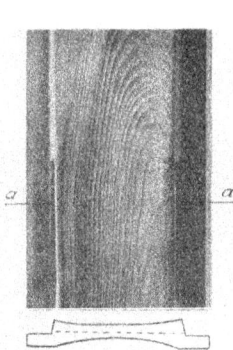
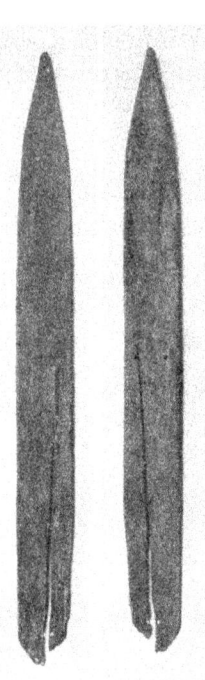
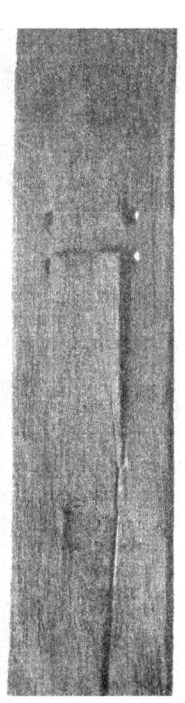

Illustrations 4

Top: Fig. 4.1
Sámi woman milking a reindeer. Female reindeer are the only females of the deer family with antlers.

Center Fig. 4.2
On the title page of the Dutch translation of Schefferus' *Lapponia* from 1682.

Bottom left: Fig. 4.4
A draft reindeer puling a Sámi pulk "reindeer sled." In Schefferus' *Lapponia*.

Bottom right: Fig. 4.5
Engraving in the Dutch edition of Schefferus' *Lapponia* from 1682.

Del av titelplanschen till den holländska översättningen av Johannes Schefferus' "Lapponia", Amsterdam 1682.

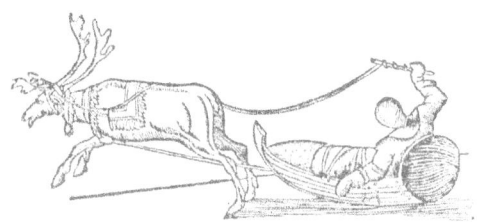

Illustrations 5

Fig. 4.6
Andr. M. Hansen's map of words for ski in the languages of Northern Eurasia, the area where skis are likely to have been used for thousands of years. In Fridtjof Nansen's *Paa ski over Grønland*.

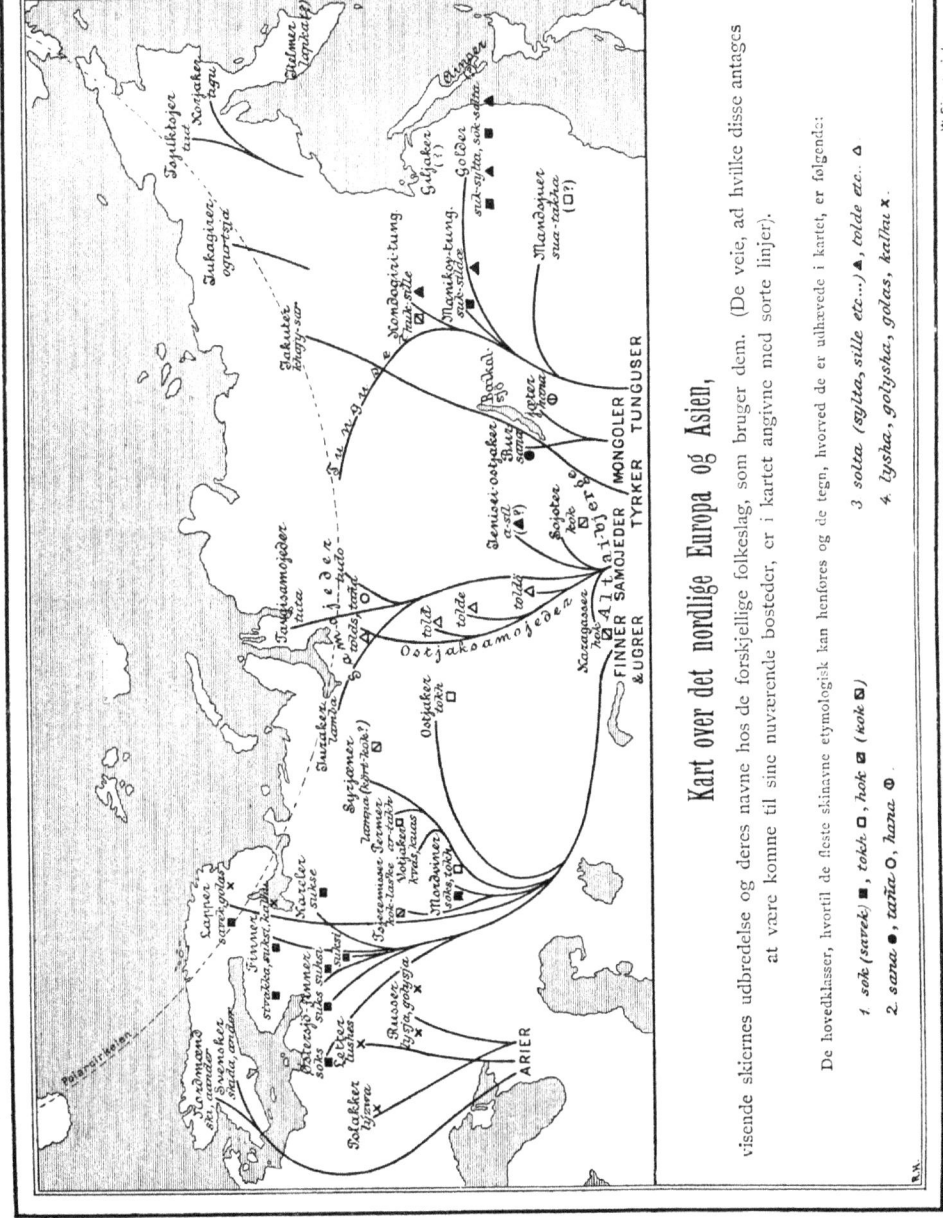

Kart over det nordlige Europa og Asien,

visende skiernes udbredelse og deres navne hos de forskjellige folkeslag, som bruger dem. (De veie, ad hvilke disse antages at være komne til sine nuværende bosteder, er i kartet angivne med sorte linjer).

De hovedklasser, hvortil de fleste skinavne etymologisk kan henføres og de tegn, hvorved de er udhævede i kartet, er følgende:

1. *sok (savek)* ■, *tokt* □, *hok* ◨ (*kok* ◨)   3. *solta (sylta, sille etc...)* ▲, *tolde etc...* △

2. *sana* ●, *taña* ○, *hana* ◉   4. *tysha, golysha, golas, kalhu* ×

Illustrations 6

Top left: Fig. 4.7
A Sámi on skis. It appeared in the text of a map of the Åsele Sámi area done by C. W. Cederhielm.

Top right: Fig. 4.8
An engraving from the 1748 German translation of Pehr Högström's book *Beskrifning öfver de til Sweriges krona lydande Lapmarker* from 1747.

Center left: Fig. 4.9
A Sámi hunting a bear on skis.

Center right: Fig. 4.11
An early picture of a Sámi ski from ca. 1650. It was reprinted in Adam Olearius' "Gottorffische Kunst-Kammer" from 1674.

Bottom left: Fig. 5.2
Hind was sacred to the Greek gods. Heracles had to fight with the gods for the beast, for example, Apollo or Artemis. This motif is seen on some Greek vases.

Bottom right: Fig. 4.5
Another Greek vase with the hind motif.

Illustrations 7

Top: Fig. 5.3
Heracles breaking off the antlers of the Ceryneian hind. Ca. 20 BCE in the style of the 5th century BCE.

Center left: Fig. 5.6
A bronze fibula from the eighth century BCE showing Heracles killing the Ceryneian hind.

Center right: Fig. 5.5
Another Greek vase with the hind motif.

Bottom: Fig. 5.9
Gold hunting on skis.

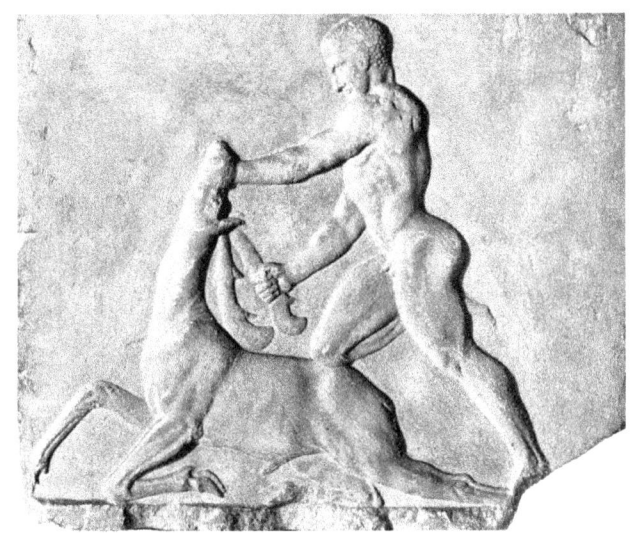
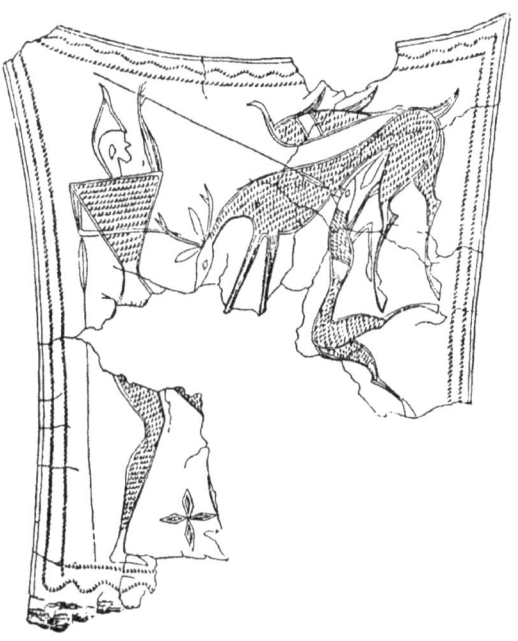

Illustrations 8

Top: Fig. 6.1
Franks Casket depiction of a scene from the Lay of Wayland from the *Poetic Edda*.

Center: Fig. 6.2
The god of skiing, Ullr.

Bottom: Fig. 6.3
Perhaps it is Ull on the famous Gallehus horn from the fifth century AD.

Illustrations 9

Top: Fig. 6.4
The ski goddess Skaði.

Bottom left: Fig. 7.2
The Arctic ski was wider than the Southern ski.

Bottom right: Fig. 7.4
A very old binding using both leather and withe was found at Mänttä, Finland in 1991 and dated at CE 530-540.

Illustrations 10

Top left: Fig. 7.5
Withe bindings with two withe loops in front and the back one bent down to go between sole and heel.

Top right: Fig. 7.8
Withe binding.

Upper: Fig. 7.9
Skis belonging to Sondre Nordheim.

Lower left: Fig. 7.18
Skis with steering ropes.

Lower right: Fig. 7.20
Children's skis found in Sweden and called *kässjor*.

Bottom: Fig. 7.19
Children's skis from Sweden.

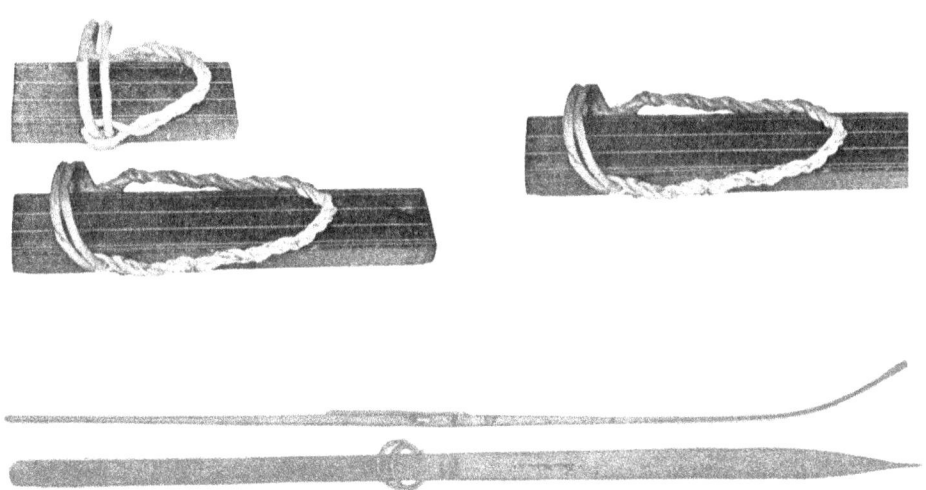

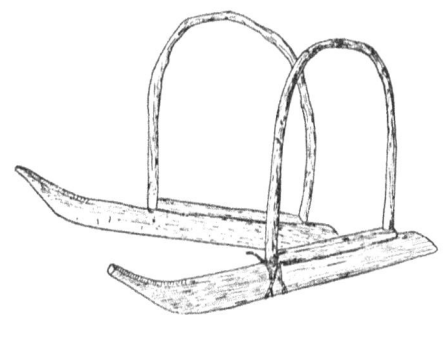

Illustrations 11

Top left: Fig. 8.2
Sámi ski (7) and a boat-shaped reindeer sleigh (6) as well as a pole.

Upper right: Fig. 8.5
Two Sámi skiing downhill with one of them picking up his cap.

Center left: Fig. 8.3
A pair of skis in Ole Worm's catalogue.

Center: Fig. 8.6
A close-up of the Ole Worm ski from 1655.

Lower right: Fig. 8.4
Part of the cover plate of Ole Worm's "Museum Wormianum" published in Leiden in 1655.

Bottom left: Fig. 8.7
A Sámi hunting with a cat.

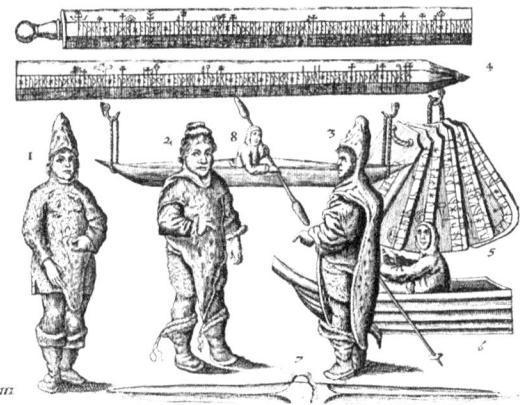

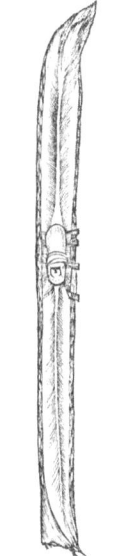

Illustrations 12

Top left: Fig. 8.8
Skier depicted on a wall in the Östersunda Church in Uppland, Sweden from the middle of the 15th century.

Top right: Fig. 9.2
Gustaf Vasa fleeing toward the Norwegian border in 1520-21 was accompanied by Lars and Engelbrekt from Kättbo in Dalarna.

Center left: Fig. 9.4
Gustaf Vasa on skis in a painting by Anders Zorn.

Center right: Fig. 9.3
Gustaf Vasa's two companions were on skis.

Bottom: Fig. 9.5
The city of Glebova where the Swedish and Dutch troops were billeted. Soldiers can be seen on patrol including two on skis.

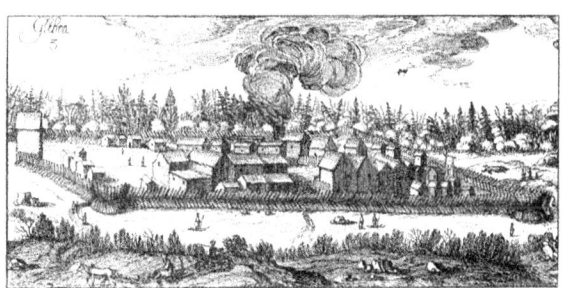

Illustrations 13

Top: Fig. 9.6
Picture from the *Schwedische Kriegs-Cronick* of March 12, 1632 of "Lapps" on skis during the time of Gustaf II Adolf.

Upper: Fig. 9.7
Another picture from the *Schwedische Kriegs-Cronick* of "Lapps" on skis.

Lower: Fig. 9.8
Norwegian Ski Corps practicing in the Trondhjem area in the winter of 1822.

Bottom: Fig. 9.9
Norwegian ski troops training on hilly terrain. The skier at the left is making "the chasseur's turn."

Illustrations 14

German artist Grüner's depictions of a ski soldier practicing.

Top left: Fig. 9.10

Top right: Fig. 9.11

Center left: Fig. 9.12

Center right: Fig. 9.13

Bottom left: Fig. 9.14

Bottom right: Fig. 9.15

Illustrations 15

Top left: Fig. 9.16
Scene from the Norwegian defeat of the Swedes at Trangen in 1808.

Top right: Fig. 10.4
Another Italian's depiction of a Sámi woman hunting with her husband.

Center left: Fig. 9.17
Another scene from the Norwegian defeat of the Swedes at Trangen in 1808.

Center right: Fig. 10.6
"Lapps" on skis.

Bottom: Fig. 9.14
A Finn [no doubt a Sámi], Torkjel, was forced to be a guide for Swedish skiers and tricked them into skiing off a precipice. This tale was made into the wonderful 1987 film by Nils Gaup entitled *Ofelaš* (Pathfinder). The Sámi boy leads the enemy *Čuđit* (Chudes) off a cliff to their deaths and saves his people.

Illustrations 16

Top: Fig. 5.1
When the demons hear what Lemminkäinen is up to, they fabricate Hiisi, a demon elk. Illustration by Björn Landström.

Bottom: Fig. 8.9
Painter Gerhard Munthe's depiction of Heming (also called Hermod) skiing away from the troll woman with the maiden on the back of his skis.

Illustrations 17

Top left: Fig. 10.8
A skier in C. C. Alanus' Report on Kemi Lappland from 1639.

Top right: Fig. 11.1
Sondre Norheim, born June 10, 1825, died in the USA in 1897.

Center left: Fig. 11.2
Sondre Norheim's withe bindings.

Center right: Fig. 10.9
Sámi wolf hunters on skis in Savolax. Note that the skiers are using two poles each.

Bottom left: Fig. 11.4
Sondre Norheim came from Morgedal in Telemark. Sondre's home is uppermost on the mountainside.

Bottom right: Fig. 11.3
Sondre Norheim as depicted by a German artist.

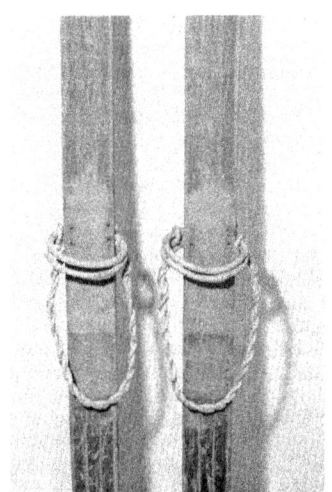

Illustrations 18

Top left: Fig. 11.8
A Norwegian skiing in Colorado.

Top right: Fig. 11.7
Sondre Norheim's memorial stone in Morgedal, Telemark, Norway.

Center left: Fig. 11.11
Pulk being pulled by reindeer. Not very realistic.

Center right: Fig. 11.5
The famous Kastedalsskotet that Sondre skied down.

Bottom left: Fig. 11.10
Pulk being pulled by reindeer.

Bottom right: Fig. 11.6
The dedication of a memorial at Sondre Norheim's grave in Denbigh, North Dakota in 1966.

Illustrations 19

Top: Fig. 11.9
A winter carnival at Minneapolis/St. Paul, Minnesota in the 1880's.

Center: Fig. 11.12
The participants in Nansen's 1887 expedition to Greenland, including two Sámi: Samuel Balto and Ole Nilsen Ravna.

Bottom left: Fig. 12.1
An old Swedish drawing of skiing in a Norwegian mountain valley.

Bottom right: Fig. 12.2
Knut Bergslien's painting "The Bird Hunter" inspired by Jonas Lie's poem.

Illustrations 20

Top left: Fig. 12.3
Hans Gude's drawing for "Berthe Tuppenhaug's Tales" from 1843.

Top right: Fig. 12.4
Artist Andreas Bohr Olsen's rendition of the poem "Knud and Birgit" (ca. 1845) drawn for the 1878 *Ny Illustrered Tidende*.

Center left: Fig. 12.6
Trysil-Knud roaring downhill and picking up the vest he had put on a bush on his way uphill. Drawn by A. Bloch.

Center right: Fig. 12.7
Bloch's drawing of Trysil-Knud on his way up a steep hill to pull off a stunt.

Bottom left: Fig. 12.8
Bloch's drawing of Trysil-Knud enjoying a new triumph.

Bottom right: Fig. 12.9
A film was made about Trysil-Knud.

Illustrations 21

Top left: Fig. 12.10
Thora Hansson as Solveig in the premiere of Ibsen's *Peer Gynt* in 1876.

Top right: Fig. 12.13
Women on skis.

Center left: Fig. 12.12
Woman on skis.

Center right: Fig. 12.11
Woman on skis.

Bottom left: Fig. 12.14
Woman on skis.

Bottom right: Fig. 12.15
Some of the skiers at the 1879 Huseby competition where the skiers from Telemark were superior to all others.

Illustrations 22

Top left: Fig. 12.16
Skiers from the four Nordic countries compared.

Top right: Fig. 13.1
Elite Norwegian army unit in the 1880's.

Center left: Fig. 12.17
Various ways to stop for those who don't ski very well.

Center right: Fig. 12.18
The national ski badge created by the sculptor Stig Blomberg on the motto "following our forefathers' footsteps."

Bottom left: Fig. 13.3
Telemark man jumping at the first Huseby competition in 1883.

Bottom right: Fig. 13.2
Telemark man jumping at the first Huseby competition in 1883.

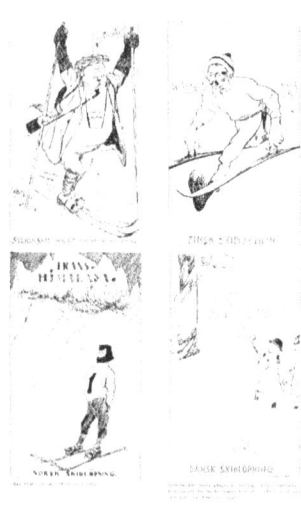

Illustrations 23

Top left: Fig. 13.4
The first ski jump in Finland won by the Norwegian Christian Nielsen.

Top right: Fig. A2.2
Skiers being pulled by reindeer.

Center left: Fig. A1.1
Map of Eurasia with Fennoscandia highlighted.

Center right: Fig. 13.5
"Skee" races in Norway and a sixty-two foot jump was published in *Scientific American* in 1895.

Bottom: Fig. A2.1
The Sámi still stitch their plank boats.

Illustrations 24

Top left: Fig. A3.1
Sandal with thong between toes.

Top right: Fig. A3.5
Birchbark canoe.

Center left: Fig. A3.2
Sandal laced on through holes along the side edges.

Center right: Fig. A3.7
In South China another peculiar device was used for crabbing in the mud.

Bottom left: Fig. Aa3.8
In Frisia a kind of mud shoe is used by peat-cutters.

Bottom right: Fig. A3.11
Sandal-boot, the forerunner of Eskimo boots.

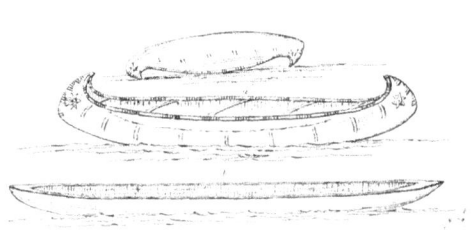
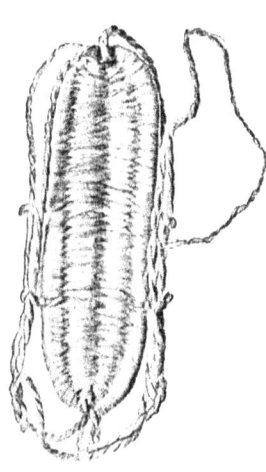

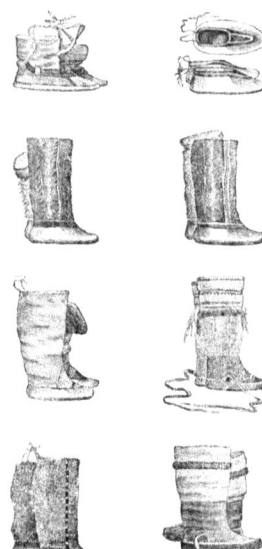

Illustrations 25

Top left: Fig. A3.16
Ladder type snowshoe.

Top right: Fig. A3.18
Frame type snowshoe.

Center left: Fig. A3.19
Frame type snowshoe.

Center right: Fig. A3.25
"Naskapi" type snowshoe.

Bottom left: Fig. A3.28
The hexagonal or "cane chair weave" occurs only in North America.

Bottom right: Fig. A3.29
The process of reeving the thongs through holes in the frame has a small distribution centered in Alaska.

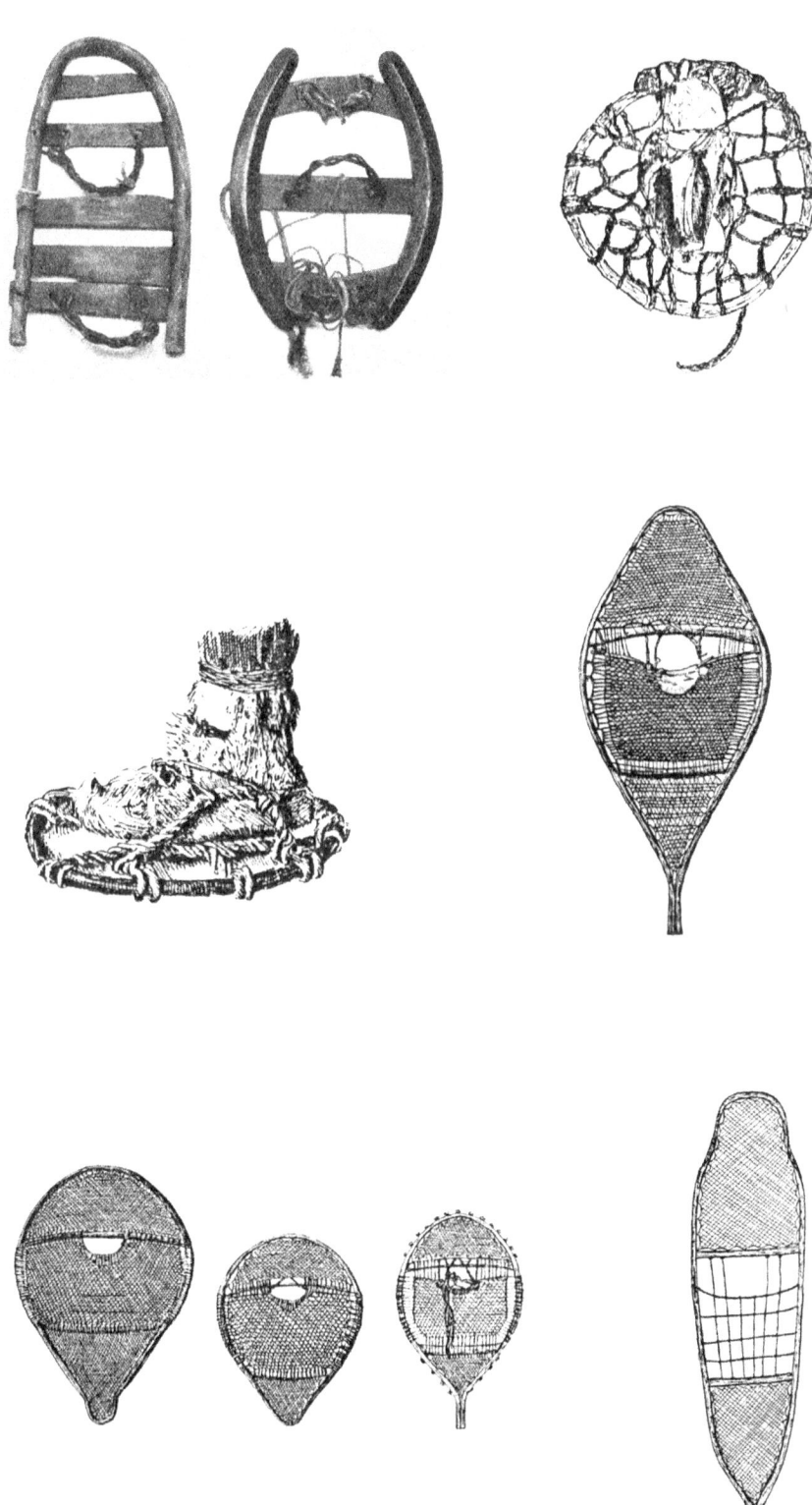

Illustrations 26

Top left: Fig. A3.33
Crossbars used in addition to the weaving to make the frame more rigid.

Top right: Fig. A4.1
Horse snowshoes.

Center left: Fig. A3.34
Square toe found in the east and midwest of North America.

Center right: Fig. A4.3
American Indians with snowshoes.

Bottom left: Fig. A4.4
American Indians with snowshoes.

Bottom right: Fig. A4.6
Johan Weichard Freiherr Valvasor, the governor of Krain (Slovenia).

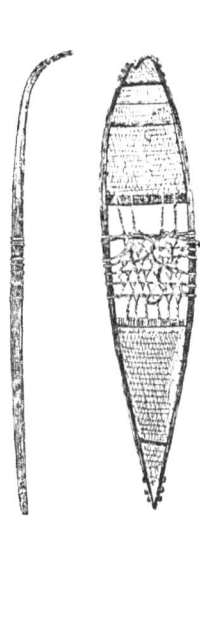

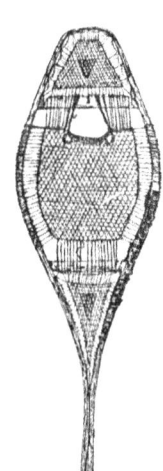

Illustrations 27

Fig. A1.2
Swimming reindeer. Lascaux, Dordogne, France. 15,000 to 10,000 BCE.

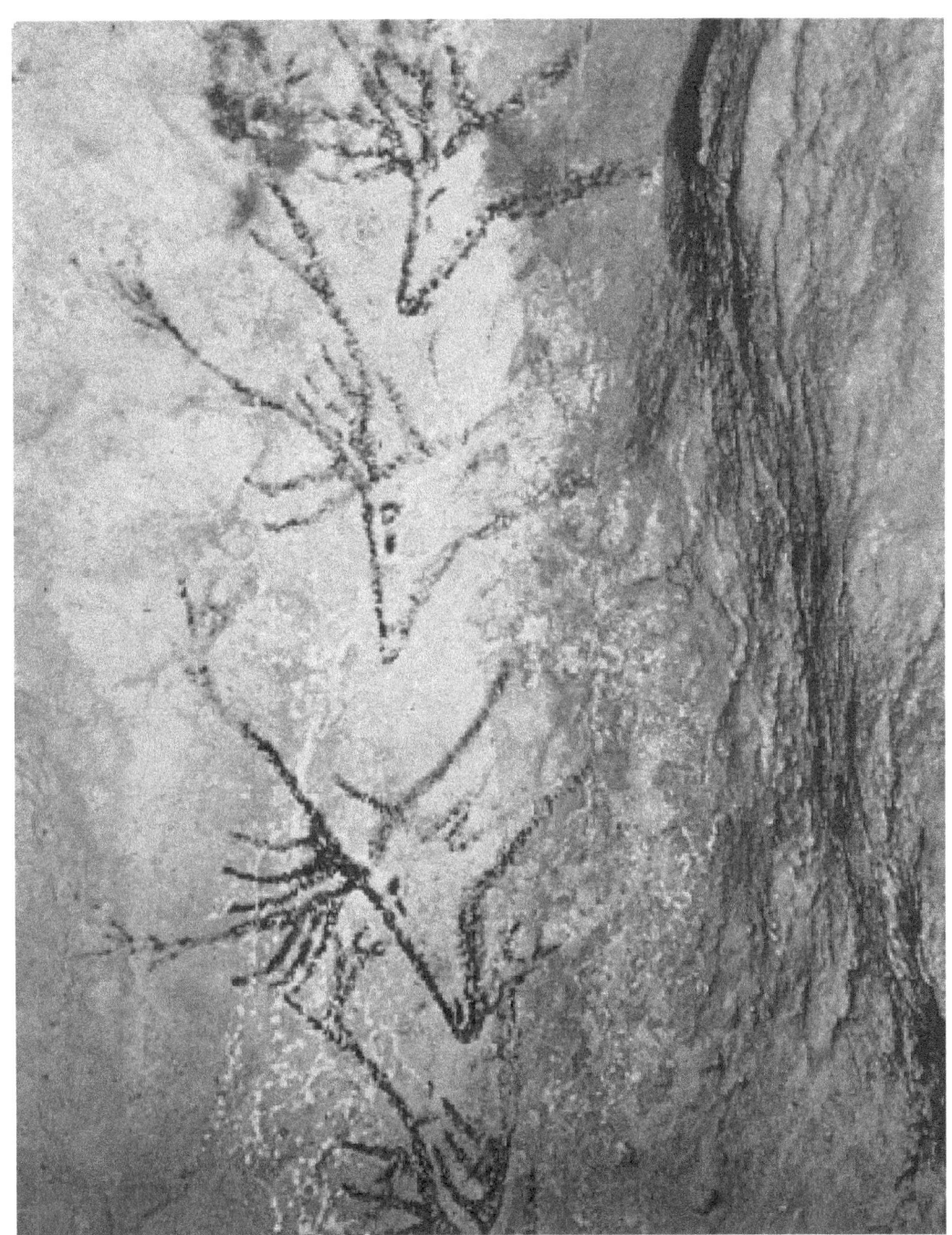

Military Use of Skis

The history of the military use of skis is largely one of missed opportunities. Remembering how it was part of the upbringing of princes during the Viking era that they learn how to ski and that skis were to be found on every farm in most of Scandinavia, it would seem that the stage was set for the employment of skis in military strategy. There are some early examples of just that. Saxo Grammaticus (see Chap. 1) wrote about a military campaign undertaken by Ragnar of the Hairy Breeches in the middle of the ninth century against Bjarmeland in what is now northern Norway. Saxo calls him Regnar. Natives of Finnmark who were on skis came to the aid of the people of Bjarmeland, and Ragnar suffered an ignominious defeat. Saxo was amazed that such well-equipped troops were ineffective against ordinary citizens on skis:[280]

> The Finns have always travelled by gliding swiftly on smooth boards and have complete control of their speed as they race along, so that men say they can be there and gone in a flash, just as they please. As soon as they have done damage to their enemy, they shoot away in the same lightning fashion as they flew to the scene. The nimbleness of their bodies and skis combined gives them a practised ease in attacking and retreating. You can imagine how aghast Regner was at being helpless to control his own fate: the vanquisher of the Holy Roman Empire at the height of its power saw himself dragged into utter disaster by an uncouth, defenceless fighting-force. So it was that the man who had superbly pulverised the glittering splendour of the imperial armies, the renowned troops of that most magnificent and clement of leaders, now yielded to a band of peasants and their miserable, flimsy equipment.

The Birchlegs

Undoubtedly the famous exploit of the two Birchlegs (the Birchlegs were one of the parties involved in civil wars in Norway during the twelfth and thirteenth centuries) Torstein

---

[280] Saxo 1999: 287.

Skjelva and Skjervald Skrukka is an example of the military use of skis. In 1206 they set out on skis with the two year old prince and later king Håkon Håkonsson, taking him through Østerdal to Trøndelag and a safe haven from certain death at the hands of Earl Skúli who himself aspired to the throne.

> "On this journey over the mountain they suffered terrible hardships due to storms, frost and drifting snow, and it was considered to be a miracle of God that a baby could endure such. One night the weather turned so bad that one didn't know where one was; they then let two of the most competent skiers in the group, Torstein Skjelva and Skjervald Skrukka [the birchlegs], set out with the boy and a couple of farmers who knew the terrain well as guides…There was no other food to give to little Håkon than melted snow. the next morning they finally came to Østerdalen, where the farmers received them in the best manner."[281]

The enemy in this case was the Bagler, the "rucksack" people who evidently had so much that they had to use rucksacks. They wanted to remove the child so that Earl Skúli could be king. Fig. 9.1 is Knut Bergslien's painting "The Birchlegs" that is Norway's best known ski painting.[282]

The best early example of the use of skis for military purposes happened prior to the battle of Oslo on March 6, 1200. King Sverre (1152-1202), who proved to be an exceptional leader and warrior, sent Pål Belte and a group of skiers from Oppland on a reconnaissance mission.[283] They were to check on the strength of the enemy who was headed toward them. The skiers soon reported that the enemy resembled nothing less than a flood. But in the actual battle King Sverre was on horseback, and there is no mention of skis being used other than for spying. *The King's Mirror* (see Chap. 8), though it has a fascinating description of skis almost as a curiosity, spends much of its dialogue on the finery of the knighthood, how to sit and fight on a horse, how to fight on land and at sea, but nothing about fighting on skis.

Wergeland

From 1855 to 1865 Lieutenant Colonel Oscar Wergeland published his *Skiløbningen, dens Historie og Krigsanvendelse* (Skiing, Its History and Military Use) as a series of fascicles in a Norwegian military journal. Wergeland, the brother of Norwegian patriot and poet Henrik Wergeland, was obviously a great devotee of skiing and as a military man deplored the fact

---

[281] Øverland: 156.
[282] Vaage 1979: 4-5.
[283] Vaage 1969: 9.

that skis had not been exploited to any great extent for military purposes in Norway for centuries in spite of conditions conducive to their use. He spent a good fifty pages lamenting the missed opportunities and even went so far as to suggest that Norway lost her independence because in winter fighting she neglected skis in favor of soldiers on horseback. There are enough grains of truth in what he wrote that it is worthwhile quoting him *in extenso*. His overall thesis is that soldiers on skis were the natural winter cavalry.[284] Even though this should have been quite apparent in the thirteenth century, it was not until early in the nineteenth century that ski troops were put to good use, by which time Norway had lost her independence, spent four centuries under Danish rule, and was about to come under the Swedish crown for nearly another century.

The same King Håkon, who as a child had been carried to Trøndelag on skis, attacked the Ribbungs (adherents of the Baglers, a clerical party in the civil wars of the thirteenth century) in 1225 with his Birch Legs. As Wergeland writes: "These horsemen were probably of the Birch Legs' old, solid stock: nobody doubts that they would have fought like bears on foot, but on heavy – perhaps not even tame – foals in snowdrifts or narrow forest roads they turned into absolutely pitiful soldiers and, following their horses' natural inclination, got into a horse race toward the rear."[285] Unfortunately, no one was able to see how effective soldiers on skis might have been.

Fig. 10.1

The old method of conscription – *leidang* – whereby each district was obliged to furnish ships, men and equipment in numbers commensurate with their size gave way to a system where people could escape military duty by paying a tax.[286] Soon there were not enough troops to occupy the forts and fortresses, and it became necessary to hire mercenaries, especially Germans.[287] But they proved to be a major problem. First of all, they drained the royal treasury, and when they were discharged after cessation of hostilities, they raised havoc around Norway, raided villages and became "Vikings" in reverse. Another problem was that sea defense took precedence over land defense.[288] Norwegians were worried by the large number of Germans in Bergen, those powerful Hanse-

---

[284] Wergeland 1865: 351.

[285] Wergeland 1865: 350.

[286] Wergeland 1865: 358.

[287] Wergeland 1865: 359.

[288] Wergeland 1865: 368.

atic merchants, and there were concerns about the Danes as well.

Another way that the national defense became debilitated was through a vast increase in the nobility. King Sverre seized feudal properties and parceled them out to his retainers and bailiffs, and these in turn no longer played much of a role in the

Fig. 10.2

defense effort. During Sverre's time commanders were usually the only soldiers on horseback, but by the time of King Magnus Lagabøter "Lawmender" (1238-80) it had become the rule rather than the exception for most soldiers.[289] And, as his name might suggest, he created legislation that gave the newly arrived foreign customs some legitimacy. This is not too surprising since the same thing had happened in neighboring Denmark and Sweden. In Denmark, for example, farmers who agreed to serve in the cavalry were exempted from all kinds of taxes.[290] By now, it was thought that a man on horse was worth more than three men on foot.[291] According to the law each farmer who owned at least 18 marks was required to have such heavy armament that he needed to be mounted.[292] Even farmers who had as much as 6 marks were required to have steel helmets and a coat of mail. But there is no mention whatsoever of skis being part of a soldier's equipment. Skiing is so different from the pastimes of a knight that it is hard to imagine a nobleman finding it fun to ski.

Fig. 10.3

The use of skis in districts of the country where they were endemic gradually went out of style, suppressed by noblemen, horsemen, German martial arts, and this development was aided by the spirit and letter of the law.[293] Skiers could not wear armor – it was too heavy. Wergeland suggests that the knife was more important to the soldier on skis than steel cloth-

---

[289] Wergeland 1865: 361.
[290] Wergeland 1865: 370.
[291] Wergeland 1865: 363.
[292] Wergeland 1865: 370.
[293] Wergeland 1865: 372.

ing.²⁹⁴ He laments the fact that there was not a Cervantes in Norway to record all this foolishness.²⁹⁵ Yet skis could be very effective for hunting during the winter. Provincial laws forbade moose hunting in the snow because the animals were helpless, as helpless as mounted troops were in heavy snow. Wergeland concludes by saying that the capability of national defense gradually declined over the thirteenth and fourteenth centuries so that Norway was no longer a match for her more powerful neighbors.

Fig. 10.5

By the thirteenth century the Russians had begun to plunder the far north of Finland, Sweden and even Norway. Sweden and Norway agreed on a mutual defense plan, and the Norwegians had to build and fortify a fortress at Vardø.²⁹⁶ Undoubtedly skiers participated in these border wars, but in Sweden it was not until the sixteenth century that skis are mentioned. Gustavus I (1496-1560) of Sweden, known as Gustaf Vasa, is famous for his alleged exploit on skis which is today commemorated in the 85 km. ski race known as the Vasaloppet. During the winter of 1520-21 Gustaf had to flee toward the Norwegian border and eventually got the Swedish people to come to his aid. He was accompanied by Lars and Engelbrekt from Kättbo in Dalarna (Fig. 9.2).²⁹⁷ It has been pointed out, though, that Gustaf almost certainly used snowshoes rather than skis.²⁹⁸ He was brought up in Uppland, an area where skis were no longer in common use. In 1518 he was taken to Jutland as a hostage, escaped to Lübeck, returning to Sweden two years later. In Dalarna at the time, unequal length skis were used, and they required special skills which Gustaf did not have. His two companions, though, were on skis (Fig. 9.3).²⁹⁹

However, Erik Geete repeated a story he heard from Fredrik Winblad von Walter that Gustaf after initially failing to gain support in Rättvik and Mora began to walk through the deep snow toward the Norwegian border. Soon a man gave him a pair of skis because he thought it a shame that such a fine person as Gustaf had to wade through the snow. According to the story: "It didn't go so quickly, for one doesn't become a skier in a day." Then Bar-

---

²⁹⁴ Wergeland 1865: 376.
²⁹⁵ Wergeland 1865: 377.
²⁹⁶ Wergeland 1965: 369.
²⁹⁷ Zettersten 1945: 284.
²⁹⁸ Zettersten 1945: 284-85.
²⁹⁹ Geete 1948: 241.

bro Stigsdotter Svinhufvud sent for Lars from Kättbo, the ski king of Dalarna, having him bring along his skis. He was to carry a letter from Barbro to a relative in Järvsö, which led to the peasants deciding to support Gustaf. Then Lars and Engelbrekt set out after Gustaf who had left several days earlier and soon caught up with him.[300]

Fig. 9.4 shows Gustaf Vasa on skis in a painting by Anders Zorn.[301]

Gustaf, however, did recognize the value of ski troops and organized a special unit of them, mostly from Savolaks and Norrbotten.[302] This occurred in 1555 after Russian detachments penetrated the Karelian peninsula and were pushed back thanks largely to armed skiers. Gustaf decided to go to war against the Russians and took his main forces to southern Finland, but for the defense of northern Finland he relied primarily on skiers. Olaus Magnus depicted Sámi ski troops in his *Historia de gentibus septemtrionalibus* of 1555. When the snows finally came in January of 1556, the king repeated his orders about skiers, and on January 27th he wrote that because of the heavy snow the enemy could not form a battle array wider than the road if he did not have skiers at his disposal. But, if the enemy had skiers, they could "be used on the snow where there were no roads as well as on the roads." He goes on to say that they are good for other purposes because they can travel thirty miles a day or more.

When the Swede Erik XIV (1533-77) fought against Norway in 1564 there was an expedition to Trondheim led by Claude Collart who had 4,000 troops at his disposal including 300 on skis.[303] And during Charles IX's (1550-1611) Polish war which was waged in Estonia, Livonia (Latvia) and Russia ski troops were often used but they were always Finnish soldiers who knew how to ski.[304] The first picture of a Swedish soldier on skis comes from this period.[305] During the winter of 1615-16 the Swede Jakob de la Gardie with assistance from a Dutch mission negotiated a peace with Russia. The Dutch steward Anthonis Goeteeris kept a detailed journal including engravings. One of them shows the city of Glebova where the Swedish and Dutch were billeted (Fig. 9.5). Soldiers can be seen on patrol including two on skis. Goeteeris wrote: "Some of the accompanying soldiers were equipped with skis, five to seven foot long or even longer and about a hand's width wide, on which they could run over

---

[300] Geete 1948: 240-42.
[301] *På skidor* 1935: 345.
[302] Zettersten 1940: 15.
[303] Zettersten 1940: 16.
[304] Zettersten 1940: 17.
[305] Zettersten 1940: 17-18.

the snow in the forests, where men and horses sank several feet deep down into the snow. The farmers here in the country benefit from skis at this time of the year."

The *Schwedische Kriegs-Cronick* of March 12, 1632 has two pictures (figs. 9.6-7) of "Lapps" on skis during the time of Gustaf II Adolf.[306] They were on German soil together with German soldiers in 1630, although the report and the pictures would seem to be pure fantasy.

One of the most remarkable feats of Swedish military skiing occurred in the seventeenth century during the Great Power Era when Swedes were fighting in Germany, Poland and Denmark where skiers would have been of no avail. In 1644 during the war against Denmark the government ordered the governor in Dalarna, Peter Kruse, to take the Särna and Idre parishes which were then part of Norway (which was under Danish rule). Since no regular troops were stationed there, there was a general call up. The local people were not unwilling to undertake the campaign, but they did not like the leader suggested by Kruse. When he asked them whom they wanted, they replied unanimously that it should be Daniel Buscovius, the chaplain in Älvdalen. He refused at first but in the end consented under pressure from the governor and bishop. On the eighteenth of March 200 men on skis left with Buscovius at the front on skis and with a large blunderbuss, his parish clerk, bible and chalice. Some of the men had rifles, others bows or spears. In just four days they reached Särna and surprised the locals who offered no resistance when told that they had to submit to the Swedish crown. They even thanked Buscovius for treating them so well. Four days later Buscovius and his skiers were able to return to Sweden having accomplished their mission without bloodshed.[307]

Fig. 9.8 shows the Norwegian Ski Corps practicing in the Trondhjem area in the winter of 1822.[308]

The Swedes continued to use cavalry for reconnaissance at the Finnish-Russian border; however, the Russians were beginning to use skiers to a greater extent, especially during the winters of 1702-04.[309] In 1689 the Norwegian general Wibe had suggested that the "fire-makers," so-named because of the long guns they used, should form a ski corps in Trøndelag during the winter.[310] They were supposed to wear white caps with green lining

---

[306] *På skidor* 1941: 281.
[307] Zettersten 1940: 19-20; Firsoff 1943: 14.
[308] Bø 1966: 33.
[309] Zettersten 1940: 20.
[310] Zettersten 1940: 20.

which they were to turn inside out in the summer. These ski troops were better organized in the early eighteenth century and, according to historical sources, performed excellently. The Norwegians have their own commemorative ski races, one of which celebrates a setback the illustrious Swedish king Charles XII (1682-1718) suffered in 1716. On the move in Norway, his troops were threatening Norwegian positions not far from Oslo. A Norwegian military unit was sent to spy on the Swedes and overheard two Swedish officers conversing in French which they thought no one else understood. In this manner, the Norwegians learned of the Swedish plans and a skier was sent to pass the information on to the Norwegian commander more than fifty miles away. The skier traveled day and night and delivered his message in time for the Swedes to be stopped.[311]

Fig. 9.9 shows Norwegian ski troops training on hilly terrain.[312] The skier at the left is making "the chasseur's turn."

There were now organized ski units in Norway, in the south made up mostly of men from Hedmark and Oppland, and in the north from Trøndelag. These units proved to be very effective in attacking the Swedish forces and inflicting considerable punishment. When the Swedish general Armfelt transferred his military units to South Trøndelag in the fall of 1718, Norwegian skiers from south of the mountains were sent to Østerdal's defense. They ran into some 70 Swedish cavalry and an amazing tree to tree fight ensued between cavalry and skiers with several men lost on either side. The Norwegian captain Emahusen was in command of the ski troops to the north. He made raids against the Swedes along the border, cutting off Armfelt's communications with Jämtland. He successfully attacked a Swedish unit in December of that year, capturing supplies, messages, and clothing. Armfelt's retreat over the mountains on New Year's day, 1719 has become legendary, at least for the Norwegians. Perhaps the proverbial "one thousand Swedes ran through the weeds chased by one Norwegian" came from here. Armfelt found out that Charles XII had fallen and immediately set out for Sweden. Many of the Swedish soldiers froze to death in the mountains because they did not have skis and because they were not familiar with the roads. Farmers in the area had warned Armfelt the night before he departed. The few Swedes who had skis survived.[313]

---

[311] Bø 1966: 29-30.
[312] Bø 1966: 37.
[313] Zettersten 1940: 22-23; Bø 1966: 30.

Figs. 9.10-15, drawn by the German Grüner, depict a ski soldier practicing.[314]

Captain Emahusen drew up the first set of rules for the military use of skis in Norway in 1733.[315] Curiously, the rules were written in German, followed by Danish versions with German commands in 1748 and 1762, and finally in 1774 a revised set in Danish. All of these were handwritten. The first printed version came out in Danish in 1804. The first regular units of ski troops date from 1742, and in 1747 the numbers increased to a battalion of three companies in the north and a battalion of three companies in the south. Toward the end of the century a "Hunters' Corps," an elite unit, was set up in which every member had to be a good skier. They were considered Norway's finest troops at the time. Not much time was devoted to training, a mere six days of winter exercises in the south and only four in the north since the troops there were presumably better trained to begin with (figs. 9.16-20).[316] Then there was training on Sundays at the local church for a few hours.

The districts that maintained soldiers supplied the equipment, and in 1798 it consisted of a pair of skis with bindings and pole, a pair of homespun gaiters, a knapsack with leather strap and a backpack also with leather strap.[317] Ten districts together had to supply a sled with skis as runners, a hand ax and a provision bag. Since there were no standards as to type of ski, the soldiers wore what they were used to in their home districts. In the south, the unequal length Østerdal skis were used. The skis were preferably made of heart pine, the harder the better. In the north Snåsa skis were used. They were lighter and were curved up at the back so that if one broke a tip the ski could be reversed and still used. Snåsa skis were usually made of hardwood such as birch or ash. It is interesting that there is no mention of ski troops coming from Telemark with their equal length skis. This is not too surprising when you consider that most of the fighting was well east of Telemark on the border between Norway and Sweden.

Organized skiing competitions find their origin in the military use of skis. Earlier on there were some individual competitions such as that between Heming and King Harald, but the military organized local competitions in the eighteenth century that became extremely popular. For example, in 1767 an invitation to a prize competition stated: "No one may be turned down, everyone must be allowed to compete with the ski companies for the above prizes, and therefore everyone must be apprised of time, place, conditions, and so on,

---

[314] Vaage 1979: 81-83.
[315] Firsoff 1943: 15; Bø 1968: 31-32.
[316] Vaage 1979: 38, 37; Luther 1942: 58, 62; Vaage 1979: 80.
[317] Bø 1966: 31.

to the extent that this is possible out in the countryside." There were to be four categories: shooting at a target at full speed (two prizes of 20 "dollars," a Norwegian monetary unit before 1875); downhill in wooded terrain (four prizes of 10 dollars); downhill without using the pole as a brake and without falling (six prizes of 4 dollars); and crosscountry on flat ground (eight prizes of 2 dollars). By 1792 these competitions had become regular events but the prize sum had been reduced to 20 dollars per company. They certainly must have stimulated the sport of skiing wherever held.

The establishment of two battalions of Norwegian ski troops in 1747 brought a response from the Swedes. The commander of the Jämtland regiment was ordered in 1749 to organize a ski corps of 200 men with requisite officers. The ski corps had some brief maneuvers in 1749 and 1753-55, but the entire corps was never assembled, and the maneuvers stopped completely after 1755. The other border regiment, from Värmland, never organized ski troops. But the Värmland "Field Hunters" were set up in 1788 and equipped with skis for border patrol during the war that had just begun.

During Gustav III's (1746-92) war against Russia several ski legions were organized for border patrol.[318] The most unusual one was at Pielisjärvi in Karelia. When pastor Stenius from this parish noticed at the beginning of 1789 that ordinary guard duty was being curtailed, he called the peasantry together. They took it upon themselves to man outposts at the border with the main watch at the church. They chose lieutenant Anders Duncker as their commander, and he trained them according to the 1774 Norwegian military ski rules. When governor Carpelan came to a general inspection on March 1st, 374 farmers marched. Then they demonstrated their drills which Carpelan wrote: "were a delight to watch."

When the main Finnish army retreated to Uleåborg in March and April of 1808 there would have been great use for experienced ski troops, had there been any, but only a small number of skiers had been selected for the companies.[319] Skiers were of more use in the Savolaks brigade. By the time the troops were assembled on February 12th of 1808 the governor had been requested to get hold of skis, and two weeks later 159 pair had been purchased. During the retreat small units of skiers were often fighting enemy forces, but not until April 20th when the brigade again advanced was a company of ski troops organized under the leadership of the infantry captain Germund Aminoff. There were to be three officers, four non-commissioned officers, six corporals, and 150 privates, all of whom were

---

[318] Zettersten 1940: 25.
[319] Zettersten 1940: 25-26.

to remain with their regular units until the ski company was to proceed. These ski troops successfully participated in the battles at Revolaks on April 27th and Pulkila on May 2nd.

Since Denmark's declaration of war was not delivered until March 14, 1808, the war along the Norwegian border became a winter campaign.[320] Norway had its experienced ski companies. In Sweden they tried to get skis for those Norrland soldiers who knew how to ski. They did not receive any special training. The results were not unexpected. When superior Swedish forces ran into outnumbered Norwegian ski units, the latter easily escaped. When Colonel Gahn of the second Dalarna battalion was surrounded by Norwegians under Captain Angell at Trangen on April 25th, it was the Hof company of the southern ski battalion that completed the enclosure even though they were the farthest off of all troops participating in the battle. Gahn himself and more than 400 men were taken prisoner (figs. 9.16-17). The Norwegians demonstrated what trained ski troops were capable of. A cease-fire prevented the Swedes from doing anything about ski troops until the summer of 1809. Swedish ski troops were largely improvisations intended to meet an inescapable need.

---

[320] Zettersten 1940: 26-27; Firsoff 1943: 16.

Skiing in Literature II: 16th, 17th and 18th Centuries

The references in this chapter range from Olaus Magnus' magnificent history of Scandinavian people to other prominent European writers mentioning of skiing. Olaus' work contains many illustrations pertaining to skiing; they are very amusing in that an Italian who had never witnessed skiing drew them.

Fig. 10.10

Olaus Magnus

The Swedish bishop Olaus Magnus (1490-1557) traveled to northern Sweden and Norway in 1518-19 and twenty years later published a map, *Carta marina* (Introduction, Fig. i.3), on which several skiers are depicted.[321] Then in 1555 in his monumental *Historia de gentibus septentrionalibus* (History of the Scandinavian People) he discussed skiing in Norway (figs. 10.1-2).[322] Here is his fourth chapter, *Om Skrickfinnarnas (Skridfinnarnas) land* (Concerning the land of the skiing Finns [Sámi]):[323]

> Scricfinnia is a province located between Bjarmaland and Finnmark, yet it stretches in a long curve to the south and down to the gulf of Bothnia, to put it simply, like an outstretched rear end. The country has gotten its name primarily from the fact that the inhabitants in order to move quickly use a sort of long and flat wooden board (ski) that is curved up in the front into a bow. These skis they tie onto their feet and take a pole in hand to maneuver with, and thereby they run easily uphill and downhill and aslant over the snowy mountains just as they wish. With these skis it can be seen that one of them is a foot longer than the other, and the shorter ski should be the same length as the skier. In other words, if the man or woman who uses them is eight feet tall, then the ski on one foot, to be of correct measure, should be just as long, i.e. eight feet, while the

---

[321] Olaus 1539.
[322] Olaus 1972: 595, 598.
[323] Olaus 1972: 13-14.

other ski is nine feet. In addition they prepare it so that the bottom surface of the ski is covered with a soft skin of reindeer calf. The reindeer is an animal which in shape and color resembles the deer, but is taller and heavier. Later in the book there will be a report about its nature. The reason why they cover their skis with such soft skin is explained by them in several ways, among others, so that they can cover the path over the deep snow much more quickly, and so that they can more agilely dodge dangerous chasms and precipices, or so that on trips up steep hills they can avoid sliding backwards: the hairs on these skins, you see, stand on end like spikes or the quills of a hedgehog and, through their peculiar nature, prevent the skier from gliding backwards. Through their skill in using such devices these people can climb mountains which otherwise would be completely inaccessible, in addition to the fact that they would race down the steepest valleys, especially during the winter. In the summer once more it goes just as easily, for even if the snow doesn't disappear, it becomes too loose and gives way to the pressure of the skis. In any case, no mountain is so steep that they do not succeed in climbing it in some clever roundabout way. Thus, when they leave the depths of the valleys, they make their way ahead in sinuous curves over the lowest cliff ledges and wend their way obliquely in a tight zigzag up the slopes, until finally over precipices and gorges they reach the top and thereby the goal they set for themselves. And this sort of exploit they carry out sometimes in the zeal of hunting, sometimes to compete with one another, since anyone wants to stand out as the best, especially since in the lists they compete to win the prize determined. Although Pope Paul III – according to the bishop of Saluzzo, Philippus Archintus, the governor of the holy state – stated that he wouldn't believe the alleged reports of the northerners' artfulness and capability in skiing, it is nevertheless the gospel truth and remains so as described above and as in the future will again be expounded.

In the fifth chapter, 'More about the country's position and nature,' Olaus mentions earlier scholars such as Jordanes and Paulus Diaconus and what they have to say about the Sámi. He cites Paulus as saying that "the *scrickfinns* have gotten their name from 'jumping' [skric-ka], for they are in the habit of hunting wild animals with jumping motions and with special tricks in that they use implements of wood, in front curved up like a bow."[324] And in the twelfth chapter, 'Concerning the Lapps' hunting expeditions,' Olaus adds:[325]

> Inasmuch as the Scrickfinns, Bjarms and Finnmarkings and their customs and life have already been discussed earlier in the book, it should only be added here how, by using curved, wide and smooth wooden slats on their feet, they have a tussle with wild animals that they hunt with bow and arrows through valleys and on snow-covered mountains and ridges, where they sweep forward at the most neck breaking speed.

---

[324] Olaus 1972: 14-15.
[325] Olaus 1972: 146.

Olaus' book was richly illustrated by an Italian artist who clearly had never seen skis, as can be seen in Fig. 10.3.[326] He misunderstood the expression "long shoes" so that his skis look very strange: they stick way out in front and come to a point as they curve up, but they end immediately behind the foot. These inaccurate drawings misled authors who discussed skis for a number of years after the publication of the book. The picture at the head of the twelfth chapter shows a woman on skis shooting an arrow, and Olaus goes on to say that the women regularly participate in the hunt as well. Fig. 10.4 is another Italian's depiction of a Sámi woman hunting with her husband.[327] Fig. 10.5 is the Olaus artist's depiction of a reindeer sleigh.[328] But what strikes the reader is that Olaus' descriptions are very accurate, for example, the unequal length skis with the shorter, right ski being fur-covered. He had visited the area and witnessed skiing firsthand.

Peer Gynt

The tales about Peer Gynt that Henrik Ibsen used as a source for his famous drama of the same name date from the beginning of the seventeenth century. Peer was a marvelous skier, as the following tale will demonstrate:[329]

> On Christmas Eve morn a man from Skoe came and asked Per to go with him to Skjerhell Hill, since Per was familiar with the route and with every route and path in that area. This man from Skoe was a lieutenant, they say. He had committed a murder and therefore he wanted to flee to Røros, which was a place of refuge at that time. The lieutenant always wanted to move quickly and directly, but he did not know the way in this case, so he wanted Per to go with him as a guide, you see. Well, Per took his skis and went with him all the way to Skjerhell Hill, from where they could see the way in to Røros. Then Per turned back and headed for home. On the steep slope above Hågå farm his skis were gliding so well that he didn't turn in to his home on the farm, but continued descending right down to the Brannvoll meadows. As he jumped a lane with a fence on both sides at the steepest part of the hill, he lit his pipe with flint and tinder, they say, but that is a bit too much to expect anyone to believe. Then he carried his skis up to Hågå, arriving just as they were putting on the pot with the milk porridge for their Christmas Eve supper. From Hågå to Skjerhell Hill is a good 4½ old miles, so he did close on 10 miles in one day.

An old Norwegian mile was seven of our miles, in other words Peer covered over thirty miles.

---

[326] Olaus 1972: 130.
[327] *På skidor* 1931: 403.
[328] *På skidor* 1931: 404.
[329] Bø 1966: 22.

Fig. 10.6 shows "Lapps" on skis. The original is in the National Museum in Copenhagen.[330]

Cervantes

Miguel de Cervantes Saavedra's fantastic adventure novel *Persíles y Sigismunda* came out in 1617, six months after his death, and deals with the endless hardships and suffering Persíles, son of the king of Iceland, and Sigismunda, daughter of the king of Friesland, must endure before they can marry one another. The action takes place partly in northern Europe, whose geography Cervantes had only vague notions about, and so his imagination was unleashed.

During a sailing voyage in the Northern Ice Ocean, Persíles' ship gets stuck in the ice somewhere outside the Norwegian coast. Cervantes in his colorful language writes:[331]

> "…we felt the sides of the ship and the keel hit what seemed to be moving cliffs, from which we understood the sea had already begun to freeze; the icebergs, which were forming under the water, hindered the vessel's movements." Finally the ship is stuck "like a rock stuck in a ring." Now there is fear of starving to death, but luckily another frozen ship is discovered, and heading a little band of his people, Persíles goes there, sliding on the ice. It turns out to be a pirate's ship, which after a short battle they take possession of. While we were examining the ship's stores, Persíles says, "we discovered unexpectedly and at an inconvenient time that from land over the ice a band of armed people, numbering more than 4,000 in all, were coming… . They were traveling on just one foot, in that with the right foot they were kicking towards the left heel, whereby they were pressing on and gliding a long way over the sea, and then they pushed off again and once again glided a long way." Soon they had surrounded the ship; Persíles and his people were taken prisoner and were dragged, together with cargo and stolen ship's stores, on ox skins over the ice to the mainland, where they were led to Cratilo, "the king of Lithuania and the ruler of these seas."

There must be a grain of truth in this fantastic description. Cervantes, living in Spain, had certainly read or heard about skiing in northernmost Europe. The devices sound like unequal length skis.

Holger Hanssøn Arctander

The next literary mention of "skirunning" in poetic form is that of Holger Hanssøn Arctander from Åfjord in South Trøndelag, Norway, a minister's son, who wrote a poem in 1625

---

[330] Wiklund 1928: 5. Joh. Rach pinx 1748.
[331] Tjerneld 1943: 314.

mentioning skiing. It is not known when he was born, but in 1624 he became a student, so he was probably born around 1600. He wrote the poem, "Encomiolon Norvegianum" (Song of Praise over Norway), in Latin while he was studying in Copenhagen and probably homesick for Norway:[332]

> See when winter comes with biting wind
> and driving snow … then the native fastens under
> the sole of each foot oblong implements
> and with them he moves
> over hill and dale as quickly as the
> fastest runner, indeed, almost like a bird
> when it flies in the air.
>
> Never is the snow so terribly piled up
> that he doesn't move forward and over
> on his hasty flight – in the snow there is
> to the extent that you can see a fleeting trace
> of the ski.

He tells about the dog that often runs ahead of him, sniffing and smelling, and chasing the game towards its enemy, the hunter:

> He comes flying forth on his willing skis
> with his hunting spear and the quick arrows
> ready for use, and the snow cannot hinder
> his strides or his forward movement
> however deep the snow is.

Arctander tells how the snow hinders the wild animals but not the hunter with his skis:

> Not even to shoot does he stop his running
> he whom Diana in mercy made a hunter
> so diligent and clever that he can
> shoot his swift arrow into
> the bird itself that flies through the air.
>
> What, I merely ask, is Acantus
> with his hunting spears, or the great hunter
> Adonis next to this one?
> Here they become small. Yes, you know it yourself,
> O great Diana.

---

[332] Vaage 1969: 108-09.

> It is not far from the truth that anyone
> native to Norway could take the prize as a hunter
> Proud of such strength he can be.

Finn Tricks Enemy off Cliff

In 1650 Jens Lauritzøn Wolff wrote (in Copenhagen) in his "Norrigi Illustrata" about a Norwegian skier who tricked Russian skiers off a precipice in the dark somewhere in northern Norway. This story appears in many variants and was made into a film in 1987 called *Ofelaš* (Pathfinder), a film both moving and austere. This is an old Sámi legend involving the Sámi and their old enemies, the Tchudes (a West Finnic group). Carl B. Roosen from Trondhjem mentioned in his 1865 book *About skiing* that a Finn [probably a Sámi], Torkjel, was forced to be a guide for Swedish skiers and tricked them into skiing off a precipice. Anders Faye localized the event involving these skiers to Tysfjord in Salten, "Mandfjordfjeldet," where human bones were supposed to have been found until as late as 1782. Faye mentions this in his "Norwegian Folk Legends" from 1844. There is a song, as well, about this migratory legend. When it was made, is not known. Here, too, the skiers are Swedish. They are coming from Jämtland in order to plunder a house where a wedding is being celebrated. A "Fjeldfin" (mountain or reindeer Sámi) whom they run into is forced to show them the way, but he tricks them in the dark off a precipice:[333]

> In Namsedal at Medjaa a wedding was to be held
> Word got around and awakened the Jämtlander's desire for plunder.
> He knew that the bridal sideboard was an old Norwegian custom.
> To it and the silver mug he directed his glance.
>
> A multitude gathered – more than three hundred
> ready to climb the high border mountains
> Although everyone was well-acquainted with the use of Norwegian skis
> they nevertheless climbed with difficulty up the steep mountain side.

In the mountains there was a snow storm, and "every single track was covered" so it was difficult to find their way:

> They now deliberated about their speed downhill
> and many a heart probably shuddered at such a daring journey.
> Then they met a mountain Finn, in his reindeer skin
> coming back from the town, heading for his hut.

---

[333] Vaage 1969: 109-10.

He was menaced into showing them the way to the place where the wedding was to be held, and he immediately made his plan as to how he would resolve the situation that had arisen:

> That advice won general acclaim, and by cheerful talk
> about how mug and silver coins would soon be theirs
> the winter day quickly slipped by. When the evening tent was raised,
> the mountain Finn stood among them with his Tyri-torch lit.
>
> "Now follow its blaze," he shouted, whoever is not afraid,
> for soon the ski will jump in more than one place,
> Steep is so many a hill, in which the mountain side sinks.
> But the Jämtlander, I know, usually stands steadily on his skis.
>
> – – –
>
> His route went to a precipice with an almost vertical mountain side
> where the jump surely led down to the pale slope.
> There he threw his torch; the flame flared vigorously,
> and down into the abyss sank the entire enemy band.
>
> Himself, he neatly stepped aside, but watched very carefully
> until each one of the Jämtlander band lay in death's arms.
> Then he took a familiar detour; the easy speed of the skis
> took him soon down the mountain to Medjaa farm.

Fig. 10.7 shows Torkjel leading the enemy off a cliff.[334]

Scheffer and Worm on Skiing

In 1655 Ole Worm, a Danish professor, wrote about skis in his work "Museum Wormianum."[335]

In 1673 Johannes Schefferus wrote in his *Argentoratensis Lapponia* (Frankfurt) that skis are covered with resin or pitch.[336] This is an early mention of treating the skis to prevent snow from sticking to them.

Petter Dass

Petter Dass (1647-1708), perhaps Norway's most prominent early writer, has nothing about skis in his major work *Nordlands Trompet*, but in the poem "Sølvbergrim" (Silver Hill

---

[334] Vaage 1969: 107.
[335] Vaage 1969: 11.
[336] Vaage 1969: 12.

Rhyme), he has:[337]

> Listen Amund Gaaskiønlie
> you who crawl in the forest
> Tie around your foot a ski
> Run and shoot ptarmigan.

and elsewhere in the same poem:

> Per Skanseng-Viskan ran
> on Andron [Andron = ondur, i.e. skis] down the stony ridge.

Egede in Greenland

The clergyman and missionary Hans Poulsen Egede went to Greenland in June of 1721. In his journal of 1722 it says:[338] "The Greenland youth had a great desire to play tricks on us. On the other hand, we could show off by skating and skiing."

Fig. 10.8 shows a skier in C. C. Alanus' Report on Kemi Lappland from 1639. It was actually drawn in 1674.[339]

Ludvig Holberg on Skiing

Holberg (1684-1754) was Denmark-Norway's finest writer during the Enlightenment. Known as the Molière of the North, he wrote many successful comedies and other dramas. He was born in Norway and, thus, had skied when he was young; but he spent most of his adult life in Copenhagen. It is not generally known that he also wrote about skiing. In 1733 he wrote a *Compendium geographiæ* which was used as a textbook in school and which touches on skiing. Here are some excerpts from the book: writing about Akershus Diocese:[340]

> In the wintertime one uses skis in order to run on the snow. The "royal" skiers (the military) have one short ski, one and one half ells long, but the other ski is two and a half ells long. These skis are covered with sealskin. A skier always has a pole in his hand to balance with…

Later on he speaks about mail delivery to Stavanger (from Oslo):

> In wintertime the mail must often be carried on skis through deep snow, since a horse cannot get through, when the local residents do not keep the road open. – In the case of

---

[337] Vaage 1969: 110.
[338] Vaage 1969: 15.
[339] Zettersten 1943: 23.
[340] Geete 1936: 354-57.

heavy snowfall certain areas are covered with snow so deep that it is not possible to clear the road except at great cost and toil. In such cases one must use *skidor* (skis) or *tryger* (snowshoes). And since here are mentioned skis that are used in Norway in the winter in order to move over deep snow, the reader should be informed about the nature of these skis.

One can walk well on a pair of skis, if one only knows how to use them correctly. This training on skis is even considered necessary. In Norway it is common for little boys to practice skiing, so that even by the coast, where one doesn't have to use them, one uses skis for the sake of amusement. A ski is a thin piece of wood, broad enough for a shoe to stand on it. In the middle of the ski there is a band or piece of leather, where the foot is put in, whereupon the ski is fastened to the foot. At the very front the ski is somewhat pointed and curved upward; it is bent with the help of fire, just as the iron on a skate is curved a little. But neither the point nor the curve is longer than a "spand" (a foot) on the ski, the rest of it is completely straight and of the same width. The width is usually 6 to 8 inches. The length is according to the discretion of the one who will use the skis. Some are not in the habit of using them except for leisure and running down a hill.

The above-mentioned skis tend to be of the same length and generally two and a half ells. When made this way, they usually are not covered with skin, but the wood is just smoothed on the bottom side, sometimes even brushed with tar, so that ice or snow will not stick to them, which would obstruct the skiing. Such skis are no good for walking uphill, as there is nothing that resists, which is why they slide back. On flat land, as well as downhill, they are, however, usable.

But the right kind of skis, such as trained people and the military in particular use, are made such that one ski is very short, about one and a half ells, the other one being two and a half ells long. These types of skis are covered with sealskin, where the foot is (underneath the ski). The fur is positioned such that when the ski moves forward, the hairs of the fur are smooth, which increases the speed. But when the ski is pulled back, the hairs go against, which keep the skier from sliding back when he goes uphill. That one ski is short and one ski long has certain advantages. For when both skis are long they are too awkward to handle, especially as they cannot go very fast, and either one has to steer them down a hill or go on flat land or uphill. When one ski on the other hand is short, one can run and steer better at the same time where that is necessary. I guess both skis could not be short, because then they would not be as secure to walk on plus they would sink down too far in deep snow. When you go up a hill you often have to make a detour when it is too steep, but when you go down a hill they could run with such speed that it's incredible, especially if the snow isn't soft but rather hard. Then the speed is such that even if one comes down on flat land, the skis still are running and could sometimes go up a hill with the same driving force.

In the hand one has a pole for help on some occasions such as balancing. When children and young people practice skiing, they use the pole such that they place it between their legs and kind of ride it, so that the end of the pole protrudes between the skis. This slows the speed considerably. Later, when they have learned to stand and run better, they hold the pole at their side and finally, when they master the art, they hold the pole in the hand, and with it they can turn out of the way or go sideways down a hill or a mountain, when they fear there could be a precipice down below. This kind of skiing has its dangers for those who are not familiar with the area, for in the mountains and hills there are sometimes openings and big holes or at least many steep, precipitous bluffs or wild "floug" as they are called in Norwegian, where one who doesn't really know the terrain, can fall down such a bluff. Across the wild mountains, when there has been a heavy snowfall, one cannot travel any other way than on skis.

Besides these skis, snowshoes (*tryger*) are used, which are of quite a different nature, as they are not made for running but only for walking, where the snow's very deep.

Fig. 10.9 shows Sámi wolf hunters on skis in Savolax.[341] Note that the skiers are using two poles each.

Hans Friis

In 1750 Hans Friis, writing under the name Petter Dass (!) produced his *Findlappers Sæder* (Elaborate, truthful description of the Norwegian Lapplanders' Customs, etc.). It was printed in Copenhagen and has among other things a little poetry where skiing is described:[342]

> When five years have passed, the young boy and girl
> On smooth, waxed skis with tender foot must climb.
> And ramble about the mountain in the deep fallen snow,
> And for speed are like the animals to behold;
> Yes, get used to it quickly, so that the dog on fast legs
> Must bend its supple back and tighten familiar tendons
> So that in full gallop it can keep up with the young Finn
> Who runs like a sailing ship in stormy downwind.

Friis became parish pastor in Aukra in the Trondhjem Diocese in 1755. Note that a girl is on skis and that the skis are waxed.

Erich Pontoppidan

In 1752 Erich Pontoppidan wrote:[343] "With these snowshoes they run just like on the ice with skates on, faster than any horse can move along."

Pehr Kalm

In 1753 the Swede Pehr Kalm told in his book *A Journey to North America* that skis were

---

[341] *På skidor* 1932: 332.
[342] Vaage 1969: 16.
[343] Vaage 1969: 16.

common in Grimstad (from where he probably set out for America). He wrote that the skis were equally long [the same length], ca. 160 cm.[344]

Nicolay Jonge

The parish pastor Nicolay Jonge published his *Geography or Description of the Earth* in 1779 under the name Ludvig Holberg – anything to increase sales! Actually much of this was directly copied from Holberg. Jonge said about the use of skis:[345] "The royal skiers had one short ski, one and a half ells long (ca 95 cm.), the other one two and a half ells long (ca. 160 cm). These skis are lined with sealskin."

About "The trips of mail and travelers in Aggershuus Stift and Parish" he wrote: "In the winter the mail must often be brought on skis due to deep snow, as a horse cannot make his way…"

He reported that skis are also used for play: "This exercise with skiing is also considered a pastime. In Norway it is common for small boys to practice skiing so that even by the coast, and where one is not forced to use them, skis are used for the fun of it."

He also discussed the waxing of skis: "The under side is rubbed with a base material so that ice or snow will not stick to it. Which otherwise would hinder them in moving along."

"When one goes up a hill, one must often make bends where it is too steep; but when one skis downhill, one can ski with such speed that it is unbelievable…"

Jens Zetlitz

A Norwegian theology student, Jens Zetlitz (1761-1821) from Stavanger, received his education in Copenhagen, which was customary at that time. He produced many poems, some of which have to do with skiing. In 1786 he wrote a hymn to praise winter, "En norsk vinter" (A Norwegian Winter). Among other things he mentions ladies on skis:[346]

> From the high mountain down its slippery side
> (My song amazes daring itself)
> On smooth skis brave Norwegians glide,
> And smilingly it goes in danger's step,
> In their hands is the steady steering pole,
> In bearskin they wrap themselves against the cold,
> Those steep declines that threaten death and grave
> By lucky turns they avoid slopes and holes.

---

[344] Vaage 1969: 16.
[345] Vaage 1969: 18.
[346] Vaage 1969: 19, 110-12.

> Onto pretty feet even Norway's daughters bind
> Smooth skis, and proud of their heroic deed,
> From high mountain to deep valley run.
> The pressure of the air brings forth happy tears.
> Far off whistles the air, and drifts of snow
> Precede the wingèd heroine,
> Who daringly hastens to compete with the men,
> and sometimes wins the prizes from them.

It sounds like there must have been prize races even then. And the skiers are turning which would have been impossible without proper bindings.

Fig. 10.10 depicts a "Lappe mit Langski und Andor" (Sámi with long ski and ondur).[347]

Lassen

In 1787 the assistant curate Lassen, born in Kviteseid, "used skis in order to get to the four churches of his parish (Bjelland) to save the expenses of a horse," wrote Andreas Faye in 1867 in the History of the Christiansand Bishopric and Diocese.[348]

Bishop Johan Nordahl Brun

At the end of the eighteenth century another minister contributed to the history of skiing, Johan Nordahl Brun (1745-1816).[349] He was born in Byneset in Trondhjem and began skiing as a child. After having received his education in Copenhagen, he worked from 1772 on in Bergen where he became bishop in 1804.

He possessed a rich poetic vein that resulted in many songs still alive today. Also, skiing played a role in many of the songs. In one of them there is a clear picture of the fact that skiing must have been quite common in Trøndelag 200 years ago:

> When I was a boy in my seventeenth year
> I skied down hills.

In the poem "My Norwegian Winter" skis are mentioned too, of course:
> Now the merry sons of the valley glide
> on skis down from the mountain side
> as quickly as the arrow through the air flies.

---

[347] Luther 1926: 508.
[348] Vaage 1969: 19.
[349] Vaage 1969: 111-12.

> He also tells how important it is to have snow:
> And mountain snow paves the road
> for the caravans of Norwegian farmers.

Norwegian clergymen in those days did not refuse a drink or two. Zetlitz was known in particular for the toasts he proposed, but Johan Nordahl Brun also thought the winter worthy of a toast:

> Another toast to Norway's mountains
> to cliffs, snow and hills!
> Hear Dovre's echo calling: "Good luck!"
> Yes, the toast three times thanks.
> Yes, three times three a toast to all mountains
> to Norway's sons shout Good Luck
> One more toast to you my mountain
> to cliffs, snow and hills.

Det Norske Selskab

At the end of the eighteenth century, with the foundation of Det Norske Selskab (The Norwegian Society) in Copenhagen in 1772, lyric and other poetry had become a popular occupation.[350] It was mostly grandiloquent, romantic poetry that came into existence. But now and then realistic and didactic poems were produced as well, some of which have been seen above.

During the next century skiing entered a new phase. Modern skiing began in the 1850's, and more and more people took it up. Thus it can rightfully be said that it had become the national sport in Norway in an epoch when the rest of the world – with the exception of a few countries – were completely ignorant of it.

Rikard Berge

Rikard Berge published "Norske Visefugg" (Norwegian Ballads) in 1904, and in this book he has a ballad from around 1800 where it says that the mountain farmers jump on skis and do slalom:[351]

> They thought that mountain farmers
> just sat around like boors.
> No, they are real fellows,

---

[350] Vaage 1969: 112.
[351] Vaage 1969: 112.

they both sing and carouse.
If you meet them at Christmas
then they are wild and happy.
In the winter they run on skis
out over high mountain peaks.

Although the hill is steep
and up so very high
that you could imagine them falling
no, they are much more clever than that.
Six ells over the cliff they jump
and stand as if it was nothing
and then they put up a turn
so that it takes your breath away.

Rikard Berge suggested that a government official wrote this song, perhaps one from Telemark. Note the turn that came at the end of the run which later on developed into the famous Telemark "sving" or Telemark turn.

Fig. 10.11 shows Sámi on skis and Samoyeds in sleighs. This German depiction of the North dates from 1712.[352]

Legends about Early Norwegian Skiers

Skis were in common use all over the country, even in Vestlandet (the western part of Norway). Among the legendary figures Vestlendinger are sometimes found, like the renowned Pilt-Ola, a mountain man of profession and passion (perhaps a Sámi). About him it is said that he skied from Ryfylke to the mountains near Røros to fetch a herd of reindeer. As for the ski trip itself he is supposed to have said that gliding over the mountain plateau was like taking a rest: "I was walking there sleeping on my skis."[353]

In Telemark there are stories about the shepherd and rifleman Jon Jonson Li from Møsstrand. He was usually called Dyre-Jon, and they said he could find his way like an animal in the mountains, but that must have been because he herded reindeer. Once when wolves had chased his reindeer away, he set out on skis and brought the animals home. This he did in two days, and it was 20 miles back and forth (200 km.).[354]

---

[352] På skidor 1939: 404.
[353] Bø 1966: 43.
[354] Bø 1966: 44.

Among the stories of early daredevils on skis there are many dealing with downhill runs with a baby on the back or with a bowl of ale in the hand. Such stories, of course, cannot be substantiated; they resemble a fixed epic formula. At the same time, though, there is something realistic in these stories, especially the ones that involve such steep and mountainous villages as are found in Telemark. There, many homes and small farms were very isolated, and they did not have horses and carriages with which to travel. But no one was so poor that he did not own a pair of skis, and that was often sufficient.[355]

Women had to learn to ski just as the men did, and often they could master difficult runs. It is related about one of them named Eli Buviki that she skied down the Breivik rocky hills with a baby on her arm. Her speed was so great that the houses at Breivik looked no larger than knife handles.[356]

The tricks performed by Trysil-Knud and others have old traditions in Telemark and elsewhere in Norway. They picked up their hats off the ground, and some could take off a coat and vest at the highest speeds. When they turned and stopped on the flatland, it was preferably to be done with artfulness. Then they would *lage hegd* "make a ring," that is, turn so that they crossed their own tracks. This was such a common trick that they never mentioned it. However, there were stories about those who managed to make two, and Dyre Vå is supposed to have managed three. Anyone familiar with this sort of thing will know that it is not easily done, unless the track ends in a slight uphill. There is probably a good deal of exaggeration in this tradition.[357]

The same is likely the case with so many of the other wild legends, such as the one about the man with the bowl of ale:[358]

> The man at Åmlid in Skafså ran from his yard down to the ice at Åmlid lake and *gjorde hegd* (made rings) around the pastor's carriage. Then he offered the pastor beer out of the bowl he had in his hands. But the pastor did not want to drink, for he was convinced that the beer had been ruined by the great speed.

From Valdres comes this legend of a skier:[359]

> At Fødnes there was once a man who was so good at skiing that there was no one like him. Fødnes lies on the hills straight up from Strønd, but the hills up are so terribly steep that it is almost impossible to crawl up there in the summer time. One winter there was pure crusted snow and ice all over the hills. Then there were some people who bet five

---
[355] Bø 1966: 44-45.
[356] Bø 1966: 45.
[357] Bø 1966: 45.
[358] Bø 1966: 45.
[359] Bø 1966: 46.

shots of liquor with Fødnes that he could not ski without poles down to Strønda farm. But Fødnes got onto his skis with a bottle of liquor in one hand and a glass that was filled to the rim in the other hand, and then he set off. When he came down to Strønda farm. the glass was just as full, that's how steadily he had skied. "But this run I'd like to do again," he said. When he had come up again to Fødnes farm he took a barrel of grain on his shoulders and set off down the hill with it. And still he stood and never faltered.

It is said that many of the best skiers in Telemark in this early period were school teachers, and some of them are named. There was Per Håkonsson (Hudsko-Per), Per Vrålsson, Knut Alvsson the sexton and from more recent times Jon Høgevoll and Olav Nape. Knut Alvsson skied from Klokkarhamaren (the sexton's crag) down to Klokkargarden (the sexton's farm), Jon Høgevoll skied from Høgevoll down the Sitje field (mountain) and all the way down to Århus. When the teachers were such masters, it is little wonder that some of the students became good skiers too.

Gaute Tinnske

In the legend about Gaute Tinnske it is said that in one day he managed to cross the Hardanger plateau:[360]

> Breakfast I ate in Harang
> the ondur went smoothly
> Then I skied the Gjeitås pass
> without thinking I did this.

Another version from Telemark is:

> Breakfast I ate in Hardang,
> and lunch I ate as I skied,
> supper I ate in Tinnsdalen,
> I hadn't planned it this way.

The complete tale goes as follows:

> Gaute Tinnske had been married and living in Tinnsdalen. But it so happened that he traveled over the mountain to "Nordlandet," in this case western Norway, and was gone a long time. After several years word spread around the villages that he was dead. Some time later his wife was to remarry. Many people came to the feast. In the evening when they led the bride in with a great procession and everyone having a good time, a man was seen skiing down the mountainside at great speed. The bride stopped in the middle of the yard and said: "No one has run down the Gaukås-pass since my husband Gaute was alive." Everyone wondered who it could be who was so daring. But when the man

---

[360] Bø 1966: 37-38; Vaage 1969: 112.

came to the farm, it was Gaute himself. He knew what was happening and recited the verse. In the verse Gaute told that he had crossed the mountains from Hardanger to Tinn in one day. He ate breakfast in Hardanger, lunch while he was skiing, and supper at home. He was in such a hurry that he could not stop and rest underway.

There is no way to know how old this verse is, or the legend associated with it, but, in any case, it was a living tradition around the middle of the last century. The same is true for the half-mythical legend about the giant track:

From the top of the Brakandal peak (Kviteseid) toward the north there are a couple of very deep mountain crevices, which are called Riselåmi "giant tracks." The legend says that a giant wanted to try to ski from the top of Brakandal down onto a bog that lies by a field in the Brakan valley. He managed the entire mountainside, but when he came down to the flatland, his rear end became too heavy. Where he landed, a deep hole was created. This is the origin of the Brakandal pond.

Sondre Norheim, Pavva Lásse Tuorda and the Birth of the Sport

Skiing competitions today include events that test a skier's reflexes, jumping ability and endurance. Of the many individuals who contributed to the rise of skiing as a sport during the 19th century two deserve special mention. Sondre Norheim[361] exemplifies that combination of skills seen in the best alpine skiers and ski jumpers today. Pavva Lásse Tuorda had the stamina and endurance that is rare even among the fastest skiers in the Vasaloppet.

Skis have been used in Scandinavia for many centuries mainly as a hunting accessory to facilitate travel over snow-covered terrain. By the nineteenth century one might suppose that the ski was on the verge of vanishing. Hunting was no longer important to subsistence and urban folk now had horses and roads. The Norwegian military, after early setbacks at the hands of the Swedes in the 16th and 17th centuries, had begun a long tradition of successful deployment of ski troops. Tales of their subsequent victories over the Swedes are legion, and at one time some 2,000 skiers were in the army. But in 1826, ski exercises for soldiers were eliminated and the ski companies disbanded.[362]

Yet skiing was perhaps more vital than ever in Norway because of the profound changes in social structure brought about by a rapidly increasing population from the end of the 18th century. The cultivation of the potato, the introduction of the smallpox vaccination, and other improvements in diet and sanitation had contributed to a falling death rate.[363] The new multitudes could not easily be accommodated in what was essentially an agrarian society. Since only 3 percent of Norway's land was arable, little new land remained to be cleared, and the destiny of most young people in rural areas was membership in the lower classes as tenant farmers, cotters, landless workers and servants. Many of these people eventually left

---

[361] Some of the material in this chapter was published in Weinstock 1983.
[362] Bø 1968: 35 and cf. Ch. 9.
[363] Semmingsen 1940.

Norway for America, yet, the rural population continued to grow and along with it rural poverty increased dramatically.

In Telemark the land was even less suitable than in many other areas of Norway; and what little clearing went on consisted of dividing up large farms and renting out portions to tenant farmers.[364] Here as elsewhere the oldest son in a large family had the right to inherit the farm, while the other sons became tenant farmers and the daughters had to be satisfied marrying tenant farmers themselves. The land available for tenant farming was often of inferior quality, away from what roads there were, and usually on hills. Torjus Loupedalen puts it nicely, "Haslaråsen, Åmlundfjøll, Kleivmånin – they all cling to the mountain or jut out from its side."[365] With little access to horses and wagons and with snow on the ground for a good five months a year the only means of transportation during winter for these people was skis, and how essential they were! "Skis are the horse and amusement of the tenant farmer."[366]

Fortunately skis were available to everyone: with plentiful supplies of wood all that was needed was time and a few tools, both of which every tenant farmer had. The wood was selected in fall, left to age, and then skis were made on winter evenings. From childhood everyone had his own skis. It is often said that Norwegian children learn to ski before they learn to walk. This was certainly close to the truth for the children brought up on the tenant farms in the hills of Telemark during the last century. Down those hills on skis they went; if they fell, the snow cushioned the fall. Some became more adept than others, but all were capable, young and old. Skis were still used for hunting, for logging and generally for anything that involved covering more than short distances. One example will illustrate this: a tenant farmer that did not possess a hay barn would cut and stack his hay in the fields or on heaths some distance away. In winter he would pile hay on a drag sled and pull it home using skis if there was not a hard crust on top of the snow. It was not easy pulling it uphill, but skiing downhill while holding onto the arms of the drag sled behind was more demanding. He had to be strong and have good reflexes; a mistake could mean serious injury. Wood was brought home in the same fashion. It goes without saying that the tenant farmers who did this were competent skiers.

They were also used to covering great distances regularly. This point is well illustrated in the story of a Christiania lawyer who was at Mogen and wanted company to Sandhaug.

---

[364] Sejerstad 1978: 121-22.

[365] Loupedalen 1947: 61.

[366] Loupedalen 1947: 88.

Kristofer, the local inhabitant who was to go with him, had just returned from the mountains and was eating porridge. The lawyer, with a superior air, remarked on Kristofer's thinness and attributed it to his diet of porridge. Kristofer picked up a sack and they started off. He had trouble keeping up for the first mile since he had a load and the lawyer did not. But as the journey progressed the lawyer fell farther and farther behind. During the second mile he came on strong, and by the third mile it was the lawyer who was behind. When they came to Sandhaug the lawyer was exhausted, while Kristofer walked just as easily as when they had begun. "Well," he said, "I guess the porridge boy was too tough for you after all."[367]

Skiing For Fun

In addition to its utilitarian value skiing was a favorite pastime in winter. A. O. Vinje, the poet, wrote in 1853, "In Morgedal people skied more than most, and not more than twenty years ago you could see grown-up men as well as small boys out skiing on Sunday."[368] Whole families would trek to church on skis and then spend much of Sunday skiing. Vinje commented:[369]

> There was another kind of life on Sundays then than now when one sits inside drinking coffee or whiskey. They ate their Sunday dinner, got their skis and went over to the ski hill. Down steep hillsides, over crags, moguls and stone piles, even off of houses they went as if glued to their ski straps. They did not become dizzy when their eyes dripped and ran, they were enshrouded in a mist and appeared like hawks through the clouds. It was a great shame to get a *møykjerring* "old maid," and you couldn't stop until you righted it. If you got too many old maids, you didn't get to dance with the girls on Sunday evening. Try to court them and they just giggled.

In fact dancing went hand in hand with skiing. Both required good reflexes, agility and endurance, and, as physical exertion, they helped to release pent-up feelings. The bitter realities of poverty and the workaday world were briefly forgotten. The dance rhythms were wild and rapid:[370]

> Boys and girls fired up by the tempos threw themselves into whirling dance tours, wild and wilder until the boy felt that he had reached the point where his body no longer resisted and the law of gravity was suspended ... For a moment, for an evening he was beyond the limit where breath and muscles could be felt ... He was released. And then

---

[367] Loupedalen 1947: 45.
[368] Loupedalen 1947: 88.
[369] Loupedalen 1947: 87-88.
[370] Loupedalen 1947: 30.

all of a sudden he was dropped back into a cold and demanding day of hard toil – red warmth dipped into cold water.

The Sport of Skiing

The roots of skiing as a sport actually go quite far back. The military started skiing competitions for soldiers and ordinary citizens in 1767 with lucrative prizes at stake in the equivalent of modern day ski-shooting, giant slalom, downhill and cross-country, and these competitions continued on a regular basis until the ski companies were disbanded.[371] Skiing, then, by the early 19th century was flourishing, at least in the rural areas of Norway, and was particularly important for the lower classes who could not afford more expensive means of conveyance. And though it was not yet a full-fledged sport, these same lower-class people derived much of their amusement in winter from skiing, and the stage was set for the emergence of skiing as an international sport.

If we take a broader definition of sport to include pastime or diversion then the roots go back much further. Part of the upbringing of the children of the earliest skiers would have been imitating their elders; this would have included skiing games.

Fig. 11.1 is a picture of Sondre Norheim, born June 10, 1825, died in the USA in 1897.[372]

Sondre Norheim Provides the Impetus

All that was lacking for skiing to become a competitive sport was provided virtually single-handedly by the exploits of Sondre Norheim from Morgedal in Telemark.[373] Three innovations have been attributed to him: 1) devising a binding that allowed sharp turning; 2) perfecting the ski shape which went on to become the model for modern Alpine skis; and 3) most importantly, bringing off feats of daredevilry on skis that left onlookers agape and turned him into a folk hero.

Ski bindings until Sondre's time came in two main varieties, both of which were toe bindings, a toe strap of rawhide or a toe loop made from a twisted willow twig known as a

---

[371] Wergeland 1865: 479-80.
[372] Vaage 1969: 273.
[373] Most of the material on Sondre Norheim comes from Pastor Aslak Bergland's collection of ballads and poems called *Lauvduskar*, which appeared in 1887, and from Loupedalen's *Morgedal*. Cf. also Vaage 1969: 272-92 and Bø 1968: 39-63.

withe or osier.³⁷⁴ In either case the shoe or boot was pushed forward through the toe binding. It was thus very easy to slip on a pair of skis and set out; however, neither binding kept the foot rigidly in place. It must have been very frustrating to have the skis come off so easily. Imagine being suspended in the middle of a jump and losing one or both skis. The rawhide strap was the older of the two bindings and was very durable but it tended to stretch when wet and was never stiff. Moreover, for the lower-class people of Telemark rawhide was expensive. Withes, on the other hand, were readily available; one simply gathered them during the summer and let them dry until winter came. Withes were quite rigid, too, but did not wear very well. A skier was wise to carry extras so as not to get stranded. Even the withe toe binding did not allow sharp turns in powder snow since the ankle could turn without the ski following. This was an age-old problem for which various solutions had been tried. Several of the Sámi groups combined the toe strap with a strap around the heel with some degree of success. The military tried this, as well as combinations of a toe strap and a block of wood behind the heel, or a withe toe loop plus a heel strap. None of these, however, was entirely satisfactory. The modification Sondre is generally given credit for was quite simple, a withe toe loop with a withe heel loop attached to it (Fig. 11.2 shows Sondre's withe bindings).³⁷⁵ Here was an inexpensive binding, which made precise turning and steering a reality, a prerequisite for the development of the sport. Birkely, though, has pointed out that Sondre may have gotten the idea for the withe heel loop from the Sámi living nearby in southern Norway whom Sondre knew and that back bindings, in any case, are mentioned by Linnæus and Schefferus.³⁷⁶

Fig. 11.3 shows Sondre Norheim as depicted by a German artist.³⁷⁷

Sondre's impact on the shape and type of the ski itself was not so decisive, for others including the Sámi produced similar skis following models that had long been available in and around Telemark and elsewhere.³⁷⁸ But Sondre did fashion some very fine skis, and the fact that he used his own skis in his remarkable feats probably had much to do with eliminating competing types. The favored type among East Norwegians and the military, as previously noted, was the so-called "unequal length" skis, a long left ski to glide on and a shorter, fur-clad right ski to push with. They were quite good for going up hill in the days

---

³⁷⁴ Cf. Ch. 7.
³⁷⁵ Vaage 1969: 275.
³⁷⁶ Birkely 1994: 87-88, 84; Linnæus 1957 and Schefferus 1673.
³⁷⁷ Vaage 1969: 283.
³⁷⁸ Birkely 1994: 88.

before the advent of waxes or the "no-wax" skis of today. Typical Telemark skis were of equal length, without fur covering, and were more suited for hilly country. In competitions early in the 19th century they proved to be superior to unequal length skis, and the latter were soon forgotten. The most important feature of the shape was the width, widest at the front, narrowing gradually toward the middle where the foot rested and then becoming slightly wider toward the rear. With the ski narrowest at the middle the withe binding did not abrade as much against the snow and so lasted longer. The extra width at the front pressed the loose snow down and created a track. More width at the back of the ski than at the footstep helped the ski steer straighter.

However, it was mainly as a skier that Sondre achieved fame not only in Telemark but also in Christiania and elsewhere in Norway. Before surveying some of his accomplishments it will be helpful to describe the terrain skiers were used to in Telemark. Sondre Norheim came from Morgedal (Fig. 11.4 is a view of Morgedal with Sondre's home uppermost on the mountainside. Drawing by Øivind Sørensen),[379] which Torjus Loupedalen called "the cradle of the sport of skiing." It lies in the heart of Telemark in an area of narrow valleys surrounded by mountain peaks, with numerous streams and tarns. There is little level ground; it is rather a question of degree of slope, with a constantly varying terrain of ridges, heaths, knolls, cliffs, scree patches and groves of trees. Land newly cleared by tenant farmers was likely to be situated on the mountain slopes, so it is not surprising that these people who relied on skis in winter were adept at getting around such undulating terrain.

There was a special jargon in Telemark for classifying according to difficulty the trails or tracks that were skied in winter.[380] The basis of these compound expressions is the second element *låm* which Ivar Aasen describes as "a track made by something that is pulled or dragged along."[381] The easiest variety was the *slalåm*, a word now in the international vocabulary. *Sla(d)* "sloping" when combined with *låm*, *slalåm*, referred to what one might today call the "baby" slopes, those used in Telemark by boys and girls not yet able to try themselves on the more challenging runs. They were told, "go ski *slalåm*." Other terms were *kneikelåm* (a course with lots of knolls), *ufselåm* (a trail off a cliff), *hopplåm* (a course with jumps along the way), *svinglåm* (a run with turns). The term reserved for the most challenging and difficult course was *uvyrdslåm*, or "daredevil" run, which contained turns, jumps,

---

[379] Vaage 1969: 281.
[380] Cf. Dalen 1997, 1998 and 1999 for more information on ski terminology.
[381] Aasen 1850: 430.

knolls, everything an expert skier could want. Occasionally a ladder was stretched from a house up the hill. When it was packed with snow it made a nice jump. Naturally, a daredevil skier had to have superior reflexes in order to turn abruptly and control the skis to avoid obstacles often unknown in advance.

Daredevil Runs

Only a rare person could ski a dangerous and complicated *uvyrdslåm* or daredevil run, and the run plus the skier who survived it became famous in Morgedal and environs. It then stood as a challenge to other free spirits in the area. Herein is found the greatest difference between top class skiing then and now. Olympic medal winners today are recognized but not so much the courses they won their medals on. To be sure there are famous runs such as the Kandahar downhill or jumps such as Holmenkollen, but countless excellent skiers have gone down them, whereas the daredevil runs of a century ago became legendary when only one or two skiers had the courage to try them. Loupedalen describes one such run that was unsuccessful:[382]

> Under a high ridge on one of the farms there was a large, bushy, two-forked aspen. A man called Gunnleik Olavsson made a dash on the ridge and put down a track so it sent him through the cleft in the tree. But he got struck with one ski and foot in the cleft. He felt pain from it the rest of his life. And he had been at war, Gunnleik, for seven years, they said.

Suffice it to say that Sondre Norheim has far more such daredevil runs to his credit than any other of the great Telemark skiers. Many of his feats were witnessed with incredulous eyes; in fact, the chance to awe beholders often stirred Sondre to action:[383]

> Sondre once took such a bold run at Åse at Flateland. At Åse there is a gorge called Årdalen. One Sunday a bunch of boys had gathered there to ski. Then Sondre came. He stood a while watching, and asked whether they wanted to bet that he could not ski off the barn at Åse, where it is highest, down to Årdal. They said he couldn't do it, but no bets were made. Nevertheless, Sondre went up and jumped from the barn roof. From there he went at wild speed, made some tremendous jumps, and landed in the deepest part of Årdalen. Everyone thought it was a splendid run. No one has ever dared it since.

One of his most memorable runs occurred when he and his cousin Tallev attempted to ski the Kastedal shoot (Fig. 11.5 is the famous Kastedalsskotet that Sondre skied down).[384]

---

[382] Loupedalen 1947: 69.
[383] Loupedalen 1947: 79.
[384] Vaage 1969: 284.

Sondre was close to fifty at the time; they were on their way home after cutting wood. Aslak Bergland described the incident in the following verses:[385]

> Tallev Kastedal and Sondre
> Once walked the timber woods.
> Both had skis and axes;
> Tallev had his gun too.
> Hard they hewed all day
> On the fat fir trees;
> Each one took down
> His dozen splendid logs.
>
> Up at Kastedal they stopped
> When at evening they headed home
> Down through the wild shoot,
> A long time they stood and gazed.
> At the top were cliffs and sloping trails,
> Then by the house it was steeper;
> There was a big knoll down at Moskei,
> Where the hill ended at the shore.
>
> "Shall we ski off here?"
> Said Sondre, teasingly.
> Tallev answered: "You go first!
> I'll follow like your shadow."
> He put the ax on his shoulder,
> Tallev put his gun at rest;
> Then both fellows glided
> Down the terrible slopes.
>
> They skied the cliff jump by jump;
> Down knolls and narrow places they flew,
> Across ridges and crevices;
> Snow like dust around them whirled.
> When they came down toward the house,
> Just where the shoot was steepest,
> Sondre kept on flying,
> But there on the slope Tallev fell.
>
> Sondre didn't stop until the tarn,
> Quickly he looked back up the shoot.

---

[385] Loupedalen 1947: 76-77. Literal translation by the author.

From the deep, where Tallev landed,
Gusts of snow flew into the air.
Up from the snow stood a pipe,
That could only be the gun.
Sondre called out to him:
"Be careful. Don't shoot me!"

Tallev freezing scrambled up;
He saw the tracks below him.
Just this last little bit
Is horrible to look at;
No one has since dared it,
Much less Sondre's path.
Never will the Kastedal shoot
Be run by another skier.

The extent of this man's achievements in his native Telemark can only be surmised. Some of the tales have grown out of proportion, and many have long since been forgotten; but the stories are remarkably uniform – this was a man recognized even by people who did not know him well as an exceptional talent.

Sondre Competes in Christiania

His fame outside Telemark had more to do with promoting the cause of skiing as a sport and did not come until he was advanced in age, at least for an activity requiring instant reactions. The chance came with a competition in Christiania arranged by the Centralforeningen for Udbredelse af Legemsøvelser og Vaabenbrug (Central Society for the Promotion of Physical Exercise and Weapon Use), one of the first official races after the military competitions were disbanded. It was to be a continuous loop of two and a half kilometers over some of the terrain of the city. More importantly though, lucrative prizes were offered, up to the equivalent of ten dollars, a considerable amount of money for poor country folk. Sondre and a couple of pals put some food in their backpacks, donned their skis, and headed for Christiania, skiing the whole way. Competitors were judged on elapsed time with points for style. The fifty-one competitors started at one-and-a-half minute intervals. The following day a newspaper reported:[386]

> Excelling especially were the men from Telemark and Trysil with the carefree confidence with which they pulled out all the stops without touching the ground with a pole. Of the entire group the winner of the first prize stood far above any of the others. There

---

[386] *Aftenbladet* February 10, 1868.

was something so remarkable about his racing and his movement on skis that one had to believe that for him it was the natural way to move."

This was Sondre, of course, now in his forty-fourth year. The city folk were overwhelmed by the ease and the elegance of form with which Sondre went around this supposedly demanding course. When Sondre returned home with his first prize money, he was asked about the great courses they had skied in Christiania. Sondre replied, "Sure the courses were great, but, you know, I could have skied them with a sack of potatoes on my back."[387]

Sondre had found friends and admirers in Christiania and a source of modest income, albeit seasonal in nature. His last Christiania race came when he was over fifty and could no longer defy the laws of nature. By then skiing was well on its way to becoming the national sport of Norway, with annual competitions in many locales and competitors from far and wide. And Sondre was now a folk hero and a legend. In the end it was his great love for skiing that stood out: even if the money had not been sorely needed, he would have gone anywhere to compete. Or as Sondre put it, "If they could ski my course at Haugliufsi today then I would go over to Kjørkjenuta and make another one for them to try to follow."[388]

Olav Christensen and Kristen Mo, among others, have shown that competitions in such places as Tromsø and Trysil preceded those in Christiania.[389] But it was the Christiania races that attracted the large crowds and it was there that Sondre's reputation spread well beyond Telemark.

Sondre Norheim: Tenant Farmer

What about Sondre the man? He was born at Øverbø June 10, 1825, up on a hill, to be sure, in an area where "only in spots does the terrain take a breather in quiet dales and hollow valleys."[390] All the children eventually had to ski down similar hills, everyone of which was a "daredevil" run. He had a brother two years older, Eivind Mostaul, who achieved fame as a skimaker. Of the two, Eivind was the easier to manage, a nice boy, while Sondre was from the beginning wild and restless. He was small in stature but tough and sinewy. One of the first things he learned was the making of weaver's reeds, which often occupied the whole family and continued to be an occasional source of income to Sondre in later years.

---

[387] Loupedalen 1947: 99.
[388] Loupedalen 1947: 46.
[389] Christensen 1993; Mo 1994.
[390] Loupedalen 1947: 61.

He also tried his hand at other types of work, carpentry, blacksmithing, lumbering, but was not always one to finish what he started, and when the call of the slopes came, he was ready to drop anything. He had plenty of older skiers to pattern himself after, and he had heard tales of the difficult runs that had been skied in the area. Before long he was excelling on the enticing old trails and making his own new ones. In many cases a run on fresh powder snow from the top of a peak down to the valley was visible to the whole village, one narrow track – good style meant skis together – broken only for the jumps. It was the long, high jumps off cliffs and crags, which amazed people and were remembered. When going off a cliff or a housetop he strove for both height and length of jump.

Many of his runs involved showing himself off, clowning around, or doing something others thought crazy. One time a bridal procession was on the way home from church when Sondre came skiing down the hillside with a bowl of beer in one hand. Bending his knees at the right times and holding the bowl at the right angle he arrived at the procession and gave the bride the first drink, all without spilling a drop. Perhaps Sondre got the idea for this feat from folklore. Good fun for one was folly for another. Consider the time he skied downhill at high speed and purposely headed toward a large sawing contraption. Everyone thought he would kill himself, but he managed to squeeze through the opening in the device and continued down the hill, making an incredible jump of thirty meters or so on the way.

Sondre worked in various villages in the area, and everywhere he had the reputation of being a first-rate dancer as well as a skier. He married Rannei Åmundsdotter in 1854. They rented and cleared some land at Sudbøkasin where they settled. He had his eye on another piece of land, but the owner did not want Sondre as a tenant because he was too openhanded. There were, naturally, many people who could not appreciate his skiing feats because they produced no income. Sondre and Rannei both worked hard to make a go of it, Sondre cutting wood, making skis and furniture, even serving as a doctor, bleeding people and treating their corns and blisters. Five years there was enough: the rent was high and the land virtually barren, so they moved on to Nordbøn. Here they could fish Breivatn, but getting grain and potatoes to grow in swamp land and gravel was no easier than in the other place. It was impossible to scrape out a decent living. They moved again, this time to a better place in the middle of the community, which they called Norheim after a large farm at Bø. One time Sondre was given a bushel of seed potatoes by the poor-relief agency. He planted them, but soon he dug them up and ate them. Sondre's excuse was that he would rather have planted turnips! When there was not enough wood to burn, Sondre tore down part of the barn, and Rannei and the children made frequent rounds begging from neighbors.

But through all the poverty Sondre did not change much; when the slopes beckoned, he was ready. It was a harsh winter when one of his sons was due for baptism. Sondre and Rannei set out on skis on the hard-crusted snow taking turns carrying the infant. Reaching a steep slope that would have been a difficult run even on powder, Sondre skied it with the boy under his arm. His love of skiing never faded. Loupedalen puts it nicely:[391]

> In Sondre the desire to ski is a quietly shining flame that burns as clearly in the grown man as in the small lad. We see him having fun on the cliffs as a ragged and happy Ashlad [male Cinderella character], we see him up in years, poor and frozen, waiting up on a hill until they shout 'Come,' – and we see him fall on the knolls, poor, gray, worn out. But we also watch the small boys picking him up, as old as he is. He gives them what he has and what he is happiest with – skiing.

He taught many to ski. He must have been quite a sight on skis, his wide pants flapping in the wind and his gray hair down to his shoulders. But if he was not there, they went to Norheim to get him, for he had much to give them.

Fig. 11.6 shows the dedication of a memorial at Sondre Norheim's grave in Denbigh, North Dakota in 1966.[392]

America Beckons

A man ahead of his time, though he became a folk hero in Norway, he could not reap the monetary gains from his fame that would have allowed him to remain there. His second oldest son went to relatives in America in 1878, and no doubt there were America letters over the next six years to Sondre and Rannei which caused them to pull up stakes in spite of their advanced age – both were 59 – and head for northern Dakota Territory with four of their six children. Though it meant leaving the beloved slopes for the flat prairie, Sondre was ready. In the end his reasons for leaving were no different from those of countless other Norwegians from rural upland areas. The New World offered hope and escape from hard times. He died in 1897 and was buried at Norway Church in Denbigh, North Dakota. That same year a ski festival was held in Morgedal in his memory. A few quotations from the memorial speech show the debt so many owed to Sondre: "The man who spent his time so that many can gather now for a celebration in the open air, for a celebration of something

---

[391] Loupedalen 1947: 86.
[392] Vaage 1969: 292.

as good and fair as skiing, his name is Sondre Norheim. He is the one who made the sport of skiing what it is now, and when one realizes that this is a happy sign of the times, a force which has brought together continents, nations, peoples and parties for peaceful competition and sacrifice, then we must say that it was a great achievement … Sondre was a pioneer. Is it possible to conceive of a Nansen voyage if there hadn't been a Sondre Norheim? … He was a skier alone, a complete, ideal, well-integrated man … No one has followed in the tracks of Sondre."[393]

Fig. 11.7 shows Sondre Norheim's memorial stone in Morgedal, Telemark, Norway.[394]

Sondre Norheim's Legacy

The development of skiing from a practical necessity in rural 19th-century Norway into an internationally enjoyed pastime was hurried along by Sondre Norheim's manifold contributions. This dual function, utility and diversion, was to continue in an America where the ski was unknown until the Norwegians arrived. The utilitarian function is best exemplified by the efforts of a Norwegian immigrant, Jon Thoresen Rue. Rue, from Tinn in Telemark, came to the Fox River, Illinois, settlement in 1837 at the age of ten.[395] Fourteen years later he was among the many Norwegians who headed for California to seek their fortunes in gold. Though he did not find much gold, he achieved lasting fame as a mail carrier on skis. Beginning in 1855 he hauled the mail over the mountains between Carson Valley, Nevada, and Placerville, California, in winter when the Pony Express was inactive. To the astonishment of the local residents he covered the ninety-odd miles each way on skis which he fashioned himself, at the same time carrying up to one hundred pounds of mail. And he continued to do it for twenty years. This was, of course, "Snowshoe" Thompson, the appellation stemming from the only similar devices Americans were familiar with. Other Norwegians who had joined the Gold Rush took to skiing when the snows arrived, and there were even some downhill races with gold for prizes (Fig. 11.8 shows a Norwegian skiing in Colorado. The drawing is from 1876. The skis were called Norwegian snowshoes.).[396]

---

[393] Loupedalen 1947: 127.
[394] *På skidor* 1945: 253.
[395] Bjork 1956: 78.
[396] Vaage 1979: 238.

The latter, sportive function of skiing in America developed strongly toward the end of the 19th century with Norwegian Americans at the forefront, and here the legacy of Sondre shines through. Only the highlights need be mentioned. In 1882 Carl Illstrup from Drammen was instrumental in founding the Minneapolis Ski Club, and the number of ski clubs in Minnesota and Wisconsin mushroomed soon thereafter. Most of the members were Norwegians, and each club had its special uniform. The Red Wing club members, for instance, were bedecked in blue pants, blue jackets and blue caps, the jackets and caps with gold trim. Speeches were held in Norwegian, and songs were sung, one of the most popular being:

> Ja, ja, vi vil ha
> lutefisk og lefse
> brennevin og snus.

Lutefisk is boiled cod that has been treated in lye, a traditional dish that dates from the time when nothing was thrown away. Lefse is somewhat more appetizing, a thin crepe, buttered and folded. Brennevin is hard liquor, and snus is snuff. Probably the latter two items helped make the first one more palatable. And regular competitions were held which soon came to include ski jumping. Forty elite immigrant skiers from Telemark were among the regular winners, and all of them owed a great debt to Sondre's pioneering efforts. The most famous were the Hemmestveit brothers, Mikkel and Torjus, who took turns pushing up the world record for ski jumping to 102 and 103 feet in 1892 and 1893, respectively. Mention should also be made of Aksel Holter from Christiania who settled in Ishpeming in the Upper Peninsula of Michigan. He ordered several pairs of skis from Norway's first ski factory in 1900, and soon he began to produce skis for Americans. He also published a yearbook on skiing beginning in 1905. Finally, Carl Hovelsen, also from Christiania, ski jumped for the Barnum and Bailey circus in 1907 and was seen by more than four million people. By the early twentieth century Americans not only knew what skis were, but the sport had established itself in the New World.

Fig. 11.9 is a winter carnival at Minneapolis/St. Paul, Minnesota in the 1880's. Norwegian skiers are coming down the toboggan slide, occasionally jumping as much as 30'.[397]

Pavva Lásse Tuorda

Sondre was only one of many talented skiers during the 19th century. Sondre's feats could perhaps be compared to the downhill or giant slalom races of today in that superb reflexes were needed to go at high speed and negotiate the difficult turns. Pavva Lásse Tuorda was a

---

[397] Vaage 79: 243.

skier of a different ilk: he specialized in endurance. He was one of two Sámi that the arctic explorer Nils Adolf Erik Nordenskiöld took along on an expedition onto the inland ice of Greenland in 1883. Nordenskiöld is best known as the first person to navigate the Northeast Passage from the North Atlantic through the Bering Strait to China (1878-80) – cf. figs. 11.10-11 from his book both showing *pulks* being pulled by reindeer, the former more realistic.[398] On a previous trip to Greenland in 1870 Nordenskiöld had only managed to go inland some 50 km since he was on foot. This time he realized that he would be able to explore a much larger area with the help of expert skiers. He selected two Sámi from the Jokkmokk area of Sweden, Pavva Lásse Tuorda and Anders Rassa, both of whom were capable skiers. Furthermore, the two Sámi could help prevent the expedition from getting lost on the vast Greenland ice sheets. Pavva Lásse had a particularly fine sense of direction.

Nordenskiöld sailed to the settled west coast of Greenland at Disko Bay from which his expedition headed eastward into the interior – the desolate and ice-covered east coast was near impossible to reach by ship. When they had moved some 120 km inland conditions worsened and Nordenskiöld decided that they should turn back. But first Nordenskiöld wanted the two Sámi to ski further inland as far as they could and return to the camp in four days. They took along what they could carry including instruments for various measurements and food. They left on the 22nd of June at 2:30 in the afternoon and were back within 57 hours. According to their own calculations they had gone 230 km further inland from the last camp. They had been forced to turn around due to lack of drinking water. They had covered, in other words, 460 km in 57 hours.[399] After the group returned to Sweden there were a number of people including Fridtjof Nansen who did not believe that anyone could have covered such a distance in so short a time. Hence, Nordenskiöld arranged the first long distance ski race the following year on April 3, 1884.

Nordenskiöldsloppet (*lopp* means race in Swedish) was to be a 220 km race through the forests of northern Sweden. Handsome prizes were offered to the top three finishers. Anders Rassa did not participate: he said that if people didn't believe what he had accomplished in Greenland that was too bad, and, besides, he had skied much further than that on some of his wolf hunting trips. Sixteen skiers started the race and of the ten who finished eight were Sámi.[400] It was an exciting race with a close finish. The man, who finished

---

[398] Nordenskiöld 1882: 67, 68.
[399] Birkely 1994: 15.
[400] Birkely 1994: 15-16.

third, Anders Ahrman, was given a flask of brandy along the route and made the mistake of sipping a little. This made him so sleepy that he had to stop and rest a while. Pavva Lásse won by a couple of ski lengths over Per-Olaf Ländta who near the end had to straighten his binding several times and thus lost a few seconds. The winning time was 21 hours and 22 minutes and this put an end to the skepticism about the Greenland exploits.[401]

Nansen wrote that in the fall of 1883 he heard someone read from the newspaper about Nordenskiöld's successful trek into the Greenland interior and the unbelievable distances covered by the two Sámi. He was so impressed that he took along two Sámi, Ole Nilsen Ravna and Samuel Johnsen Balto, on his expedition four years later that was the first to cross the interior of Greenland beginning from the east coast and using skis.

Fig. 11.12 shows the participants in Nansen's 1887 expedition to Greenland. The two Sámi are wearing their traditional caps, Ravna on the left and Balto on the right.[402]

---

[401] Birkely 1994: 16-17.
[402] Vaage 1969: 32.

Skiing in Literature III: 19ᵗʰ Century

In chapter 11 we saw that skiing very nearly died out in Scandinavia around the beginning of the 19ᵗʰ century, surviving in only a few areas. On the contrary more and more writers began to write about skiing.

Henrik Wergeland

Henrik Wergeland (1808-45) was Norway's first writer of international stature. He is perhaps best known for his romantic poetry. He was also an enthusiastic skier. It is known that he relaxed with a daily ski trip at Eidsvoll, where his father was pastor, during the winter of 1829, when he was putting the finishing touches on the gigantic poem: "Skabelsen, Mennesket og Messias," (The Creation, Man and Messiah), a poem of 720 pages. Then a good ski trip could be beneficial!

He also touched on winter, which all Norwegians appreciate more than people of other nations:[403]

> I do not wish for a foreign spring
> my Norwegian winter to exchange.

Fig. 12.1 is an old Swedish drawing of skiing in a Norwegian mountain valley.[404]

Gjest Baardsen, Master Thief

The master thief Gjest Baardsen tells in his autobiography (1835) about a ski trip from Bjerkreim in Rogaland via Sirdalen to Setesdal:[405]

---

[403] Vaage 1969: 116.
[404] Vaage 1969: 17.
[405] Vaage 1969: 21-22.

> With my knapsack on my back, dressed like a merchant, and with two watches in my pocket, whose broad silver chains dangled down my pants, I journeyed up Jederen. Soon I left the King's road, bought myself skis and took to the mountains in the upper Birchrem parish in order to go over to Sirdalen. Here I came upon a snow storm, which caused me almost to freeze to death in the mountains, as I had to stay in the mountains and lie in the snow a whole night.

On the road to Setesdal he tells:

> …I quickly glided on my skis over the snow-covered mountain plateaus. Darkness, however, came upon me before I could reach that farm which someone had told me about, which was supposed to be in a valley, which was separated from Setesdal itself by a small mountain …I let 'er rip and skied down the steep mountain sides, and was more than half-way down into the valley when I suddenly felt that I was no longer touching the ground with my feet, and thus had gone over a cliff.

He lost one ski in the "jump" and didn't find it again in the dark, but when he heard a dog bark he found his way down to the nearest farm.

Jonas Lie

Jonas Lie (1833-1908), Norwegian novelist, playwright and poet, says about O. T. Krohg, the founder of the newspaper *Tromsø Tidende* in 1838, that "No one threw snow balls or skied like he did."[406] Lie enriched Norwegian literature with a ski poem, based on Knut Bergslien's painting "The wild bird hunter." It goes like this:[407]

> Frosty clear is the day, down snow white hillsides
> home over the high mountain they travel on skis.
> The old man carefully watches out with his pole,
> Other than the cliffs the boy manages without it,
> Snow drifts and snow piles, they stay on their feet,
> it's healthy to travel in winter blue.
>
> The wood grouse they shot on the Hallingdal side
> beyond the mountain on the fir tree hill,
> The white ptarmigan they took on the crusty snow
> Their skis swiftly carried them close to the hare.
> Glittering winter and ruddy cheeks
> down the slopes flying like the wind.

This poem was probably written in the middle of the 1860's. Note that they used the pole (just one) if the downhill speed became too high.

---

[406] Vaage 1969: 22.
[407] Vaage 1969: 116.

Fig. 12.2 is Knut Bergslien's painting "The Bird Hunter" inspired by Jonas Lie's poem.[408]

Asbjørnsen and Moe

Peter Christen Asbjørnsen (1812-85) and Jørgen Moe (1813-82) did for Norwegian folklore what the Grimm brothers had done in Germany. They traveled around the countryside, collected tales and published them. Both were very fond of skiing, and both have described skiing and told about trips on skis, which they themselves have made.

In the introduction to "Berthe Tuppenhaug's Tales" from 1843 (Fig. 12.3 is Hans Gude's drawing for these tales),[409] Asbjørnsen wanted to write about and describe a ski trip he himself had made. The description became a frame for Berthe's tales. After a successful fox hunt he was offered a ride home:[410]

> It was an honorable offer, but since the road was twice as long, I preferred to return the way I had come, on skis. With the fox skin and my rifle on my back and the ski pole in my hand I glided off. Skiing conditions were excellent; the sun had been shining during the day, and the evening coldness had covered the deep snow with a light crust; the moon shone in the sky, and the stars twinkled. What more could I ask for? It went like the wind down the hills, over the fields, and through the groves with their erect birch trees, whose crowns formed airy, glimmering silvery domes, under which the owls sat telling frightful stories out into the quiet night. The hare shrieked 'hutetutuhu' over the February cold and the nasty owl chatter; the fox was out on his romantic adventures, arguing with his rivals and uttering scornful screams.

But it didn't end so well:[411]

> I let 'er rip down the hill; whizzing by in the shadow of the fir tree woods, the alder thickets slapped me on the ears; but due to the incredible speed it was impossible to see any object, and before I knew it I crashed hard against a tree stump, broke one of my skis and lay on my head buried in the snow.

In *Billedmagazin for Børn* (Illustrated Magazine for Children) Asbjørnsen wrote in the fifth issue of 1839:[412]

> …The mountain farmer binds the long smooth skis on his feet, and over the deep snow, where there is neither road nor path, he runs along as quickly as the falcon, who hunts ptarmigan on his mountain. At Christmas or the other holidays, when the roads are impassable, both men and women ski to parties; the wives follow with their babies on their

---

[408] Vaage 1969: 117.
[409] Vaage 1969: 16.
[410] Bø 1966: 46-47.
[411] Bø 1966: 47.
[412] Vaage 1969: 22.

backs. The quick mountain farmer sets off on his skis over the big wide mountain (such as the Dovre mountains and Filefjell (File mountains) to distant villages, he goes on his skis to put out traps for the ptarmigan, which he often catches hundreds of; on skis he pursues, overtakes, and kills the reindeer, the moose, the wolf and the bear, which could not be overtaken by the fastest horse, and many a hunter has only a couple of really frail pieces of wood to thank for the fact that he is still alive.

The clergy seems to have had a great predilection for expressing themselves in poetry about skiing. Moe, who became bishop in 1875, was known to be a competent skier. His love of nature often shines through in his poems, and he does not forget the national sport, either. In "Bjørneskytten" (The Bearhunter) which must have been written about 1840, he paints a picture of the hunter on skis:[413]

> Now the spruce stands stacked with snow
> Up on the hillside
> Nowhere can the hunter see
> Traces of the path.
> Far and wide
> To glide
> He wants on his skis.

In the poem "Knud and Birgit" (ca. 1845) he tells of a rather anxious young man who has difficulty expressing the words he more than anything would like to tell his sweetheart. Not until he gets her behind him on his skis, and feels her heart beat, does he gather his courage:[414]

> Laughingly she thanked
> Stepped behind me onto my skis
> And down we flew like the bird
> On its windy path.
> While tightly she threw around me
> Her round soft arm.
> And tighter she squeezed and faster it went
> I felt her heart beat – tick, tick, tick!
>
> I thought of how cute she
> In her fear certainly must look
> And asked, before I knew it,
> "Dear beautiful one, be my bride!"
> I was about to turn my head

---

[413] Vaage 1969: 22, 115.
[414] Vaage 1969: 22.

In order to see the girl's answer
And – oops! there we both lay
In the deep cold snow.

He finds out that winter is not the right time to propose, least of all when one is skiing. Spring is not a good time, either. But only when summer comes, will his chosen one be willing. Fig. 12.4 is artist Andreas Bohr Olsen's rendition of the poem drawn for the 1878 *Ny Illustrered Tidende*.[415]

In 1850 Moe wrote the poem "Furudalskastet" (The Fir Valley Leap) according to which a rich young girl loves a proud, but poor young man:[416]

> Certainly no one made such leaps
> on the dance floor among the villagers
> and no one stood as steadily and erect
> on skis from the mountain down the hill …

Skien, Norway

The Norwegian town Skien where Henrik Ibsen was born has a pair of skis in its emblem. There is an interesting explanation for the origin of the town's name, which, in fact, means "the ski." In Andreas Faye's *Norske Folkesagn* (Norwegian Folk Traditions) from 1844 the following passage occurs:[417]

> One winter when the ice lay thick, a speedy bear hunter came skiing down the so-called Pastor's hill, which now leads from the Pastor's farm up to the church. His speed took him out onto the ice, where he stopped by that cliff on which the church is situated. He goes up there and finds a bear lair, kills the bear and then travels back to his home village, where he announced the fortunate location of the place. A city was then built there and a church built on the cliff, which is why for a long time it was called "The Bear Skier's Church."

Åsmund Olavsson Vinje

Aasmund Olavsson Vinje was one of the two great nineteenth century Norwegian writers – Arne Garborg was the other – who wrote in Norway's new official language, *nynorsk*

---

[415] Vaage 1969: 111.
[416] Vaage 1969: 24.
[417] Vaage 1969: 22, 24.

(New Norwegian) which had been created by Ivar Aasen from Old Norwegian and western dialects. In an article in the newspaper *Drammens Tidende* in 1853 he wrote about how one and all found amusement on skis on weekends when conditions were right:[418]

> So they live even today
> in many a lonely farm;
> every Sunday young people get together
> to practice ski-running.
> The greatest fun they know
> is to ski down the big ski track with ease.

But he ends up by saying that there probably wasn't anyone who could measure up to the master Sondre Norheim:

> Among Telemark's mountains and steep bluffs
> you can find many a good skier;
> But no one has possessed such skill
> that they mastered Sondre's runs.

Chapter 11 presented Sondre Norheim and his contributions to skiing.

Bjørnstjerne Bjørnson

Bjørnstjerne Bjørnson (1832-1910) was one of the major figures of nineteenth century Norwegian literature. He was a political leader, a brilliant journalist, and he had great influence in a Norway that was striving for independence. He promoted Norwegian as a literary language as opposed to the Dano-Norwegian in sway in the major cities. One of his poems became the national anthem. Bjørnson often deals with skiing in his poetry. In the poem "Der ligger et Land mot den evige Sne – i revnerne kun er der vaarliv at se" (There lies a land against the eternal snow – only in the crevices can spring life be seen) are the well-known lines:[419]

> She scattered her snow over mountain-steep hill
> and then bade her boys to ski down it.

Before he heard of Sondre Norheim's feats, Bjørnson tells about boys playing on skis on steep hillsides and about their competitions with each other. It was important to be best, something which is at the heart of all sport, to give the best one can. Later in the poem "Norway, Norway" he has the famous lines which are probably most quoted in Norway to

---

[418] Vaage 1969: 115.
[419] Vaage 1969: 24.

prove that skiing was commonplace a hundred years ago:

> Norway – Norway
> the radiant land of the skihill race.

In 1870, before skiing had really become a competitive sport in Norway, he wrote the play *Arnljot Gelline* about the Swedish skier mentioned in the previous chapter. The poem "The ski trip" begins with the familiar lines:[420]

> Isn't it dashing
> Isn't it smashing,
> three men standing on one pair of skis,
> forest roads, mountain roads, villages passed
> in the middle of Christmas
> clear weather and wind –
> the valley with light below them.
>
> Isn't it dashing
> Isn't it smashing,
> the one on whose skis they stand,
> bewildered and afraid, they barely come up to his shoulder,
> and when they tire
> again he goes
> twisting and turning, as were he skiing alone.
>
> Isn't it dashing
> Isn't it smashing
> downward now in gusts and snow,
> no one can see them, nor do they see themselves,
> only trolls and animals
> they see, but they fly …
> Halt! A house is hidden in the woods.

Fig. 12.5

For Bjørnson to conjure up such images as skiing in the dark – at the end of the year there is very little light in Scandinavia, skiing in the mountains and all that that entails, would not have been possible unless he was familiar with the use of skis in the everyday life of that part of the country where he lived. Fig. 12.5 is a caracature of Bjørnstjerne Bjørnson and his wife Caroline skiing by Olaf Gulbransson.[421]

---

[420] Vaage 1969: 115-16.
[421] Vaage 1979: 40.

Trysil-Knud

In 1861 Bernt Lund published an epic poem about Trysil-Knud. The poem provides a good description of how multifaceted skiing was in Norway even before Sondre Norheim demonstrated his feats of daredevilry. Moreover, the poem has had an enormous impact in Norway down to the present day. The legendary Trysil-Knud is a fascinating figure in that Lund has created him with possible historical connections. It will be fitting to consider some of these aspects before presenting the poem in its entirety. Fig. 12.6 shows Trysil-Knud picking up the vest he had earlier put on a bush while roaring downhill – drawn by A. Bloch.[422]

"Trysil-Knud" was first printed in the New Year's edition of the *Illustreret Nyhedsblad* (Illustrated Newspaper) in 1861. Two years later, Dr. Morten Andreas Aabel alluded to it in his poem "Der Øst ved Grensefjeldets Side" (East at the Edge of the Border Mountains):[423]

> That if one day at a solemn council – the old Norway calls out,
> we will then meet with courage and skill – standing as steadily as Trysil-Knud.

In the 1870's many people became acquainted with Trysil-Knud through H. M. Dahl's *Smaastykker af Norske Forfattere* "Excerpts of Norwegian Authors" which was read in school, and a few years later the entire poem appeared in A. E. Eriksen and P. A. Paulsen's *Reader*.[424] School children had to learn the poem by heart; it was read aloud on festive occasions and enthusiastically received everywhere. Later other readers included the poem, and it remained popular among schoolboys. Jacob Vaage reported some fifty years ago having spoken with older people who still remembered having had to memorize "Trysil-Knud." Fig. 12.7 is Bloch's drawing of Trysil-Knud on his way up a steep hill to pull off a stunt.[425]

In 1897 Abel's Kunstforlag published the poem in an illustrated booklet with beautiful color sketches by Andreas Bloch, further contributing to making the ski larger in people's minds. In 1906 the poem appeared in Chr. A. Winterhjelm's anthology *Norsk Lyrik* "Norwegian Poetry." Then in 1909 Ole Haugen published a novel by the same name replete with a number of new exploits for Trysil-Knud. According to the novel he started skiing when he was three years old. At age eight he was hunting white grouse with his father, using one long ski and one "andor" (the andor was the shorter half of a pair of unequal length skis which were used in eastern Norway in the eighteenth century; the andor often had a fur

---

[422] Vaage 1969: 89.
[423] Vaage 1969: 117-18.
[424] Vaage 1969: 85.
[425] Vaage 1969: 90.

covering) on his feet. One time while jumping on skis he grabbed a cap in the air and put it on his head. As the novel progresses, Knud's feats become more and more supernatural. He shoots and hits the same hole made by a bullet already sitting there. He performs heroic deeds in the war with Sweden in 1814. His farm becomes a cultural center in the village when he joins those who support Henrik Wergeland's national views and fight for popular education. The novel, even if fantastic from beginning to end, helped make Trysil-Knud a national hero.[426] Fig. 12.8 is Bloch's drawing of Trysil-Knud enjoying a new triumph.[427]

Melvin Simonsen published a *Community Song Book* in 1943, and in it he included the poem with an old Trøndelag melody so that school children too could sing it. The melody Simonsen got from Olav Gulvaag. The students enjoyed singing it because they found the ballad exciting even though there were many stanzas. But, the first person to actually write music for Trysil-Knud was the German ski historian and Holmenkollen skier Carl J. Luther. He took part in Holmenkollen in 1909 and became so enthusiastic about Norwegian skiing that he taught himself Norwegian. When P. Chr. Andersen then sent Luther the illustrated booklet mentioned above, he composed a melody to it in 1920. It should be mentioned that Luther was a strong opponent of the Nazis. He was arrested by the Gestapo and so mistreated that he went blind in one eye. When he came out of prison after the war, his vision was so bad that he had to give up skiing. But he continued to write about skiing in *Der Winter*, which he edited, from 1906 to 1938.[428] Even a film was made about Trysil-Knud (Fig. 12.9).[429]

One historical incident helps to show why many people believed that Trysil-Knud himself was a historical person. When the Norwegian Ski Museum at Holmenkollen opened in 1923 it was reported that one of Trysil-Knud's skis could be found on a farm in Ringebu in Sør-Fron. The Ski Association made a number of efforts to acquire the ski through the sports dealer P. T. Helleberg in Lillehammer, who had provided the museum with many valuable old skis from Gudbransdalen. Helleberg said that if he couldn't get the ski in another way he might simply 'steal' it. The owner of the ski would not part with it because of an old tradition that on a farm what belonged to the old folks should remain untouched. Helleberg thought he could eventually get hold of the ski if he could "thaw the wife." That

---

[426] Vaage 1969: 85-86.
[427] Vaage 1969: 91.
[428] Vaage 1969: 86.
[429] Vaage 1969: 87. Johan Trondsen stands in for Alfred Maurstad in the film *Trysil-Knud*.

never happened. Helleberg did not believe the ski belonged to Trysil-Knud anyways.

Just who was this Trysil-Knud who inspired a poem of 31 stanzas? Consider first the author Bernt Lund.[430] He was born in Solør in 1812, and after having studied theology for three years at the university, he transferred to the Military Academy and became an officer in 1837. He had artistic talent and began to paint landscapes, studied with among others Thomas Fearnley and Hans Gude. An eye disease forced him to give up painting. From 1853 he was employed as an inspector in the highway department and traveled around Norway for many years, from one road construction site to another. He died in 1885.

Lund also had a lyrical vein, which came to the fore during the last 25 years of his life. It began when he wrote "Trysil-Knud." Eventually there were many poems. Some of them he published in 1882 when he was 70 years old in a collection called *Some Poems*. In the 1850's and 1860's a number of articles by Lund appeared in Christiana (Oslo) newspapers, dealing with a wide range of topics.

In the *Illustreret Nyhedsblad* where the poem was printed there were also poems and articles of Henrik Ibsen, Bjørnstjerne Bjørnson, J. S. Welhaven, and Ivar Aasen, so he was in good company.[431] There is no doubt that the editor, the well-known Pål Botten Hansen, thought it to be a good poem. Otherwise, he would hardly have found it worthy of being printed in this exclusive little book containing exquisite bits of Norway's most famous authors.

In 1882 when Lund had "Trysil-Knud" reprinted in his *Some Poems* he divided it into three sections. The first, which deals with Knud's feats in the ski company, has five stanzas, the second which tells about the competition with Ole Kynsberg's trotter, consists of eight stanzas, and the last part about the "slalom run" in Vestlandet has 17 stanzas. He deleted one stanza from the original version, which had nothing to do with skiing, and he made minor improvements in a few places.

Who then was this Trysil-Knud? Most people who have read the poem believe he was one of the ski soldiers from Østerdal Ski Company in the eighteenth century. In *Trysil Book* there is a long story about him:[432]

> Linnes is one of those places, which the many legends about Trysil-Knud designate as his home, and Trysil-Knud would then be identical to Knut Knutsen who came to Linnes sometime around 1780. (He was born in 1748 and died in 1830). No attempt

---

[430] Vaage 1969: 88.

[431] Vaage 1969: 88.

[432] Vaage 1969: 88-89.

will be made here to determine whether there even lived a man like Trysil-Knud or whether the qualities of many men from the Trysil area – both real, wished-for and possible qualities – have been invested by legend and tradition in a single character. It is not inconceivable that Skår-Knut, as Knut Knutsen Linnes was known in his older years, could have had at least some of the qualities attributed to Trysil-Knud and, for that matter, could be behind the origin of the character. Ole Kynsberg was a historical person, fond of horses and a merchant. That Skår-Knut and Ole Kynsberg lived at the same time means that one cannot definitively exclude the possibility that Trysil-Knud was a historical figure who lived and executed the deeds the poem refers to.

Kynsberg was a rich merchant who came to Elverum in 1790 when he was 41 years old. He soon owned the best trotters. Bernt Lund certainly heard many stories about Ole Kynsberg and his trotters. But there are historical data that Kynsberg is supposed to have had a race with a skier. This can be found in the Grong village book. In Grong there lived a man called Lars Åsmulen (1790-1880) who, according to historical accounts, raced with horses many times.[433] Bernt Lund is supposed to have visited Grong in the 1860's, so people have assumed that he got the idea for the contest between horse and skier while there. Since the road construction work in the area did not begin until two years after the poem was published, the idea must have come earlier. It turns out that Bernt Lund and his family, nevertheless, lived in the area from 1850-55. There is even a painting of Småsvannet by Lund, a lake not far from Grong. It is, therefore, quite likely that Lund got the idea for the race between horse and skier from Lars Åsmulen's feats. The exact same story (as in the poem) is discussed in the Grong village book. Lars Åsmulen once raced the sheriff's trotter: When the sheriff arrived in Solum, Lars was standing in the yard to greet him and help put his horse in the stable.

There are many reports that the men of Trysil were good skiers 150 to 200 years ago, something, which Bernt Lund must have known, having been born and raised in Solør. Yet, the Trysil men used the so-called Østerdal skis, one long ski and one short ski. Would it have been possible to jump with unequal length skis? Lund probably had heard about the Telemark man Olaf Rye, who later became a general and fell in Denmark in the battle at Fredericia in 1849. In Major Jens Edvard Hjort's handwritten memoirs Rye's jumping skills were mentioned in 1808: "Rye was highly praised by his comrades as the best of all skiers … in a jump competition arranged in a deep valley (in Eidsberg) where there was built up a snow bank, he remained standing on his skis, as he made a strong run and a jump that took him on his skis 15 ells from the ground (ca. 13 m.)." Word of Rye's jumping feats must

---

[433] Vaage 1969: 89.

have spread and may be the first real information there is about ski jumping. Historically, it is known that in 1767 the ski companies competed in downhill racing and target shooting while skiing. The "Description of Trysil Parish" (1784) by Pastor Axel Christian Smith may have given Lund the idea of using the name Trysil in the name of the skier he praised in his poem, in that there was no end to what these Trysil-men could accomplish:[434]

> After the shooter has risen from his seat and stretched half a score times, slowly lit his pipe and just as slowly smoked it, he stands up and ties his sack to his back, throws the rifle on his shoulder, puts his feet on his skis, and woe to the moose, the bear or other wild animals whose tracks can be picked up! Our slow Trysil-man now sets off with the speed of one of Jehu Nimfi's sons. Like the arrow he flies through forest and field … In races, in a game, a wedding party or other fun gatherings, the heavy and stiff Trysil-man makes bends and turns like a theater dancer, he throws himself with speed over a high pole … runs after loose timber logs.

This was before the people of Telemark had shown their ski tricks. For most people the Trysil men represented the best skiers in the country before 1850. Since he himself was half "Trysil," it is no wonder that Lund chose Trysil-Knud as his hero.

The last part of the poem where Trysil-Knud demonstrates his skiing ability in Vestlandet by picking up objects lying in the snow while he zooms down hill, is known in Telemark from old.[435] Also well known in Telemark is the feat of skiing down a steep hill with a bowl of ale filled to the top without spilling a drop (cf. p. 213). Studies show that there is no place in Vestlandet named Vigeland, and what is Bergensleden? From articles in *Morgenbladet* more than 100 years ago it appears that Bernt Lund was inspector on the road construction between Mandal and Vigeland in the 1860's, and he may have been there as early as in the 1850's. That the words Bergensleden and Vigeland fit in with the style and rhythm of the poem explains why they were used.

The best proof that Trysil-Knud is not a historical person comes as early as 1865, only four years after the poem was written.[436] That year General Oscar Wergeland published *Skiløbningen, dens historie og krigsanvendelse* (Skiing, its history and military use). He writes that skiing has deteriorated much since the end of the ski companies (in 1822). "Now (1865) people are found in sleds, and Trysil-Knud asks for a ride or goes third class on the railroad." Trysil-Knud had been dead for many years, so when Wergeland used this name,

---

[434] Vaage 1969: 91.
[435] Vaage 1969: 91.
[436] Vaage 1969: 91-92.

he was referring to Norwegian skiers in general. They were now choosing what was comfortable, taking horse and sled and railroad instead of using their skis.

The poem can be interpreted as an effort at getting ski competitions renewed. It was no longer just the military, it was just as much a national sport. Here then is the poem:

I
Among the Østerdal ski corps
once was heard so great a story
about Trysil-Knud who skied
in the Bratberg battle and Glommeli.

In prize runs and in drills
it was Knud who won the first prize
He was number one, wherever it was,
and stood, where the best would fall.

The gigantic hill one picked out
was still too little for Trysil-Knud.
He made a jump in the middle of the hill
under it twelve men were lined up.

And Knud flew over, to the sound of hurrahs
while he cheerfully shot off a round.
It was a jump worthy of a story
even within this ski corps.

And far and wide his reputation spread
it became an honor to be like him
And if a skier receives distinction
one still calls him "a boy like Knud."

II
Mr. Ole Kynsberg kept a trotter
of which he was more than a little proud.
Twelve miles to town in the same day
was nothing with it pulling the sled.

A trip like this Mr. Ole intends
and horse and sled stand ready at the door.
Then Knud comes on his skis
and lifts his cap and wants to pass.

But Ole greets him: "Good Day, my friend
out so early – where are you going?"
"To town I plan to go by evening."
"Oh?" says Ole, "I do, too."

"If you can follow me to Minne-Sund,
then you will own your farm and land;
and if you can follow me all the way to town,
I'll even rebuild your house."

Off he went, he didn't hurry
as one, who is sure of himself.
Where Knud took off went unnoticed;
he always went his own way.

When Ole stopped at Minne-Sund
Knud had just left a short while ago!
When Ole traveled over the Aker River
then Trysil-Knud himself met him.

"I wish you welcome!" he said dryly.
"You have driven quite soundly.
I am now, you see, on my way home
Shall I give them your greetings?"

The word got around about Trysil-Knud.
He didn't take the farm but traveled out.
It was thought he wooed and got turned down
and no one knew where he went.

III

At Bergensleden not far from the coast
there lies a farm named Vigeland.
There a merry group had gathered
for a wedding feast one winter day.

They saw a fisherman row toward shore
and take the road toward Vigeland.
And the young people in the group were about
to play some tricks on the fisherman.

"Listen here, you Stril! and you'll see
a vessel made for sailing in the snow!"

That was clever teasing,
when they showed him a pair of skis.

"Oh, my! It would be so much fun
to get to try such an art once!
I wonder if one of you will show me
how sailing in the snow is done?"

And they told him: "Stand this way,
and let 'er run straight down the hill!
But first take the vessel with you up
on that highest, round top!"

And the man from Stril calmly took pole and skis
and wandered up the steep hill.
It was a walk that was pretty long:
for the hill was both steep and high.

He walked with the skis under his arm.
You could see that the walk made him warm.
For soon he removed his cap,
left it behind on his pole.

Then he climbed further up;
that was a real persistent guy!
But it seemed to cost him his warm sweat;
for now he threw off his coat, too.

And upward, upward without pause;
he gained on the hill with incredible haste,
now he threw off his vest too in the end,
and hung it on a fir tree branch.

But still higher up he went
and he became tiny to everyone's eyes,
Finally they saw he had come up;
he could be seen on the mountain top.

And everyone thought it would be fun
to watch the Strilen man's snow sailing trip.
"He'll be falling soon – and all for the best;
for otherwise he would kill himself.

So, there he comes and with such speed!
He didn't fall so soon after all.
Often he was hidden behind the cloud of snow
but immediately shot forth as an arrow again.

And just as the speed was best of all,
he took again from the branch his vest
and pulled it on, as is only proper;
– he had tried sailing before.

And when he came to where his coat was
he picked it up and pulled it on.
And the speed increased; it went like lightning
before the eyes of the amazed men.

Then he took the pole and waved his cap
and greeted the group one more time;
and steered straight down to the boat
and shot off from land and was on his way.

They stood there staring; they wanted to know
that this really hadn't happened.
And some thought he was a troll
and threw fire and steel after him.

Then they found something black in his track;
and carefully they took hold of it.
And it was the kerchief of the troll;
on it was sewn "Trysil-Knud."

Henrik Ibsen

Norway's great dramatist, Henrik Ibsen (1828-1906), mentions skiing only once in his entire authorship, but then he spent nearly three decades in exile in Italy and Germany. In the third act of *Peer Gynt* Solveig enters the stage on skis and when she reaches his cabin, she says:[437]

> On skis I have run;
> I have asked my way;
> they asked where I was going;
> I answered: "I'm going home."

---

[437] Vaage 1969: 27.

Fig. 12.10 shows Thora Hansson as Solveig in the premiere of Ibsen's *Peer Gynt* in 1876.[438]

Ski Jumper

In 1883 the artist Andreas Bloch drew a picture of a ski jumper pulling up in the air (the style then) and to this picture the author Kristoffer Randers composed a poem:[439]

> Now it's time to give it a try
> on arrow-fast skis over layers of snow drifts
> exerting oneself is good for the body.

He also touches on hunting and playing on skis:

> It is not a game to clamber on skis
> after the reindeer herd's tracks and on the bear's path.
> But what a delight to feel so free
> and bathe one's chest in the air!

and then the skier comes to a jump:

> Onwards it goes. There is no stopping
> before you go out over the ledge.
> The house sits between the tops of the cliff
> until you slam into the ground. –
> The skis glide. The supple body
> squeezes together and then straightens itself up.
> – He who can stand after such a jump
> he will not fail us, when it counts.

A constant theme – one often heard now at the end of the twentieth century – was that those who took care of their bodies and who did not sit inside in the oven corner when it got cold, had what it took and were capable of more than most others. But there was no shortage of challenges. In a poem by an unknown author the following tirade occurs:[440]

> When the snow covers valley and mountain
> and the cold happily crackles,
> to crawl under a warm sheepskin
> seems to suit many well,
> to sit cozily in the corner by the stove
> and let the fire burn,
> and drowsily leaf through a book,

---

[438] Vaage 1979: 31.
[439] Vaage 1969: 119-20.
[440] Vaage 1969: 120.

perhaps feels awfully good!
But I know a better way, however,
to use the time well:
On skis out on a merry trip!
You can warm yourself later.

When you have become old and gray
and your limbs are stiff,
then you can get under the sheepskin
and stay in the corner by the stove.

Arne Garborg

Arne Garborg (1851-1924), the other of the two great nineteenth century *nynorsk* writers – Vinje was mentioned above – made a contribution to the history of skiing with a little poem. To him it was essential to get the young people out into the fresh air, even if it bit your nose:[441]

In the living room air and in the corner by the stove
There shudders our decadent present
But at the hill on skis and dancing on skates
That's where the Norwegian future grows.

Knut Hamsun

Knut Hamsun (1859-1952), Nobel Prize winner in literature in 1920, was himself an enthusiastic skier in his younger days. He wrote a poem called "Snow:"

And the skis are strapped onto toes familiar
and skiing conditions are first-rate crusty snow.
In the hill there are swarms of all kinds of folk
Small boys are heard humming.
They darken the countryside like an army of birds
And no one is spared the joy that exists
A divinity has touched everyone.

Women on Skis

Women on skis are present in the folk tradition and are portrayed in romantic poetry, especially the village woman who could ski well because she had to.[442] Skiing for pleasure was

---

[441] Vaage 1969: 116.
[442] Bø 1966: 97-98.

something else (Fig. 12.11 shows a woman on skis).[443] One of the first female skiers mentioned was Ingrid Olavsdotter Vestby from Trysil, only sixteen when a ski meet was held in her village in 1862. She competed with the men in the jumping competition, staying afoot where "so many a spry lad lost his balance." Toward the end of the century women began to participate regularly in ski meets. Of course, there were many who were opposed to such "unfeminine" behavior as entering skiing competitions against men. A woman's place back then was in the kitchen! Nevertheless, the women persisted and started their own ski clubs.[444] The first club was founded by the women of Steinkjer and was called Skade after the ski goddess of the same name. An unmarried lady protested in vain against the name: "Skade was so daring that her reputation was far from untarnished. She had married Njord, but had had a son with Odin, and even though this was a great honor, it was, in her opinion, a less than noble affair. And her son Sæmund was, by the way, a real wild boy, too."

People were aghast at boys and girls beginning to ski together; women's ski suits – more and more available – were criticized; but, most of all, some people did not like to see the Nordmarka peace disturbed in that women tended to howl and shriek when they fell.[445] Knut Hamsun rebutted this view in *Dagbladet* wondering why women shouldn't be allowed to scream a little when they went onto their heads in a pile of snow. An attorney, Axel Huitfeldt, carried on the battle for a while. He described the ladies at Frognerseteren, who could drink two beers, who put their feet up close to the fireplace to warm them, even crossing their legs, and breaking the laws of femininity in other ways, by drinking cognac for example under the ski jump, and so on. This is the reply he got:[446]

> It has been written, among other things,
> about a sight so horrible
> as "women folk" out skiing.
> "No, please, spare us!"
> Great "harm" have those ladies done (harm in Norwegian is *skade*)
> to our noble sport
> yes, really spoiled it.
>
> When earlier we went out skiing
> we were so wonderfully safe
> from seeing ladies

---

[443] Bø 1966: 45.
[444] Vaage 1969: 120.
[445] Bø 1966: 99.
[446] Vaage 1969: 120, 122.

out in the deep snow.
But now it is crawling and swarming
in the mountains, in the woods and bogs
with these "pests!" (pest in Norwegian is *skadedyr*)

Fridtjof Nansen's wife Eva now intervened. In a famous newspaper article she described the joy and exhilaration of skiing and the outdoor life compared to the paleness and misery of the girls who go from ballroom to ballroom. She did not fear moral decay:[447]

> Can anyone seriously claim that women will become more immoral from skiing, even if it takes place together with gentlemen? Does anyone believe that Kristiania's ballrooms, streets, cafes are, morally speaking, healthier places for young girls than the fields and woods around Kristiania?
> Even if the worst should happen, and they are not home before dark or they go out one evening, such a ski trip through the woods, be it by moon light or by torch light, is an experience that I have difficulty believing will offend anyone with a heart and with feelings.

The skiing of women came to play a role in their emancipation. They even had parties alone without men, and that was wrong according to the custom of the day:[448]

> But "Skade's" ladies who've
> had parties with song
> and lots of speeches
> without male chaperones
> what will become of them?
> To thus completely
> forget themselves
> and meet in a hotel,
> O, femininity, farewell!

The following lines come from another song from the 1890's in Steinkjer:

> And the skis carried them with joy and delight
> all the way under the steepest hills.
> With heroic courage they passed their test.
> They did not bite the dust.

Figs. 12.11-14 depict women on skis toward the end of the nineteenth century and suggest that skiing was becoming a popular pastime for them.[449]

---

[447] Bø 1966: 99-100.
[448] Vaage 1969: 122.
[449] Vaage 1979: 12; Vaage 1979: facing 49; Egnell 1979: 21.

Ski Songs

Not many of the ski poems were set to music, but in the 1880's and the 1890's when the fight for independence from Sweden was heating up, Jørun Telnes wrote a catchy battle song with skiing as its main theme:[450]

> When Norway in her silver coat gleams
> then we strap skis onto our feet.
> We swarm in flocks up from the valley
> and then we boys meet on the hill.
> …
> And though icicles form on our shirts
> our cheeks are in the most fervent glow.
> Down from cliffs and bluffs we run
> so we stand in a drift of snow.
> And then we do a jump
> and with our skis and with our bodies
> we fly up so it sighs at the top.
>
> But if the boy should happen to tumble
> he again sets off just the same.
> He learns the slowest, he learns the best he who should
> when he thinks he stands there he falls!
> …
> Let the little boy be baptized in the snow
> so he will show when the boy grows up,
> "the young Heming" can still ski!
> Let us sing his song in the north!

In the last stanza the real intent of the song comes out. Norway should become a free nation and the skiers should play a role in the liberation:

> When the old folks have the army arrow cut
> yes, then the boys will show up keenly,
> for skis could carry them so well
> where the enemy got stuck in the snow.
> Let us run on skis!
> Let us shoot ourselves free!
> Let us love our Norway all our days!

---

[450] Vaage 1969: 122.

Theodor Caspari wrote a ski song in the 1890's with a fine melody: *Der står en lystig Herreferd* "There is a merry train of men." In one stanza it says:[451]

> You silently hid your warm soil
> with the white waves of snow;
> we run like a flock of birds
> through your woods.
> "Look up! On your way!
> Hurrah! Hurrah!
> Thus we sail
> thus we rush
> on light skis
> through your woods!"

Laila, the main character in the book *Laila* by Jens Andreas Friis, had a song composed about her by the Swedish author, Daniel Fallström:

> Fast is the ski and sharpened the spear
> which he tightly holds in his hand.

Before the turn of the century there are some lively children's songs by Margrethe Munthe:[452]

> I tie my sack, I strap on my skis
> the hills are shining so beautifully.
> Away form the stove corner! So happy and so free
> toward the big white forest I set out.
> Those wings on my feet give life and joy and courage
> now I am heading towards the highest top.
> Everything heavy and everything sad, everything petty and gray
> rushes and flies away with the wind.

Ski Humor

When the sport of skiing began to take off there were many opportunities for humor, especially when less skilled skiers competed against the best.

Fig. 12.15 depicts some of the skiers at the 1879 Huseby competition where the skiers from Telemark were superior to all others.[453] Fig. 12.16 compares skiers from the four Nordic countries,[454] and Fig. 12.17 shows various ways to stop for those who don't ski very well.[455]

---

[451] Vaage 1969: 122.
[452] Vaage 1969: 123.
[453] Vaage 1979: 130.
[454] Egnell 1979: 57.
[455] Egnell 1979: 240.

Bertel Gripenberg

Gripenberg (1878-1947) was a Finland-Swedish poet, perhaps best known for his erotic poetry. That skiing interested him is evident from the poem "Ett ensamt skidspår" (A Lone Ski Track):[456]

> A long ski track wending
> off into the woodland depth,
> a lone ski track bending
> forth over ridges and slopes,
> over bogs where snow's awhirling
> and stunted pine stand thin and short –
> it is my thought slipping
> further and further away.
>
> A frozen ski track fading
> in the solitude of the forest,
> a human life ebbing away
> on paths known to no one –
> the answers remained in the distance
> to questions borne by the heart
> my erratic wandering was
> a twisting track on the crusty snow.
>
> A lone ski track ending
> before a suddenly treacherous cliff,
> where a windworn fir leans out
> over the edge of the rock –
> how coldly the stars gaze
> how dark the forest's shadow
> how lightly the flakes fall
> on snow-covered tracks!

Fig. 12.18 shows the national ski badge created by the sculptor Stig Blomberg on the motto "following our forefathers' footsteps."[457]

---

[456] Gripenberg 1911.
[457] Egnell 1979: 137.

Skiing Spreads Around the World

As has already been demonstrated, skis are very old – a good 8,000 years or more. They spread outward from central Asia toward the northwest and northeast, reaching most of the circumpolar areas of Eurasia where they are still in use. There were periods when skiing flourished, for example, among the Sámi in Finland, Norway and Sweden in recent centuries or, to some extent, among the military in these countries and Russia during the sixteenth to early nineteenth centuries, especially Norway where military ski competitions were open to the public.[458] But, by the time Sondre Norheim was making a name for himself, skiing was on the wane in many areas. Undoubtedly, the small populations of circumpolar people of northern Asia would have continued to use skis for utilitarian purposes; however, it is highly unlikely that many outsiders would have been aware of this. People had reverted to their older habit of hibernating during the winter when snow made communication difficult.[459] Skiing might simply have died out had it not been for the people of Telemark and other rural areas who not only kept skiing alive and fostered its development but provided the necessary foundation for skiing to become a true sport.

Jakob Vaage described the beginnings of the sport of skiing in his book *Norske ski erobrer verden* (Norwegian skis conquer the world) from 1952.[460] It will be sufficient here to sketch the main lines of the explosive growth of skiing toward the end of the nineteenth century and early in the twentieth century. Vaage, in a bit of hyperbole, says that Norwegians have had wanderlust in their blood since the Viking era. Beginning in the eighth century Scandinavian Vikings headed abroad in their long ships not only to plunder neigh-

---

[458] Firsoff 1943: 14-16.
[459] Vaage 1952: 5.
[460] Vaage 1952.

boring countries but also to seek land on which to settle, including Iceland, Greenland and even Vinland. The next great wave of Scandinavians leaving their homes came in the nineteenth century when many emigrated to America and elsewhere in search of land and a better life than they lived on their small tenant farms at home.[461] The third wave came when Norwegian students and professional people went abroad to study or participate more fully in the industrial revolution on the continent of Europe and elsewhere. It was this last group that was to some extent responsible for the spread of skiing as a sport, in a way paralleling the much earlier spread of skiing as an accessory to hunting.

These Norwegians who spent time abroad either took their skis along or sent for them or made skis themselves following the patterns they remembered from home. Imagine the impression it made on people who had never heard of skis to suddenly see someone skiing down a hill or attempting a jump. This happened virtually everywhere there was plenty of snow in the winter and Norwegians to take advantage of it. Vaage mentioned that in Japan a group of soldiers had died on a mountain after getting stuck in the snow (1901) and that in Algeria the same thing had almost happened (1904). In both areas, Norwegian consuls showed how skis might have prevented catastrophe.[462]

In America, Australia and New Zealand it was Norwegian immigrants who introduced skiing during the gold rush.[463] Even if these Norwegians did not find gold they had something to amuse themselves with during the winter. In central Europe is was Norwegian students who introduced skiing to Switzerland, France, Germany and Austria. Norwegian engineers did the same elsewhere in the world. Certainly the greatest individual contribution to the then nascent sport of skiing was the publication of Fridtjof Nansen's book *Paa ski over Grønland*, which appeared in Norwegian in 1890 and then in English, French and German editions the following year.[464] It is difficult to overemphasize the sensation this book made on so many people. It was stated in the introduction that this book took the first systematic look at the history of skiing. More importantly it demonstrated to many what could be accomplished on skis. After reading the book some people even wrote to Norway in an effort to purchase skis. But first of all, the huge success of Fridtjof Nansen's book *Paa*

---

[461] Semmingsen 1940.
[462] Vaage 1952: 7.
[463] Vaage 1952: 7 and Bjork 1956.
[464] Nansen 1890; Vaage 1952: 7 and articles by Allen, Eichenberger, Ueberhorst and Ulmrich in Goksøyr 1994.

ski over Grønland in Europe and elsewhere cannot be underestimated, nor the enormous influence it had in aiding the spread of skiing. This created an interest in skiing around the world and made people receptive to this "new" idea.

But why was it primarily Norwegians who were responsible for the spread of skiing and its growth as a sport? This question has already been answered in the chapter on Sondre Norheim. Through his competitive efforts he showed the world what could be done with a pair of skis. His heel binding made sharp turning possible. In other areas such as Finland and Sweden where only toe bindings were available, skiing remained an accessory to the hunt or a means of transportation during the winter. The basic shape of the Telemark ski was also a factor. This shape – widest at the front, narrowing to the footrest, and then getting wider toward the back – was an old pattern in the Telemark area. Sondre is usually given credit for this, but what he more than anyone else did was to help this shape become the standard outside of Telemark. By the turn-of-the-century the Norwegian ski industry was producing these skis in record numbers and exporting many of them.[465]

Mountain hotels that had been in the habit of closing for the winter now remained open as more and more people took up skiing.[466] Although it was Norwegians who spread skiing around the world, the natives soon took over in their respective countries and helped turn skiing into a boom industry. Skis began to be produced in other countries as well. Even Norwegian ski terminology was exported, most notably the word ski but also other words such as slalom, Telemark turn, and Christiania turn (Christie).

It will be helpful to look more closely at the special cases of Sweden and Finland, since many of their inhabitants already knew how to ski. In Sweden skiing was not as widespread as in Norway or Finland. As early as 1840 the four Swedish princes received gifts of Norwegian skis and, with some help, learned how to use them. Perhaps the most significant factor in the introduction of the sport of skiing to Sweden was that the Norwegian *Jægerkorps* "sharpshooters" were stationed in the Stockholm area from 1856-88 (Norway was under Swedish rule at this time).[467] Fig. 13.1 shows this elite Norwegian army unit in the 1880's. The illustration is from the *Illustrierte Zeitung* in Berlin in 1886.[468] They did a lot of skiing and some jumping in the 50's and 60's and must have made a big impression on the Swedish population. The first Huseby competition in Oslo had come in 1879 before 10,000

---

[465] Vaage 1952: 9.
[466] Vaage 1952: 9.
[467] Vaage 1952: 13-14.
[468] Vaage 1979: 220.

spectators (Huseby was the forerunner of Holmenkollen). That same year the Swedish Ski Club was formed, and competitions were held in the Stockholm area. Figs. 13.2-3 show a Telemark man jumping at the first Huseby competition in 1883, in the air in a painting by Gustav Lærum and landing in a Christian Krohg painting.[469] The Swedes had been taught by the Norwegian sharpshooters. At these early competitions the prizes were won exclusively by Norwegians. In 1883 Åmund Oppebøen from Telemark came to the Jægerkorps in Stockholm.[470] He was a very good skier and had to perform for King Oscar. He also taught many Swedes to ski and stayed ten years in the Stockholm area as a ski instructor after the sharpshooters returned to Norway in 1888. In Gothenburg, it was Norwegian students who brought skiing in 1894; here the snow does not remain on the ground as long as further to the east.

Fig. 13.6

Finland had a tradition of skiing competitions, but they were quite different than what was developing in Norway. They had only crosscountry races run around a triangular course on a frozen lake.[471] They mainly stood on their narrow skis with toe bindings and used their poles to push themselves around. Finns and Norwegians met as competitors for the first time in Stockholm in 1892. In 1881 a Norwegian by the name of Petter Fredheim went to Helsinki and brought ski jumping with him. He got the sons of the owner of the company where he worked interested in jumping.

Fig. 13.7

He was shown a trove of Finnish skis, which he tried, breaking eleven pair in a short time. Finally, he got hold of some ash and made his own pair. Soon he began to import and sell Norwegian skis. Finland-Swedes and Finns adopted the Norwegian bindings and took to jumping and crosscountry on hillier courses in no time (Fig. 13.4 shows the first ski jump in Finland won by the Norwegian Christian Nielsen).[472] The same story repeats itself in every country to which Norwegians brought skiing.

Fig. 13.5 showing "skee" races in Norway and a sixty-two foot jump was published in *Scientific American* in 1895.[473]

---

[469] Vaage 1979: 27, 47.
[470] Vaage 1952: 16-22.
[471] Vaage 1952: 131-32.
[472] Vaage 1979: 22.
[473] *Scientific American*. Supplement No. 1007, April 20, 1895: 16099.

More than a century later skiing has become an extremely popular pastime for many and a competitive sport on the highest level. Witness the winter olympics where the following ski disciplines are contested: crosscountry (three distances plus a relay for women and men and skiathlon with two different styles), jumping (large and small hill; small hill for women), biathlon (a continuation of the military use of skis, with points awarded for speed of skiing and accuracy of shooting), Nordic combined (crosscountry plus jumping), Alpine (downhill, slalom, giant slalom, super giant slalom), ski cross (mass start, just pure speed down a steep slope) and freestyle (moguls, half-pipe, aerials, slope style). Ski flying off of huge ski jumps with distances approaching 700 feet is a discipline that has not made it to the Olympics yet. The ski "industry" has become a multinational endeavor with companies annually turning out new equipment and stylish apparel. Ski resorts thrive even in areas of marginal snowfall thanks to snow machines. In figs. 13.6-8 are Norwegian stamps issued for the 1966 World Championships.

Fig. 13.8

What would the Rødøy skier from some 4,000 years ago have thought?

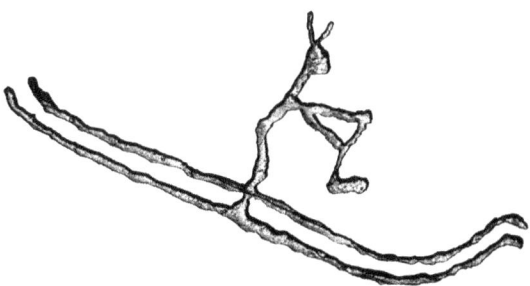

Appendices

1 – The Evolution of Humans to the Late Stone Age

2 – The Reindeer Hunters of Post-Glacial Scandinavia

3 – Winter Travel in the North: Snowshoes

4 – Literary References to Snowshoes

The Evolution of Humans to the Late Stone Age

Much of the cultural evolution of man[474] took place during the geological epoch known as the Pleistocene. This epoch of climatic fluctuations between cold and warm periods differed markedly from the preceding relatively more equitable Pliocene epoch. Present estimates put the duration of the Pleistocene at about one and one half million years ending some 12,000 years ago when the most recent glaciation ended, and the large glaciers began to melt rapidly from the face of the earth. On such a grand time scale the invention of the ski came quite recently, only after the northern portions of Eurasia had opened up to human settlement. By then man had already been a highly skilled hunter-gatherer for about a million years, and the material culture associated with this late Paleolithic hunter was very advanced technologically. Since it was these Paleolithic hunters who most likely invented the ski and who brought the ski to Fennoscandia (Fig. A1.1),[475] it will be helpful to survey briefly the evolution of man down to the Stone Age and thereby gain a glimpse of the people responsible for this technological achievement.

What was this late Paleolithic hunter like, and how had he evolved from his earlier ancestors? The ancestors of man were subject to manifold and far-reaching changes, the end result of which was "rational man," *Homo sapiens*. When the climate deteriorated millions of years ago and the plush forests began to diminish, being gradually replaced by savanna, the forebears of man moved onto new surroundings and adapted to new conditions. Since then man has always possessed a remarkable ability to improvise and adapt to new conditions and environments and to change behavioral patterns accordingly, and this is what distinguishes man from all the other animals and their highly specialized life patterns. Man cannot see as well as the hawk, pick up scents like the bloodhound or hear like the deer.

---

[474] The words "man, he, his" should be read as gender-neutral and representing humankind.
[475] Map of Fennoscandia.

The gazelle runs swifter and the porpoise swims faster, but man has all of these senses and abilities in a fine balance.

These pre-humans had become adept at moving about in trees. Rather than digging into branches with claws as squirrels and raccoons do, they grasped the branches using pressure between thumb and fingers.[476] They had eyes facing forwards, which gave them partial stereoscopic vision and fine depth perception. Good eye-hand coordination was a must, for a missed branch might have meant a fall from the trees. But soon they had to leave the trees. At that time, perhaps as recently as one and one half million years ago, came one of the most far-reaching changes to have affected mankind, a change that accounts for the uniqueness of man among his closest of kin in the animal world. Mankind became omnivorous; he became a hunter, a predator, a scavenger and a meat-eater.[477] This drastic change in basic pattern of subsistence from vegetarian to omnivore did not occur overnight, but was a long, slow process. Man had to pre-adapt to the hunting life before he could leave the trees and survive on the savanna. The savanna offered plentiful food supplies with fewer primates competing for them, but there were perils in the form of new and physically stronger predators such as the carnivorous ancestors of lions. Though man's two-legged gait freed his hands to fashion tools, wield weapons and carry things, it would be a long time before his weapons became efficient enough to master large game.[478] Therefore, the key to survival lay in social organization. These pre-humans had to learn how to cooperate, something seen only rarely among primates, but the rule among such predators as wolves, and for the ancestors of man this was a fundamental change in behavior. But these pre-humans were quite intelligent. They were curious animals with good memories, and they were able to alter their behavioral patterns when confronted with new threats and challenges. This was an auspicious development for the future of mankind. This union of the intelligence of the primate with the carnivorous way, catalyzed by the worsening climate, would eventually lead to that highly intelligent and unique species, *H. sapiens*.

The most remote ancestors of man are perhaps the *Ramapithecines*, who inhabited the sub-tropical forests of East Africa, Southern Europe, and Southwest Asia. Since these forests were not fertile year round, there were perhaps periods when *Ramapithecines* had to hunt for nuts and roots and take to eating meat just as the chimpanzee does today. This would ac-

---

[476] Farb 1978: 80.
[477] Ardrey 1976.
[478] Farb 1978: 25, 77.

count for their teeth and jaws, which differed from those of other contemporary primates. *Ramapithecines* had disappeared by eight million years ago.

Some of the major characteristics of man that set him apart from the other primates are:

- A larger brain
- The use of tools
- Spoken language
- The sharing of food
- The female tied to a home and children

All of the complexities of advanced cultural and behavioral patterns called for a bigger brain, and brain size increased steadily and gradually until relatively recently. The sharing of food was part of group living that was necessary on the open savanna. Hunting in groups was much more successful. Prey could be pursued, encircled and slain, with the kill being distributed afterwards. Larger prey were scavenged because they were beyond the capabilities of these early hunters. Group living also assured the individual of security in numbers. The female became less mobile and multiple births became uncommon (they are uncommon in all of the apes), because the transmission of a complex culture from one generation to the next required longer periods of infancy, juvenility, and adolescence. Free hands were soon put to use with the invention of tools and better weapons. Finally, large quantities of information were acquired, stored, exchanged and eventually passed on. Symbols facilitated the transmission of information, and ultimately human language evolved.

The first true large-brained hominid, *Homo habilis*, appeared about two million years ago. A close cousin, *Australopithecus africanus*, is well represented from this period. *A. africanus* was already a hunter-gatherer, subsisting on meat, bone marrow and what could be gleaned from the savanna. His brain was about 30% the size of modern man's, and his habitat was still quite limited, mainly to central and northern Africa. *A. africanus* became extinct more than one million years ago. His tools were crude, satisfying only the need to cut and break. But what is significant is that an implement was produced with a special use in mind, and this shows that current wants could be projected into future events and needs. Chimps do this as well. Scavenging the carcasses of large animals required crude tools if the bone marrow was to be exploited, and these tools had to be carried to the site of the carcass. Two such implements are choppers and flakes. The choppers consist of pebbles on which only one edge has been modified. Striking one piece of rock against another, which results in a very sharp edge, produces a flake, a huge advance. Though peoples with this basic tool kit survived into the late Pleistocene in a few areas, more advanced tools began to appear in the early Pleistocene. It was then that the process of retouching came to be used. Retouching involves removing small flakes along an edge so as to make the edge less brittle. By retouching both surfaces of a thick flake a biface or hand axe was produced, and this replaced the choppers in many areas, so that by the end of the Lower Pleistocene the biface/flake cultures known as Acheulean were widespread in Africa and Europe.

Homo erectus appeared in the Middle Pleistocene beginning 1.5 million years ago and spread throughout much of the Old World. Early examples of *H. erectus* such as Peking man or Java man now had a brain some 60% the size of modern man's. By the time *H. erectus* vanished, some 250,000 years ago, brain size had further increased to 75% of modern man's, although the areas of the brain having to do with speech, memory and thinking were perhaps not as well developed. There are traces of right-handedness, which suggests an increase in dexterity and more specialized brain-hand function. *H. erectus* was a meat- as well as plant-eater, and his prey may have included big game animals. He knew how to control fire that had been produced naturally, for example, by lightning. Fire was perhaps first controlled (obtained and kept burning) around one half million years ago. It is not certain for what purposes he used it. It could have been used for cooking, to break down the tissue of tough meat, to kill parasites and to allow for longer storage, or it could have been used to provide heat and light and protection. Fire may even have been used to round up game and stampede them into an entrapment for the kill. It was probably also used to oust larger animals from caves which then provided shelter for them. But *H. erectus* did not know how to make fire himself. The major weapon was probably the wooden spear equipped with a fire-hardened tip, so tempered to give a better penetration capability, though the archaeological record does not attest to this. This was not a long distance weapon, however, and was used primarily to stab with. Animals were also captured in traps, pits, or by running them off cliffs. Their multi-purpose tool was the bifacial hand axe used for digging, cutting up game and shaping wood.

Then in Europe and around the Mediterranean the Acheulean cultures disappeared and the Mousterian cultures began to emerge in the early Upper Pleistocene. Tool making became more advanced. Tortoise-shaped cores were prepared from which a series of flakes could be systematically struck from one face. These flakes were retouched to produce a number of different tools such as side-scrapers, points, and blades. It was at this time – over

200,000 years ago – that Neanderthal man emerged.[479] He pushed the frontiers of human habitation into the new ecological zones of the northern forests and the arctic tundra where his stocky build helped him to conserve heat in these colder climes. Animals he hunted included the wooly rhinoceros, musk ox, mammoth, cave bear, and reindeer. He was one of the first to make use of "unearned" resources, i.e. mammals that had grown fat on food obtained outside of the normal Neanderthal environment and that were killed as they passed through on their seasonal migration routes (the wildebeest also migrates through Africa). The teeth of Neanderthals were similar to those of modern Eskimos and show that they chewed animal skins to soften them. Scrapers were used for cleaning hides, stone knives to cut them, and gouges to make holes for sewing with rawhide thread. Animal skins were sewn into clothing and perhaps also tents. The clothing had a number of functions: for carrying things such as infants, food and tools, for protection from the cold and for the sake of vanity. They lived in caves during part of the year. Evidence of care of the elderly suggests that they lived to a fairly advanced age, and whereas *H. erectus* had practiced ritual cannibalism, Neanderthal man seems to have buried the dead, often with tools, food, jewelry or wreaths of medicinal flowers. Man had by now learned that death was inevitable. The brain of Neanderthal man was as large as or slightly larger than that of today's human being.

In the latter half of the Upper Pleistocene, some 45,000 years ago, Cro-Magnon man, immediate ancestor to modern man, appeared. Arising concurrently in the Near East, Southeast Asia and Europe, Cro-Magnon man may have been responsible for the disappearance of Neanderthal man from the earth some 40,000 years ago.[480] This could be the first example of large-scale warfare among the ancestors of man. Or, Neanderthal man may have been too specialized in his adaptation to the fringes of the ice-sheet, or Cro-Magnon man survived because of better tools. The stocky Neanderthal man was at a disadvantage in the use of the spear; Cro-Magnon man with his long, slender-body could hurl a spear better. Or, Neanderthal man may have simply evolved into the Cro-Magnon man. The two types of *Homo sapiens* do not differ greatly from one another anatomically, and there are wide ranges within each group. In any case, recent genetic evidence suggests that Neanderthal and Cro-Magnon people may have interbred before 45-50,000 years ago.[481] Modern Eurasian genomes include up to 4% Neanderthhal DNA and up to 6% Denisovan DNA.

---

[479] Gore 1996: 4. Cf. revolvy.com on Neanderthal/Cro-Magnon.
[480] Gore 1996: 4.
[481] Cf. Neanderthal genome project.

Fire making was now a reality; it made nightlife possible, which in turn stimulated verbal communication. Cro-Magnon man also seems to have had a conception of an afterlife. By now man had begun to spread rapidly over much of the earth reaching the New World and Australasia before the end of the period, so that most of the world was colonized by man while he was still a hunter. Noteworthy of Cro-Magnon man was a less robust skeleton, a lighter jaw, and smaller teeth. His tool-kit was much more complex. Bone and antler were now frequently used as the raw materials for tools, being made into awls, needles, and points, and also into some of the first art objects. Fishhooks and harpoons show that the resources of the sea were being exploited as well. The process of polishing stone implements resulted in their increased efficiency and longevity. Hafting – attaching handles to stone blades or axe ends – produced lances, harpoons, barbed weapons, and spear throwers. And by the beginning of the Mesolithic era the bow and arrow were in use in Europe. Pulling the bow required the broad-shouldered, thick arm muscle build typical of the Cro-Magnon man. In areas lacking caves, earth huts or tents of skin supported by poles provided shelter. There is evidence of music in the form of percussion instruments and art in the magnificent cave paintings and sculpted figurines, showing that man had become artistically creative and had learned how to abstract from everyday life to the symbolic realm (Fig. A1.2).[482] Eventually the highest form of symboling – human language – evolved. From this point on, cultural evolution through language predominated over biological evolution. Advanced Paleolithic culture culminated during the final stages of the Pleistocene (17,000-12,500 BCE), and on the European continent at this time the Magdalenian reindeer hunter flourished.

The stage was now set for the ice sheet to recede and for the hunters to pursue their prey northward. If winter hunting was to become more effective, snowshoes and skis were needed to facilitate travel.

---

[482] Kühn 1971: Plate VII.

The Reindeer Hunters of Post-Glacial Scandinavia

One hypothesis for the origin of snowshoes and skis has the following general outline: the glacial period ended causing the wild reindeer herds to move north. Then, hunters who lived throughout the year primarily on reindeer followed them north, but were impeded during the winter by the deep snows of the boreal forests. And since "necessity is the mother of invention," snowshoes and skis were created to aid the hunters in seeking their prey. In order to test the validity of this hypothesis, it will be necessary to consider in some detail the reindeer and its importance to early hunters. The magnificent cave paintings of the Magdalenian hunters of the Upper Paleolithic (ca. 14,000-ca. 9,500 BCE) and the enormous piles of reindeer bones left in caves the hunters inhabited show that the reindeer was essential to their subsistence. During earlier periods, other animals may have predominated in the hunters' quarry, but the reindeer was the ideal prey, providing meat for the diet, skins for clothing and tents, sinews for thread and lines, bones and antlers for tools and weapons, and teeth for ornamentation.

What was *Rangifer tarandus* like, the reindeer, the animal that helped make it possible for early men to push the frontiers of human settlement to the north?[483] With regard to demographic characteristics and behavioral patterns the reindeer hunted by Stone Age men was essentially the same as the wild reindeer and caribou of today so that what is known about wild reindeer of the twentieth century will generally hold for the late Stone Age. They are members of the deer family, distinguished by their tolerance and even preference for cold climates, and by their gregarious nature. They are herbivorous, eating plants in the summer and lichen under the snow in winter. They are usually found together in numbers of fifteen or more, and at certain times of the year in herds numbering into the hundreds or thousands. They are not dangerous to humans and are often quite easy to kill, being ex-

---

[483] For more information on reindeer cf. Laufer 1917, Manker 1953 and Clark 1966.

tremely unwary at times. Both sexes carry antlers, the male shedding his after the rut in late autumn, the female shedding hers after calving in spring. The female needs antlers during the winter when she is pregnant so she can access the lichen beneath the snow. Their skins provide extremely good insulation from the cold because the outer guard hairs contain vacuolated, keratinized cells, which resemble balloons. As a result of this, reindeer float when killed in water. These skins were one of the many features that made them desirable as a human resource so early.

Typically, reindeer are in the habit of migrating seasonally. They are on the move at all times, spending the late spring and summer on the arctic tundra and moving south to the boreal forests of the taiga for the winter. There are many factors which may in part account for these migrations: 1) the forest provides better shelter during the bitter winters; calving is preferable on the tundra rather than in the still deep snows of the taiga; 2) the reindeer are plagued by mosquitoes and other insects during the summer, and there are fewer insects on the tundra; 3) the constant search for food and hormonal changes are others.

It has generally been assumed that the early reindeer hunters more or less followed the herds closely in their seasonal migrations, but this has been discounted of late. The reindeer are simply too fast to follow: they are capable of trotting up to 25 mph for long periods and have been known to cover 500 air miles in six weeks over all sorts of terrain. It had also been thought that they generally follow the same routes in their annual migrations, but this is usually not so. The fact that they tend to travel in single file leads to deep paths being worn into the countryside, which in fragile environments may last for decades even though the reindeer do not traverse them again in the interim. Only deep winter snow slowed them down, as indeed it did the early hunters. Moreover, during the winter the reindeer were warier than at other times. This would seem to suggest that they were easy prey only during portions of the year, e.g. when they could be expected to pass north or south during the spring or fall migrations or near bodies of water where they tend to congregate. Hunters could hunt reindeer in several ways: by enticing them into pitfalls, driving them into entrapments or over cliffs, or employing the chase, i.e. tracking and pursuing and getting close enough to slay them with weapons such as the spear thrower or bow and arrow. The method depended on the season. Hunters such as the Magdalenian groups of the Upper Paleolithic may have shifted base-camps twice a year in the spring and fall, carrying with them their collapsible tents of skins and poles. At other times, when the reindeer were relatively sedentary, the hunters could make expeditions from base-camps and employ search-and-destroy tactics. This worked especially well during the summer fly season or during the depths of the winter assuming the hunters had either snowshoes or skis to traverse the snow. In any case, a thorough knowledge of the animal's habits, the terrain, and the climatic conditions was necessary at all times.

One might expect that large numbers could be killed during the migrations and preserved for lean periods. This was to a certain extent true, but there were storage problems: specifically, a limit to the length of the frost season, and the difficulty of drying meat during the summer due to insects. Thus, very few of the peoples living off reindeer hunting could get by without some other means of subsistence. Sea mammals, stranded whales, or fish made up much of the diet during the warmer months of those living in coastal areas; however, most reindeer sites are inland. It has been estimated that a family of four would need 250 reindeer per year to satisfy all needs of food, clothing and shelter; this number, however, would seem to be too high. By the late Upper Paleolithic (ca. 40,000-ca. 10,000 years ago) the reindeer was the most important resource on the European continent during at least part of the year.

The Magdalenian hunters occupied caves, some in winter and others in summer. Caves in the Pyrenees Mountains between Spain and France suggest winter occupancy because the bones found there were from fish and fowl types caught in winter. On the other hand, there are caves in Switzerland with the remains of reindeer including some only a few days old; this would imply summer occupancy since calving occurred in late spring or early summer. The usual interpretation has been that the hunters more or less followed the reindeer in their migrations spending the winter in caves in Southwest France and Northern Spain and the summer in the higher altitude Alpine area caves. This would mean incredibly long semi-annual journeys for these Stone Age hunters with families and possessions and without transportation aids. More likely, though, such long treks were undertaken only when other means of subsistence did not appear. László Vajda, who investigated the domestication of reindeer, saw an analogy between the Magdalenian hunters and the Caribou Eskimo who hunt caribou in summer but live off of fish in the winter and grouse in the spring before the return of the caribou.[484]

Further to the Northeast were other groups of Upper Paleolithic hunters who subsisted on reindeer during much of the year. The hunters of the Hamburg culture, moving into Northern Germany some 15-18,000 years ago upon withdrawal of the ice cover, were summer reindeer hunters, but the rise in temperature which began around 9,000 BCE, called

---

[484] Vajda 1968.

the Allerød warming, was calamitous for the reindeer.[485] The hunters of the Bromme culture from this period who were just south of the ice sheet in Jutland, Southern Sweden, and Northern Schleswig-Holstein were advanced Paleolithic peoples who used flint and antler extensively in their tool-making. Though there were no flint axe blades yet, tanged points (a point with a projection for attaching a handle or shaft) were used in weapons, on projectiles, and as arrow tips, as can be seen from reindeer bones with deeply embedded flintheads. This was near the end of the glacial period and reindeer were already becoming scarce.

Typical of the Allerød warming were July temperatures of ca. 13-14° C and a rapid withdrawal of the ice sheet. Mixed forests of birch and pine had replaced the tundra and with them came the fauna associated with the forest, viz. elk, beaver, wolverine, and horse, but few reindeer remained. By now the hunters knew how to use harpoons on sea mammals in the summer and ringed seals in the spring. Some reindeer returned in the winter, and the beginnings of a new complex economy based on fishing and sea mammal hunting in the warmer parts of the year, plus the hunting of hoofed animals, began to take shape.

The Allerød warming was followed by a somewhat colder period, called the Dryas oscillation, of the late glacial period (ca. 8,500-8,200 BCE) and the reindeer returned to Northern Germany in number. The hunters of the Ahrensburg culture from this period were again summer reindeer hunters. But the temperatures began to climb around 8,000 BCE, the tundra was replaced again by the forest and the reindeer either had to move north as some undoubtedly did, or perish in the new environment.

It is possible that much of the reindeer population in this area died out in the first (pre-boreal) phase of the post-glacial era, since at this time Fennoscandia was an island separated from the European continent by a sea called the Yoldia sea. It would have been difficult for the reindeer to cross the sea on their move northward. They were replaced by other hoofed animals that preferred the forests, such as elk, aurochs, and deer. Some scholars have suggested that the reindeer hunters followed the reindeer north, but this is unlikely. More likely they blended with post-Magdalenian peoples to produce Mesolithic groups whose hunting was more local and who were consequently more sedentary, and a specialization in reindeer hunting such as seen in the Magdalenian, Hamburg, and Ahrensburg groups was not to be seen again in Europe.

Similarly, further east in the South Baltic area there were probably also reindeer hunting specialists until the end of the Pleistocene. What should be stressed is that reindeer

---

[485] Clark 1975: 37-44.

hunters were prevalent in the cooler areas of Europe until the glaciers began to recede. They concentrated on reindeer hunting especially during the summer months, and relied on fishing and bird hunting for subsistence during other times. They did not generally follow the migrating reindeer, and when warmer climates brought in mixed forests the reindeer disappeared. These hunters adapted to the new conditions and their economy gradually became more complex: summer fishing and hunting of sea mammals along the coast in the summer, winter ice fishing and hunting. The elk was now the most important animal hunted, followed by the aurochs and deer.

From Eastern Europe on into the Urals and Northern Asia there was an entirely different situation during the Upper Paleolithic: the inhabitants of these areas lived only in the southernmost range of the reindeer. The reindeer did play an important part in their subsistence patterns, but there is no evidence of a reindeer hunting specialization such as in Western Europe during the late-glacial period. This was mainly mammoth hunting territory. The hunting and slaying of a mammoth required a greater expenditure of energy, a highly organized hunt with many participants and hunting sites, and different methods, to wit, close-in killing. The mammoth may have become extinct from overkill but, in any case, died out as the average temperatures climbed.

By ca. 7,750 BCE the ice had pretty well disappeared from Scandinavia, all of which had been covered save for a few ice-free areas along the Arctic and Atlantic coasts. Much of Eurasia had been ice-free during the last glacial period. Middle and Eastern Siberia were ice-free up to the mountainous regions and strips of land near the Pacific coast. And in the areas of the Altai and Sayan Mountains and Lake Baikal there were only sporadic glacial formations. Much of Northern Eurasia other than Fennoscandia could conceivably have been occupied during the Upper Paleolithic era though human settlement went no further north than 65º north latitude in the area of the Urals and not even that far north in Siberia. But under the new Holocene (post-glacial) life conditions man began to move into the north and a new economy developed which became the basis of the Mesolithic and Sub-Neolithic cultures throughout the area. Its main characteristics were that it was much more sedentary, oriented around fishing on the banks of rivers or along the coasts with subsistence patterns determined by the rhythm of the seasons. Land hunting was important for the diet of both coast dwellers and inland groups, but the animals hunted were mainly elk and in the south deer, neither of which moved about in large herds. The deer were in small bands and the elk preponderantly alone. This sedentary fishing-hunting culture was to become the rule throughout the circumpolar area.

Many of the surviving hunting peoples live in the northern climes, the Eskimos of Alaska and the Sámi of northern Scandinavia for example. They as well as the Stone Age hunters of the north have a great deal in common in the way of cultural connections, the causes of which certainly have something to do with the northern environment. Gutorm Gjessing in his *Circumpolar Stone Age* has concluded that the cultural forms of the modern circumpolar peoples are similar because they are built on the same foundation, viz. that of the ancient Stone Age culture.[486] For them life in the north was more difficult than in the temperate zones. More heat was required to warm the body and to keep it warm, and it was only after fire making was mastered that man could inhabit the cold zones. Clothing of various types helped to preserve the heat. Furthermore, shelter of some kind was needed to protect the body while sleeping. And with less sun in the north it took much larger areas to support flora and fauna.

Some of the features shared by modern circumpolar peoples are the following:
- They live either on the tundra (arctic region) with its scanty vegetation or none at all, or
- They live on the taiga (sub-arctic region) with its coniferous, boreal forests plus some birch and willow.

Permafrost, which hinders the growth of trees, is found in both areas. The boundary between tundra and taiga is the tree line. Winters are long and cold with little snowfall, but the snow accumulates over time. The summers are short and cool, though they can be quite hot inland. Ecologically the land produces little food because of the low energy from the sun; the sea on the contrary is relatively rich in marine life. Most significantly they, like their Stone Age relatives, are hunting peoples who do not resort to agriculture, and it was agriculture that made population explosions possible. Accordingly, the populations of the various modern day circumpolar peoples are small, numbering in the thousands or fewer, and all of them – until recently – still use snowshoes or skis to get about during the winter.

Anthropologically, there is a good deal of racial variation around the circumpolar zone, though with the exception of the Sámi all of the peoples are Mongoloid (characterized by yellowish-brown to white skin pigmentation, coarse straight black hair, dark eyes and prominent cheekbones). Subsistence comes from fishing, sea mammal hunting, and land

---

[486] Gjessing 1944.

hunting, and in Eurasia reindeer herding as well. Hunting techniques are similar throughout the north: until the advent of firearms from the south, the spear and the bow and arrow were the major weapons, though the latter reached North America no more than 1,500 years ago. For hunting, traps, snares and large game corrals were also used, and for fishing, traps, leisters, and weirs. Because of the similar resources throughout the circumpolar area cultural characteristics do not differ greatly: tailored skin clothing is widespread as are semi-subterranean housing and skin tents. For transportation by sea skin- and bark-covered boats such as the *umiak* are common. The Sámi, though they no longer use skin-covered boats, preserve the tradition of having had them, and they still stitch their plank boats (Fig. A2.1).[487] Over land, sleds are used on the tundra pulled by dogs or in Eurasia by reindeer (Fig. A2.2 depicts skiers being pulled by reindeer).[488] On the taiga toboggans are found, and either snowshoes or skis. Skis are important today even for those Sámi who use snowmobiles to herd reindeer during the winter.

Food sharing is universal among circumpolar peoples. Another important feature is the seasonal migrations, which allow different means of subsistence to be exploited at the most opportune times. There are a myriad of peoples and different languages. The language families are Eskimo-Aleut, Na-Dene, and Algonquian in North America, Palaeo-Siberian and Ural-Altaic in Eurasia, and most of the linguistic relationships are obscure.

As a part of the hunting life these peoples display a tenacious conservatism. They may not have been overly inventive but were certainly very resourceful. Cultural impulses under arctic conditions were until recently spasmodic at best. As an example of this conservatism may be mentioned the dented-comb pottery that reached Western Siberia during early Neolithic times and which survived virtually unchanged for a good 3,000 years until the Viking Age. These then are the people whose forebears followed the reindeer and other prey north as the ice sheets receded and during those periods of the year when there was snow cover made use of snowshoes and skis to facilitate hunting and transportation.

---

[487] Vorren 1988: 95.
[488] Egnell 1979: 19.

Winter Travel in the North: Snowshoes

The ski is a very special device indeed, its use limited to areas where there is snow cover during some portion of the year. But the ski is only one of many devices with the general function of facilitating communication between individuals and peoples. The Danish ethnologist Kaj Birket-Smith notes that "life is activity." Travel for many earlier peoples was an essential part of their lives, and any device that could aid them was most welcome. The shoe, snowshoe, sled and boat all helped in supporting and conveying humans and their burdens over various kinds of surfaces. Earliest is a covering for the foot to provide protection from sharp objects in, for example, volcanic regions, from hot desert sands and from the bitter cold. The anthropologist Otis T. Mason called the shoe "an accessory of travel," saying "it belongs on the road." Foot coverings were not essential until man began to travel and to move beyond the temperate zones. Mason also said, "the shoe is a sandal that has grown up over the foot." The sandal was the first foot covering and is found in two main types: one with a strap or thong between two toes (Fig. A3.1)[489] and another laced on through holes along the side edges (Fig. A3.2).[490] The laced sandal is common throughout the circumpolar regions.

When it came to transporting possessions Stone Age people either carried or dragged them. The skin of a newly slain animal could be used to drag the meat back home, or a tree trunk with branches removed could have been similarly used. Pulling a tree trunk over ice or snow is an earlier stage of the sled, the development of which in fact followed three different paths. The trunk was hollowed out to form a trough with the sides possibly extended upward yielding a boat-shaped sled common among the Sámi and various Siberian tribes as well as among Scandinavians and Finns for hauling manure. The Sámi *keris* or Finnish *pulk*

---

[489] Mason 1896: Plate 18b.
[490] Mason 1896: Plate 16.

dates back to the Stone Age (Fig. A3.3).[491] Secondly, instead of hollowing out the trunk it could be shaped like a board, and when several such boards were connected at the sides and curved up in front it yielded the toboggan as found throughout the Canadian woodland zone. Thirdly, the tree trunk could be shaped like a primitive runner or crude ski. The simplest form of the sled consisted of several of these runners connected with crossbars. Sleds of this type are even found outside of the Snow Belt, for example, in ancient Egypt where they were used to move heavy stone blocks. When the load was lifted up off the runners by means of uprights the sleigh evolved.

As to the age of the various sled types: the sleigh is most highly developed and of smallest distribution, and accordingly of most recent vintage. This distributional argument will be used again. According to it, features or traits of culture or language that tend to spread geographically through contact can be mapped to determine their relative chronology. Features found at the periphery are generally older than those found at the center. The boat-shaped sled and the toboggan are found over wide areas of the Old World and North America respectively and both of them in the boreal forests where there is plenty of soft snow. These two types are associated with the snowshoe culture of the circumpolar Stone Age. The simple runner sled would tend to sink in deep snow and was therefore better suited to ice and, in fact, is found at the extremities of the circumpolar area. It was an element of the Stone Age ice-fishing culture. A wooden runner found in Finland and dated to the Ancylus lake period of ca. 6,000 BCE may perhaps be the runner of a sled used on snow (Fig. A3.4).[492] South of the snowy terrain is found the travois of the American Indians, a kind of slide-car consisting of two poles lashed together at the front and spreading out toward the rear and pulled by either dogs or horses. But what is important is that the gliding principle necessary for the invention of the ski finds one of its predecessors in the runner and the idea of dragging things over the snow, of getting them to slide.

The boat too finds its origin in the tree trunk. Trees uprooted during a flood provided salvation for those who could not swim. Several trunks tied together made the first raft. In areas where very large trees grew the trunks were hollowed out and the dugout canoe was created. If large trees were unavailable, other means had to be found. The earliest boats in the far north were skin-covered. Highly developed skin-boats are found among the Eskimos: the open *umiak* for traveling and hauling and the closed *kayak* for hunting, both very

---

[491] Schefferus 1973: 299.
[492] Clark 1975: 230.

light and seaworthy. They date back to the Stone Age in the circumpolar area. As mentioned in the previous appendix, the modern day Sámi though they do not use skin-covered boats maintain the tradition of having once used them. These boats are one element of the ancient "ice-fishing" culture. Later on they were replaced by the main boat of the snowshoe culture, the birchbark canoe, which had a framework like the skin-covered boats but a different covering (Fig. A3.5).[493] The birchbark canoe has a similar distribution to the early runner-sled.

As the glaciers receded large areas were opened up to migratory animals such as the reindeer, caribou, mammoth, etc., and Stone Age man followed the animals north. The earliest stage is the so-called "ice-fishing" culture. Animals could be pursued and killed in the summer, but when the snows came man was greatly restricted in movement and thus had to spend the winter on the coast or near lakes or streams where fish provided their sustenance. The animals too were greatly confined by the deep snows but safe for the time being from man who had no means of transportation over the snow.

The sandal had come north with man, and for protection from the cold in winter was combined with the stocking which in its earliest form may simply have been a skinned leg hide of one of the larger animals. Extending the sole of the sandal in snowy terrain created the "snowshoe" which in turn was always used with a stocking which itself had evolved into the moccasin. Snowshoe and moccasin, hand in hand, provided Stone Age man with the means to exploit the vast inland boreal forests of the circumpolar area with the abundant game therein. Perhaps he took a cue from the varying hare, or "snowshoe" rabbit as it is commonly called. Through biological adaptation the snowshoe rabbit acquired large, hairy back feet enabling it to bound over the snow with ease. It also had "ice-creepers," long nails giving it good traction on ice or hard snow. At winter's end the tufts of hair on the back feet were lost and the rabbit changed color from white to brown only to await the onset of another winter.

The extension of the sole could take many forms. The most primitive consist simply of anything that could make the sole larger and permit more weight to be supported: sacks, pieces of oxhide, wooden wheels, round wickerwork, boards, snow-baskets, bundles of sticks, and so on. Many of these examples are quite old; in fact it will be shown later on that they go back to the early Stone Age. Combining the literary references to snowshoes with their distribution in the present century it can be said that snowshoes are found throughout

---

[493] Catlin 1857: 240.

the Northern Hemisphere wherever there is enough snow during a significant portion of the year. In other words, they are found throughout the circumpolar area as well as further south in the mountainous areas of the Temperate Zone (Alps, Carpathians, Armenian plateau, Caucasus, Korean and Japanese Mountains). Snowshoes do occur outside this area, though, as the writings of Rosales and Gusinde indicate (cf. Appendix 4); and there is no possibility of their having been introduced from outside. This suggests that the snowshoe was not invented only once as the anthropologist D. S. Davidson thought in his 1937 study of snowshoes,[494] but rather that primitive snowshoes were invented independently in a number of areas. The very simplicity of an extension of the sole as well as the multiplicity of forms possible would seem to support this.

Snowshoe-like contrivances, it turns out, have been used outside the Snow Belt to support humans on other kinds of surfaces such as swamps for example. The Klamath Indians of Oregon use their snowshoes for marsh wading. They are widely distributed and suggest a closer relationship between boats and skis, of which more later. In 1922 a Korean hunter was observed running a trap line in the Yalu river delta between China and Korea, an area consisting mostly of clay banks. The hunter was moving along on a pair of canoe-like skis as if he were on the finest snow (Fig. A3.6).[495] They were miniature versions of dugout canoes, ca. 1.5-2 m. long and wide enough to fit snugly on the foot. The side walls were thin except where the binding was. The astonished Swede who saw them in use described them as similar to the smallest sampan, or canoe. The Korean hunters in this area were then on the point of disappearing, harassed in turn by the Japanese and Chinese and decimated by opium and narcotics, and the canoe-like skis with them.

And in South China another peculiar device was used for crabbing in the mud (Fig. A3.7).[496] Typologically this device seems to be about half way between the Korean canoe-like skis and a real dugout canoe with the "rower" on one knee and using the other leg to push with. Something similar is or was found in the area of the Frisian Islands along North Holland, West Germany and the southwest coast of Jutland, viz. a mud-sled used to examine the osier baskets in which fish were caught. These mud, clay and sandbanks are covered with water when the tide is in but muddy and soft at ebb tide. And also in Frisia a kind of mud shoe is used by peat-cutters (Fig. A3.8).[497] In Ireland there are also mud shoes

---

[494] Davidson 1937: 157.
[495] Wiklund 1931: 47.
[496] Wiklund 1933: 23.
[497] Berg 1953: 171.

called "scooches" which are used for hunting and spearing eels (Fig. A3.9),[498] and on the island of Fårö northeast of Gotland similar shoes are used for egg hunting (Fig. A3.10).[499] In Iceland, though, it is safe to assume that no such devices were known. Witness the well nigh impassable swamp in *Hrafnkels saga* that contributes to the murder of Eyvind:[500] "There is a swamp there, and one has to ride through watery slush, with the mud reaching up to the horse's knee or mid-leg, sometimes even up to its belly." Snowshoe-like devices were once widespread throughout the Northern Hemisphere and they go back a long way in time.

The snowshoe as one usually conceives of it reached a peak of development in North America. In order to illuminate the relationship between the ski and the snowshoe it will be necessary to look in some detail at the development of snowshoes and also the moccasin, which evolved side by side with the snowshoe. When the French-Canadians borrowed the snowshoe they were obliged to adopt the moccasin too, for snowshoes require a pliable, stocking-like kind of footwear. That snowshoes and moccasins belong together can be seen from their respective distributions: in areas where snowshoes are highly perfected one also finds highly developed moccasins or "transformed moccasins" (boots with flat sole of moccasin-like pliability). On the other hand the most highly developed moccasins occur in areas of highly developed snowshoes. The anthropologist Gudmund Hatt refers to two different cultural complexes in the north:[501]

- Complex A with pancho, leggings plus a genital cloth, and sandals
- Complex B with kaftan, breechcloth trousers, and moccasins

The most highly developed forms of moccasins in Northern Asia are found where complex B clothing is found. Cultural complex A is older and is found on the periphery, that is, the eastern and western extremities of Eurasia, whereas cultural complex B is younger and occurs in continuous distribution in between. Of the elements in Complex B the kaftan has the smallest distribution, and the moccasin the widest. All of the items of complex B are found in the area where the Tungus live with no trace of Complex A elements, so this may be the area of origin.

There were probably two cultural waves, the first being the coastal or "ice-fishing" culture which is most highly developed among Eskimos. They had no snowshoes and were confined to coastal areas, nor did they have moccasins. When the Eskimos of Point Bar-

---

[498] Berg 1953: 169.
[499] Berg 1955: 182.
[500] *Hrafnkels saga* 1971: 65-66.
[501] Hatt 1916.

row travel on snowshoes, they wear heavy skin stockings rather than their boots that have the stiff, sandal-like sole. The second wave was a younger, inland or snowshoe culture that spread over most of the circumpolar area. There are other important differences between the two cultures: the snowshoe culture made use of a double-handled scraper, smoking of skin and fat for tanning, conical lodge (tepee), cradle-board, birchbark canoe, hunting of reindeer and moose on snowshoes. Some aspects of the circumpolar inland culture never reached North America, viz. the ski and reindeer nomadism; thus the inland culture reached North America early, before the advent of the ski and reindeer nomadism, judging from the highly developed snowshoes and moccasins and the diversity of terms for them. Accordingly, Eskimo culture, which is older, must have been in America even longer. The parallel distributions of moccasin and snowshoe have been mentioned. The oldest moccasin was a form of skin stocking and it is found among the Ainu from Yezo in Northern Japan where it is used with snowshoes, and the whole moccasin group with few exceptions consists of highly developed skin stockings. The exceptions are some moccasins from Europe and South America, which developed from primitive sandals in areas where snowshoes were not used.

The evolution of the moccasin and snowshoe went as follows: the sandal already in existence was taken north into the colder regions and used with a wrapping of the foot or stocking. These two elements fused and developed into the sandal-boot, the forerunner of Eskimo boots (Fig. A3.11).[502] But at a later date in areas where there was a lot of snow, the sole of the sandal was extended into a primitive snowshoe, and on top of this primitive snowshoe a stocking was used rather than another sandal because of the flexibility needed. As the snowshoe improved so did the stocking, evolving into the moccasin. Then when American Indians, for example, moved south of the Snow Belt they abandoned their snowshoes but kept the moccasins as their main footwear.

The main features of a moccasin are its being made of one or more pieces of skin including the piece covering the bottom of the foot. It is turned up along the sides and gathered at the heel into a vertical seam that is shaped like an inverted T. True moccasins are found throughout North America but in Eurasia only among the Sámi and Amur at the western and eastern extremities respectively. However, in between most of the boot forms of the circumpolar area (soft leather boots, legskin boots) have this T-shaped heel seam and thus derive from moccasin-boots, i.e. a combination of moccasin plus legging. Thus, the

---

[502] Mason 1896: Plate 4.

moccasin or derivatives of it are found throughout the circumpolar boreal forests, precisely the area as will be seen where snowshoes and skis are found.

At this time more precise definitions of the terms snowshoe and ski are needed. By snowshoe is meant any device attached to the foot which facilitates "walking" on top of a snow surface; it does not include ice skates or ice creepers (crampons) though Strabo's tambourine-like snowshoes had spikes attached to them (cf. Appendix 4). The "ski" is also a device for moving over the snow, the essential difference between it and the snowshoe being that one does not generally walk on skis, one *glides*. This definition holds true even today: the two skiing disciplines, cross-country and downhill or Alpine – though they differ in many respects – both require the gliding or sliding motion over the snow. Modern snowshoe racers who can move at considerable speed still "run" on their snowshoes, that is, they lift their snowshoes with each step usually dragging the tail end. Cross-country racers also lift their skis, but the front ends always maintain contact with the snow as they glide along. There are also functional differences between snowshoes and skis that will be taken up later.

The snowshoe was one of the most important inventions in the history of transportation allowing large numbers of Stone Age peoples to exploit the vast circumpolar inland areas, abetting contacts between humans and promoting the exchange of ideas. Hatt and Birket-Smith see the snowshoe as the fundamental element in the culture of the inland peoples of northern Eurasia and of the American Indians. In Eurasia eventually it also allowed reindeer nomadization, though this did not spread to North America. The concept of domestication came from the south, however; the southern animals could not have survived the circumpolar winters, so the aboriginals domesticated the reindeer herds and followed them in the winter on snowshoes or skis. Snowshoes and/or skis are found wherever there is enough snow to impede travel, over the entire circumpolar area as well as two examples from South America (cf. Appendix 4). Curiously the Sámi never had snowshoes until relatively recently when they were used with horses. Skis are found throughout Eurasia, but not in North America until Scandinavian immigrants brought them in the nineteenth century. After people learned how to use skis, they crowded out snowshoes in many areas because they were much more efficient for hunting.

Primitive snowshoes as already seen came in a variety of forms, some of which can be seen as prototypes of or as contributing features to the more advanced forms. There are three advanced forms from which all the more sophisticated snowshoes and the ski derive, the wooden snowshoe, the ladder snowshoe, and the bearpaw snowshoe. The wooden or solid snowshoe in its primitive form will be seen (Appendix 4) in Strabo's "round plates" and the boards of Thomas Arcruni. In North America they are found mainly in the eastern half among the Algonquians, Cree, Eskimo, Naskapi, Ojibwa, Penobscot and Asulteaux. Some examples are shown in Figs. A3.12-14 of which that of the Caribou Eskimo is most primitive in that it does not have any of the improvements that were made on the bearpaw snowshoe other than the basic oval form and tapering towards the rear.[503] They were tied on with thongs through vertical holes in the snowshoe. Davidson has shown that the Caribou Eskimo did not originally have this snowshoe but borrowed it from Algonquian tribes to the south before they were separated from them by the Chipewyan wedge. The other tribes are all Algonquian language speaking. It should also be noted that all of these tribes possess the more advanced frame snowshoes. It would seem then that the ancestors of the Algonquian Indian tribes brought the wooden snowshoe with them over the Bering Straits and moved east with it. Later on they borrowed better snowshoes, maintaining their wooden snowshoes as relics. In Eurasia no wooden snowshoes are found but only the younger descendent thereof, namely the ski.

The ladder-type snowshoe represents an advance over the solid variety in that a weight saving was effected. The ladder-type is found in the central portions of Norway and Sweden, Czechoslovakia, Austria, Slovenia, and Switzerland, and among the Basques in the Pyrenees. These consist of two parallel pieces, two curved pieces, or one curved piece connected by two or more crossbars (Fig. A3.15-16).[504]

The third type, the bearpaw, is by far the most important in terms of distribution and as being the prototype of the finest North American frame snowshoes. Its fundamental features are a frame, a filling in the middle – usually plaited, plus a way of attaching the filling to the frame. It therefore represents an additional advance since a very light, non-rigid filling led to an even lighter snowshoe. The ladder-type can be viewed as a bearpaw snowshoe without the frame, that is, a filling alone, lighter than the solid snowshoe, yet rigid enough to carry the weight. The frames could be made from one or two pieces of wood. Examples of the one-piece round or oval frame snowshoe (bearpaw) are shown in Fig. A3.17-19.[505] The ends of the single piece were either tied parallel to each other or overlapped and tied. This bearpaw type is found at the extremities of the Eurasian-North American snowshoe

---

[503] Davidson 1937: 141, 142, 141.
[504] Davidson 1937: 49; Zettersten 1933: 100.
[505] Davidson 1937: 27, 26, 28.

area as can be seen from the map (Fig. A3.20).[506] An unusually large (40" by 16") bearpaw snowshoe found in west central Honshu, Japan was attached under a smaller snowshoe, the *tsurukanjiki* for use in deep snow (Fig. A3.21) and because of its size lifting ropes connected to the front were needed to make progress over the snow.[507] The Ainu of Hokkaido created a derivative of the bearpaw, which is called the "hourglass" snowshoe because the sides are pulled in at the middle (Fig. A3.22).[508]

Davidson makes use of distributional theory to determine the relative chronology of the snowshoe types and traits.[509] In other words, he assumes that a certain trait is invented and then diffuses outward from the point of origin. Thus, traits found most widely separated from one another are assumed to be the oldest, and traits with smaller, more local distribution younger. Davidson has been attacked for relying too heavily on distributional criteria, and rightly so, for it has been shown above that the snowshoe or sole extension concept was invented independently more than once. One problem with distributional theory is that a particular cultural item may have many features or traits, and, depending on which traits one emphasizes, one can arrive at different conclusions. When technologically advanced features are considered Davidson's distributional arguments and unique origins make much better sense. This distribution on the periphery as well as its relative simplicity attests to the great age of the bearpaw.

A step forward came by bringing the heel to a point, which allowed the tail end to be dragged more easily. Examples are given in Fig. A3.23.[510] Frames that consist of two U-shaped pieces tied together are 1) the "telescoped" variety as seen in Fig. A3.24 and found among the Ainu, Japanese and in the Caucasus,[511] 2) the "Naskapi" type as seen in (Fig. A3.25), both "beavertail" and "round end" each spliced at the sides and found among the Naskapi-Montagnais Indians of Labrador[512] and 3) the Athabaskan type with the two pieces joined at toe and heel in Fig. A3.26,[513] with pieces brought together and spliced in the former and overlapped and spliced in the latter.

---

[506] Davidson 1937: 24.
[507] Davidson 1953: 59.
[508] Davidson 1953: 46.
[509] Davidson 1937: 157-61.
[510] Davidson 1937: 53.
[511] Davidson 1953: 48.
[512] Davidson 1937: 67.
[513] Davidson 1937: 72.

With regard to the filling or netting Davidson distinguished three varieties: unsystematic, rectangular, and hexagonal. The unsystematic filling has no consistent arrangement of strands as can be seen in Figs. A3.17-19. This type is found only with the bearpaw frame. The rectangular weave of warps and woofs at right angles is limited mainly to North America and among the Chukchee of northwest Asia and in Sweden. Examples are seen in Fig. A3.23 and in Fig. A3.27 with rectangular weave only in the center.[514] The hexagonal or "cane chair weave" occurs only in North America. Examples are given in Figs. A3.26-28.[515] The relative chronology is in the order presented with the unsystematic filling going along with the oldest frame type, the bearpaw, and the most complex and strongest, the hexagonal, having a central distribution.

With regard to the method of attaching the filling to the frame, the third fundamental trait of frame snowshoes, there are three methods: thongs wrapped around the frame, reeving of the thongs through the frame, and attaching the thongs to a selvage thong. The first method is seen clearly in Fig. A3.23. As with the unsystematic filling, wrapping thongs around the frame is found exclusively with the bearpaw frame snowshoe, and has the widest distribution and is therefore the oldest. The process of reeving the thongs through holes in the frame has a small distribution centered in Alaska but extending eastward and westward somewhat and always occurs with rectangular weaving. Examples are seen in Figs. A3.29-30.[516] Most such examples have reeving only near the footstep with hexagonal weaving elsewhere attached to a selvage thong as in the Kutchin snowshoe (Fig. A3.29), or on the periphery, no filling or netting whatsoever at the toe and heel space as in the Athabaskan snowshoe (Fig. A3.30), where it is assumed hexagonal weaving had not yet arrived. The number of reeving holes had to be kept to a minimum because they weakened the frame.

The selvage thong is found throughout North America except in some of the peripheral areas, and it is used only for the toe and heel spaces, with wrapping or reeving being retained for the foot space because of its greater strength. A thong runs along the inside of the frame to which the hexagonal weaving is attached as seen in the Cree snowshoe in Fig. A3.31[517] with wrapping and in the Eskimo snowshoe of Fig. A3.27 with reeving. Its distribution is contiguous and within that of hexagonal weaving and thus of recent vintage, perhaps even after the introduction of European knives which would have allowed the manufacture

---

[514] Davidson 1937: 85.
[515] Davidson 1937: 92.
[516] Davidson 1937: 94, 75.
[517] Davidson 1937: 57.

of much finer thongs. The snowshoe, once in North America, was subjected to a great deal of technological development, which led to the highly perfected snowshoes of today. This development was enhanced by the fact that there were no skis in North America; no one had conceived of adding the gliding motion to the wooden snowshoe. In Eurasia, however, skis evolved very early and replaced snowshoes in many areas; this is why only relatively primitive snowshoes are found in Eurasia.

Among the secondary traits Davidson includes the crossbar, which is widely distributed. But he fails to distinguish between the crosspieces that are part of the filling as is the case with all ladder-type snowshoes and with those of the Ainu of the Kurile Islands (Fig. A3.22) and from Slovenia and Spain (Fig. A3.32)[518] and the crossbars used in addition to the weaving to make the frame more rigid as in Fig. A3.33.[519] The latter usage is clearly a secondary trait and found only in North America. An examples of multiple crossbars is seen in Fig. A3.33. The crossbars are attached by means of thongs or mortised into the frame, mortising making for a stronger structure. The latter method of attachment is seen in the snowshoes of Labrador tribes and the Eastern Cree Fig. A3.31 and carries with it an upgrading of quality. Variations on the rounded toe are the bent toe and the square toe found in the east and midwest of North America alongside the round toe snowshoe (Fig. A3.34).[520]

A trait of much greater significance is the toe-hole, an opening in the mesh located just behind the front crossbar or crosspiece. It permits the toe to go through the snowshoe on that portion of the walking or running where the leg is behind the center of gravity of the body. Without the toe-hole it would be analogous to trying to walk on a pair of modern Alpine skis with a binding fixing the foot firmly to the ski. All one can do is to trudge along, lifting the whole ski with each step. The toe-hole along with the pointed heel made running on snowshoes possible. It is found throughout North America on the more advanced forms, but not in Eurasia except in Siberia by diffusion from North America. It is probably of Athabaskan provenance, though possibly Algonquian. Examples are in Fig. A3.34.[521]

The finest snowshoes have a filling or netting throughout, but it can be assumed that the netting was originally limited to the foot space as in the Koryak snowshoe (Fig. A3.35)[522] and then extended. The turned-up toe was an improvement in the snowshoe having a paral-

---

[518] Gunda 1940: 233.
[519] Davidson 1937: 71.
[520] Davidson 1937: 91.
[521] Davidson 1937:
[522] Davidson 1937: 75c.

lel with the ski: the turned-up toe allowed more rapid movement just as a ski with a turned-up toe is the only conceivable form. This trait is Athabaskan in origin and found throughout their territory (Fig. A3.30). Other secondary snowshoe traits are the making of rights and lefts (Fig. A3.36),[523] and separate snowshoes for men and women. Most of the advanced snowshoe traits are Athabascan in origin, though the Algonquians may have come up with the hexagonal weave and the selvage thong. That the bearpaw frame snowshoe was brought with the Athabaskans on their migration to North America over the Bering Straits is supported by a number of arguments:

1) All Athabaskan tribes living in areas of considerable snowfall have frame snowshoes, none save the Eyak have wooden snowshoes.

2) The Athabascans have been responsible for most of the technological advances.

3) Athabascan tribes living in areas of little snowfall possess the older bearpaw snowshoe.

4) The remains of a bearpaw snowshoe among the cliff dwellers of the Southwest have been dated by dendrochronology to a minimum age of 1000 years; it was probably brought in by Athabascan invaders.

5) As will be seen later on the bearpaw snowshoe was in Asia before the Athabaskans became the last Indian group to come to the New World.

Summing up then, it seems likely that because of their respective peripheral distributions the primitive wooden snowshoe and the crude bearpaw snowshoe both originated in an area in between these extremities. Gudmund Hatt has suggested the area where the Tungus are located, near the northern boundary of Mongolia south of Lake Baikal (map in Fig. A3.37)[524] as possibly the area where the moccasin and the inland cultural complex B originated. If this is true, wooden snowshoes and bearpaw snowshoes probably had their origin nearby too. The wooden snowshoe by virtue of being simpler than the bearpaw is undoubtedly older and probably coexisted with the bearpaw for some time as both began to spread throughout the circumpolar area, the wooden snowshoe preceding the bearpaw over the Bering Straits with proto-Algonquian Indians, and the bearpaw reaching Europe first. The superiority of the frame snowshoes brought to North America by proto-Athabaskans soon made itself evident, and the tribes possessing wooden snowshoes not only adopted frame snowshoes, but applied the advanced traits from the frame snowshoe to their wooden ones. It is important to note that once the crucial step of going from a solid snowshoe to one with frame and filling was made, the possibility of adding a gliding motion and creating a ski

---

[523] Davidson 1937: 72.
[524] Davidson 1937: 150.

was precluded. The Algonquian wooden snowshoes were inferior to the Athabaskan frame types which the western Algonquians came in contact with, so the toe-hole for example was borrowed, and gliding was no longer an alternative. With no competition from gliding, the snowshoe was perfected over a very long period of time.

Literary References to Snowshoes

There are literary references to snowshoes, some of which go back more than 2000 years. Earliest is the report of Xenophon (ca. 434 BCE-ca. 355 BCE) in his *Anabasis*. Xenophon, who was a historian and a well-to-do young acquaintance of Socrates, left Athens to join the Greek mercenaries, called the Ten Thousand; they were serving under Cyrus the Younger of Persia who had rebelled against his elder brother Artaxerxes, the legitimate heir to king Darius. Artaxerxes learned of the plot, gathered his forces, and defeated Cyrus in the battle of Cunaxa in 401 BCE Cyrus lost his life and the Persians killed the Greek generals. But the Ten Thousand, rather than surrender, chose Xenophon as their leader, and he led them on a heroic retreat over the Armenian highlands to the Black Sea during the winter. In his account of the retreat Xenophon reports that many soldiers either froze in the snow or lost toes because they kept their boots on at night rather than removing them so that they could keep the blood circulating. The snow blinded many because they did not put anything black in front of their eyes. And then in Book IV, Chapter 6 there is:[525]

> So for the present Xenophon then went off, taking the headman back with him to his household and friends. He also made him a present of an oldish horse which he had got; he had heard that the headman was a priest of the sun, and so he could fatten up the beast and sacrifice him; otherwise he was afraid it might die outright, for it had been injured by the long marching. For himself he took his pick of the colts, and gave a colt apiece to each of his fellow-generals and officers. The horses here were smaller than the Persian horses, but much more spirited. It was here too that their friend the headman explained to them, how they should wrap small bags or sacks round the feet of the horses and other cattle when marching through the snow, for without such precautions the creatures sank up to their bellies.

---

[525] Xenophon 1969: 143.

This is the first literary reference to a device having the same function as a snowshoe and it was used on horses – in this case something to make the horses' hooves larger so as not to sink in the snow (cf. Figs. A4.1-2).[526]

So eminent a poet as Vergil (70 BCE-19 BCE) makes an indirect reference to snowshoes in Book 3 of his *Georgics* (30 BCE), in which he looks favorably on rural life and work on the farm. In discussing the terrible Scythian winter, which surely must have been frightful for a Roman, Vergil mentions that the livestock have to remain in the stables, that the snow lies seven ells deep (one ell = 45 inches) and that the wind blows continually. Where ships sailed, now wagons travel, for the waves have turned to ice, wine is not poured, but cut apart with axes – it is frozen and even the brass containers are burst by the ice, clothing stiffens in the frost even on a warm body, icicles form on men's shaggy beards. Then in ll. 367-75 Vergil writes:[527]

> Meanwhile the body of the air is snow;
> The sheep are choked; the mighty bulk below
> Of beeves stand overwhelm'd amid the drift;
> The huddled stags the numb weight cannot lift,
> And scarce the top tines of their antlers show.
> These, not with any toils, or slip of hound
> Or scare of purple feather, they surround;
> But, while they breast the mountain-drift in vain,
> The hunters close, and cleave their necks in twain;
> In spite of all their piteous roars, they slay
> And shouting gladly carry home their prey.

Fig. a4.2

Though he does not make explicit mention of snowshoes, it would have been impossible for the hunters to get so close to the deer in such deep snow without some aid to travel over the snow. Vergil does not use the term "snowshoes" because he was not familiar with the word. After all, Vergil had not visited Scythia, a remote and exotic area that extended from the Danube to the Don and the Altai Mountains. A fifth century BCE source has been assumed for Vergil at this point, the same source that Hekataios presumably used for his report on the Ionians.[528]

There is a striking parallel to the Vergil report in Schiller's poem "Indian Threnody" from 1797. The relevant passage is:[529]

---

[526] *På skidor* 1938: 388; *På skidor* 1929: 20.
[527] Vergil 1931: 86.
[528] Meuli 1975: 762-63.
[529] Jantz 1959: 72.

> Where the eyes whose falcon glances,
> Reindeer's tread could see
> Marked upon the grassy billow,
> On the dewy lea?
>
> Where the legs which did more nimbly
> Travel through the snow
> Than the stag, the twenty-tinèd,
> Than the mountain roe?

Here too, such swift movement over snow would be unthinkable without some type of snowshoe or ski (Figs. A4.3-4.4).[530] Schiller was probably not much more familiar with the snowshoe than Vergil. Goethe – an ice skating enthusiast – admired the poem and may have provided Schiller with his source, Jonathan Carver's *Travels through the Interior Parts of North-America in the Years 1766, 1767, and 1768*, a popular work running to at least 32 editions. Carver, an American explorer, was hired to journey to the Indian tribes of the Middle West. His book was the first English account of the upper Great Lakes and Mississippi area. In the second part of the book, "Of the Origin, Manners, Customs, Religion, and Language of the Indians," he describes a funeral speech where the following words appear: "why are those feet motionless, that a short time ago were fleeter than the deer on yonder mountain?"[531] Again there is no mention of snowshoes.

Carver undoubtedly witnessed such funerary ceremonies when he wintered with the Indians; however, when he decided to provide a written account of his travels a decade later, he borrowed a passage from Baron de Lahontan's *New Voyages to North-America* (1703) describing such a ceremony. As in the Vergil there is no mention of snowshoes in the Schiller or the Carver, yet it is inconceivable that an Indian could be swifter than a deer other than in deep snow and with the aid of snowshoes. Lahontan has a wonderfully detailed description of snowshoes elsewhere in his book. In letter X from July 8, 1686 Lahontan wrote:[532]

> The hunting of Elks is perform'd upon the Snow, with such Rackets as you see design'd in the annex'd Cutt. These Rackets are two Foot and a half long, and fourteen Inches broad; their ledges are made of a very hard Wood, about an Inch thick, that fastens the Net just like a Tennis Racket, from which they differ only in this: that those for the Tennis are made of Gut-strings, whereas the others are made of little thongs of the skins of Harts or Elks. In the Cut, you may perceive two little spars of Wood, which run across to ren-

---
[530] Catlin 1857, Vol. I, No. 109; Catlin 1857, Vol. II, No. 243.
[531] Jantz 1959: 71.
[532] Lahontan 1905: 103-04.

der the Net firmer and stiffer. The hole that appears by the two Latchets, is the place in which they put the Toes and forepart of the Foot; so that 'tis tied fast by the two Latchets, which run twice round about the Heel, and every step they make upon the Snow, the fore-part of the Foot sinks into that hole, as often as they raise their Heel. By the help of this Contrivance they walk faster upon the Snow, than one can do with Shoes upon a beaten path: And indeed 'tis so necessary for them, that 'twould be otherwise impossible not only to hunt and range the Woods, but even to go to Church, notwithstanding they are so near; for commonly the Snow is three or four Foot deep in that Country during the Winter. Being oblig'd to march thirty or forty Leagues in the Woods in pursuit of the above-mention'd Animals, I found that the fatigue of the Journey equal'd the pleasure of it.

Though the modern game of lawn tennis dates from 1873 it is clear that the game is much older than that.

A description of another snowshoe-like contrivance comes from the Greek geographer and historian Strabo (63 BCE-21 CE) In his *Geographia* (Il, 5, 6) he writes about the people living on the highest slopes of the Caucasus (where there is a great deal of precipitation):[533]

> The summits of the mountains are impassable in winter, but the people ascend them in summer by fastening to their feet broad shoes made of raw ox-hide, like drums, and furnished with spikes, on account of the snow and the ice.

The broad shoes furnished with spikes are called *plateia* in Greek, literally "round plates" and the word from which the English word *plate* is derived. These devices doubled as ice creepers. Similar tambourine-shaped snowshoes found in the Seven Mountain section of the Carpathian Mountains are called the Hargita type. Strabo continues:

> They descend with their loads by sliding down seated upon skins, as is the custom in Atropatian Media and on Mount Masius in Armenia; there, however, the people also fasten wooden discs furnished with spikes to the soles of their shoes.

The first evidence of plaited snowshoes comes from Flavius Arrianus (second century CE) the Roman historian, philosopher and general whose main work dealt with Alexander the Great. The reference was in his history of Parthia which is now lost; however, excerpts were quoted by the tenth century Byzantine scholar Suida in his *Lexicon*. Here is the entry for Λύγος, which is a pliant twig or willow branch:[534]

> And Arrian: "When the crossing appeared to them impossible, Brutius gathered together the native people and bid them lead the way, since they were accustomed to exchanging visits among themselves during the winter season. And they fitted circles of willow twigs (Gk. Κύκλους ἐκ λύγων) on their feet and without injury traversed the

---

[533] Strabo 1928: 241.

[534] *Svidae Lexicon* 1967: 292.

snow, which the circles pressed down; and they created an easy passage for the Romans. The snow was often sixteen feet deep."

In other words, the Armenian natives tramped out a path for the Roman army to make the crossing easier. And in May of 710 Leo III of Isauria who was later to become Byzantine emperor crossed the Caucasus on "hoop feet" (Gk. κύκλοπόδων).[535] In the tenth century the Armenian historian Thomas Arcruni writes: "but because of the weight of the moving snow which all at once falls from the clouds in huge quantities, they have contrived boards which they tie onto their feet with thongs like yokes, and run as easily over the snow as over firm ground."[536]

The Japanese use the term *kanjiki* for snowshoe, and the word has a curious origin or, for that matter, origins since there are a number of versions in the folklore.[537] According to one, Yoshire Hachimantare (d. 1106 CE) was escaping from a feud on a warm day in June when his rival, Sadato Abe, conjured up a snowstorm to delay him. Yoshire took a branch of fir and invented a snowshoe which he called *anzuki* (< an "idea" + zuki "to contrive") and later *kanjiki*. Another version has *anzuki* coming from the observation of a sparrow being thrown into the air after lighting on a supple branch over the snow. *Kanjiki* is mentioned in Japanese literature as early as 912 CE when Tashihito, a military hero of the Fujiwara period, won a great military victory by equipping his troops with snowshoes.

Fig. a4.5

Secondary sources from around 1600 have a picture of a *kanjiki* and a sleigh (*sori*) beside a man, the sleigh included since its Chinese character was used in the written word for snowshoe.

Olaus Magnus the Swedish bishop of Uppsala in his famous *Carta marina* (1539) described snowshoes for horses and men and included an illustration of them drawn by an Italian who undoubtedly had no more firsthand knowledge of winter culture than Vergil (Fig. A4.5).[538] The thirteenth chapter of the fourth book has the title: Concerning the travel of horses over snow-covered mountains and begins as follows:[539]

---

[535] Theophanes 1982: 86-87.
[536] Arcruni 1874/76: 107.
[537] Davidson 1953: 47-50.
[538] Berg 1950: 38.
[539] Olaus 1972: 147.

The above picture of a man with a horse who is travelling as if on military shields is to be explained in the following manner. The high mountains which make up the border between the Scandinavian kingdoms of Sweden and Norway and which are called the Dovre mountains and others like them are covered during the winter by such thick and deep masses of snow that it is not possible for wayfarers to travel in the usual way there on a firm path. Meanwhile the native merchants with the help of common sense seek to overcome such difficulties and find a way to carry their loads more easily. For this purpose they tie onto their own and their horses' feet wickerworks or laths bent together with a grating of light and broad filaments of linden bast, and so equipped they can tramp on the snowdrifts without having to fear sinking down, even though they are heavily loaded; and in this way they cover a day's journey, i.e. two mountain miles (which is equal to 12 Italian miles), this because the days are so short. At night, on the other hand, when the moon is out they can cover two or three times as much.

Snowshoes are also found in the Southern Hemisphere. In 1650-53 the historian Diego de Rosales visited the Pehuenche who were living in the higher valleys between the two main ranges of the Andean cordillero where they remained for much of the year in spite of the heavy snowfall. In his *Historia de el reyno de Chile*, 1674, Rosales reported that in deep snow the Pehuenche warriors traveled around "putting on shoes which they make of *coleos*, large (or broad) like (a) *chapin*, with which [shoes] they go around, when they wish, without sinking in the snow."[540] *Coleos* are grasses with thick reed- or bamboo-like stems. The *chapin* was a clog worn at the time in Spain under the sole of ordinary footwear for walking on wet or muddy ground. Rosales is an extremely reliable source for ethnology. There is no reason to suspect influence from early Spanish colonists, nor does Pehuenche culture show many traces of European culture.

In Turkey the inhabitants of Ulu Dagh, the Asiatic Olympus at 2,500 m. elevation near Bursa (the old Prusa), were supposed to have come to the market at Bursa on snowshoes in the seventeenth century. These travelers were called *Ivikciler* and their trip *Ivik kaymak*. In modern Turkish, skiing is called *Kayak kaymak*, which according to scholars is the same thing. There is also mention of snowshoes being used in the Turkish districts of Kars, Erzurum and Tunceli at the same time. It is doubtful, though, that the devices referred to here were skis since after this skis are not again heard of in Turkey until World War I when they were introduced from Europe. Nevertheless, the Turks may have brought skis with them when they migrated from their homeland around Mongolia.[541]

---

[540] Cooper 1945: 63-64.
[541] Riedel 1942: 61.

Johann Weichard Freiherr Valvasor (Fig. A4.6)[542] the governor of Krain – known as Slovenia today – published a beautiful four-volume work entitled *The Honor of the Duchy of Krain* in 1609. Under the heading "snow-baskets" is found:[543]

> When in winter time in the high Alps a thick snow falls and the roads are buried to the extent that one cannot walk, because everything breaks through and a man sinks down quite deep, the people take small baskets plaited from fine, small twigs of which some are also plaited with twine and tie them on their feet. Then they walk on the snow safely and without danger of breaking through the snow. Even if the snow is soft and fresh, these broad baskets hold the person up so that he does not fall through the (snow).

Josef Schiffner in his "The Giant Mountain Range and Its Supposed Inhabitant-Riebenzahl" (1805) says that the inhabitants of the snow-rich portions "use so-called 'hoop-shoes,' a kind of sled-shaped sole, which they tie on their feet and know how to glide from one place to another with much agility over the drifted depths."[544] What these hoop-shoes looked like is not certain, but von Schollmayer-Lichtenberg points out in a little booklet "On Snowshoes" from 1893 that this type of snowshoe or ski is used in the area of Reifnitz. He says that these devices are produced along with the household production of sieves by working light sieve hoop pieces (sieve edges) into snowshoes. The hoop-shoes would therefore be snowshoes out of sieve hoops and not snowshoes resembling those of the American Indians.

Richard Blackmore (1825-1900), English novelist, gave up a career as a lawyer because of bad health. His reputation largely rests on *Lorna Doone* (1869), a romantic novel about the outlaws of Exmoor. In the chapter "The Great Winter," Lizzie who is well read tells the narrator how people in the far north cope with the deep snow:[545]

> For seeing how the snow was spread, lightly over every thing, covering up the hills and valleys, and the foreskin of the sea, they contrived a way to crown it, and to glide like a flake along. Through the sparkle of the whiteness, and the wreaths of windy tossings, and the ups and downs of cold, any man might get along with a boat on either foot, to prevent his sinking. She told me how these boats were made; very strong and very light, of ribs with skin across them; five feet long, and one foot wide; and turned up at each end, even as a canoe is. But she did not tell me, nor did I give it a moment's thought myself, how hard it was to walk upon them, without early practice ... Therefore, I fell to at once, upon that hint from Lizzie, and being used to thatching-work, and the making of traps, and so on, before very long I built myself a pair of strong and light snow-shoes,

---

[542] Luther 1942: 39.
[543] Valvasor 1609: 583.
[544] Mehl 1964: 27-28.
[545] Blackmore 1930: 7-9.

framed with ash and ribbed of withy, with half-tanned calfskin stretched across, and an inner sole to support my feet. At first I could not walk at all, but foundered about most piteously, catching one shoe in the other, and both of them in the snow-drifts, to the great amusement of the maidens, who were come to look at me. But after a while I grew more expert, discovering what my errors were, and altering the inclination of the shoes themselves, according to a plan which Lizzie found in a book of old adventures. And this made such a difference, that I crossed the farm-yard and came back again (though turning was the worst thing of all) without so much as falling once or getting my staff entangled… And so I took her at her word, which she was not prepared for; and telling her how proud I was of her trust in Providence, and how I could run in my new snow-shoes, I took a short pipe in my mouth, and started forth accordingly.

In the following chapter there is:[546]

Through the sparkling breadth of white, which seemed to glance my eyes away, and past the humps of laden trees, bowing their backs like a woodman, I contrived to get along, half sliding and half walking, in places where a plain-shodden man must have sunk, and waited freezing, till the thaw should come to him … in this state of the weather, and knowing that no man could catch me up (except with shoes like mine), I even resolved to slide the cliffs …

Another report of snowshoes being used in South America comes from Martin Gusinde the Austrian expert on Tierra del Fuego who says that the Ona Indians in order not to sink into very loose, deep new snow when traversing it, tie onto the sandal a small bundle of thick sticks and call this *xo she ke xami* "snowshoes."[547] A similar type of snowshoe is shown in Fig. 10 of Ch. 3.

---

[546] Blackmore 1930: 10.
[547] Gusinde 1931: 215.

Bibliography

Aasen, Ivar. *Norsk ordbog*. Kristiania, 1850.

Adam of Bremen. *History of the Archbishops of Hamburg-Bremen*. Tr. with an Introduction and Notes by Francis J. Tschan. New York, 1959.

Aftenbladet (Christiania), February 10, 1868.

Aikio, Ante (Luobbal Sámmol Sámmol Ánte). "An essay on Saami ethnolinguistic prehistory." *A Linguistic Map of Prehistoric Northern Europe*. Edited by Riho Grünthal & Petri Kallio. Société Finno-Ougrienne, Helsinki, 2012.

Alfred: *The Whole Works of King Alfred the Great*. London: Bosworth & Harrison, 1858.

Allen, E. John B. *From Skisport to Skiing: One Hundred Years of an American Sport, 1840-1940*. U. of Massachusetts Press, 1993.
    "The World Wide Diffusion of Skiing to 1940." In Goksøyr 1994.

Alsvik, Elling. "En helt annen verden? Om skihistorie i Sovjetunionen." Trøndelag Folkemuseum, Sverresborg, Årbok 1991: 41-58.

Altheim, Franz. *Weltgeschichte Asiens im Griechischen Zeitalter*. Halle/Saale 1948.
    Niedergang der Alten Welt. Vol. I: *Die Außerrömische Welt*. Frankfurt am Main, 1952.

Amundsen, K. Vilh. *Skiløpning*. Kristiania, 1924.

Angell, Kaptein H. *Norsk skilauparsoga: Øystredølarne*. Kristiania, 1908.

Appelgren-Kivalo, Hjalmar. "Muinaisajan suksista." *Suomen museo* 18, 1911: 7-16.

Arcruni, Thomas. Brosset, *Collectiones d'historiens Arméniens*. St. Pétersbourg, 1874/76.

Ardrey, Robert. *The hunting hypothesis: a personal conclusion concerning the evolutionary nature of man*. New York, 1976.

Baudou, Evert. *Norrlands forntid – ett historiskt perspektiv*. Wiken, 1992.

Beowulf and Other Old English Poems. Tr. Constance B. Hieatt. Odyssey, 1967.

Berg, Gösta. "Förhistoriska skidor i Sverige." *På skidor* 1933: 142-169.
    "Skidslöjden hos dolganerna i Jenisejska provinsen." *På skidor* 1940: 341-343.
    "De båda stavarna och våra skidtyper än en gång." *På skidor* 1944: 89-94.
    "Den bottniska skidtypen och dateringen av ett finskt myrfynd." *På skidor* 1946: 276-278.
    Finds of Skis From Prehistoric Time in Swedish Bogs and Marshes. Stockholm, 1950.

"Nya fynd av förhistoriska skidor i Sverige." *På skidor* 1951: 181-186.
"Snöskor och trygor." *På skidor* 1953: 167-71.
"Nya rön om snöskor." *På skidor* 1955: 179-82.
"Skidor." In *Kulturhistorisk leksikon for nordisk middelalder*, vol. 15. Stockholm, 1970: 496-500.

Berg, Karin. *Ski i Norge*. Oslo, 1993.

Bergland, Aslak. *Lauvduskar*, 1887.

Birkely, Hartvig. *"I Norge har lapperne først indført skierne."* Idut, 1994.

Birket-Smith, Kaj. *Geschichte der Kultur*. Zürich, 1946.
The Paths of Culture. Madison, 1965.

Bjaaland, Olav S. and Jakob Vaage. *Den moderne skiidrott hundre år, 1866-1966*. Telemark, 1966.

Bjork, Kenneth. "'Snowshoe' Thompson: Fact and Legend." *Norwegian-American Studies and Records*, 19. Northfield, Minnesota, 1956: 62-88.

Blackmore, Richard D. *Lorna Doone*. New York 1930.

Blumenschine, Robert J. and John A. Cavallo. "Scavenging and Human Evolution." *Scientific American*, vol. 267, no. 4 (1992): 90-96.

Bogoras, Waldemar. *Chukchee Mythology*. Reprint from Vol. VIII, Part I, of the Jesup North Pacific Expedition. *Memoirs of the American Museum of Natural History* Vol. XII, 1910.

Brennu-Njáls Saga. Ed. Einar Ól. Sveinsson. Reykjavík, 1954.

Burch, Ernest S., Jr. "The Caribou/Wild Reindeer As a Human Resource." *American Antiquity*, vol. 37, no. 3, 1972.

Burov, Grigoriy M. "Some Mesolithic Wooden Artifacts from the Site of Vis I in the European North East of the U.S.S.R." In *The Mesolithic in Europe* ed. Clive Bonsall. Edinburgh, 1985: 391-401.

Bø, Olav. *Norsk skitradisjon*. Oslo, 1966.
Skiing Traditions in Norway. Oslo, 1968.
På ski gjennom historia. Oslo, 1992.
"Skiing Throughout History." In Goksøyr 1994.

Carver, Jonathan. *Travels through the Interior Parts of North-America in the Years 1766, 1767, and 1768*. London, 1778.

Catlin, George. *North American Indian Portfolio, Hunting Scenes and Amusements of the Rocky Mountains and Prairies of America*, 1844.
Illustrations of the Manners, Customs, and Condition of the North American Indians: with Letters and Notes. Vol. I London, 1841. Vol. II London, 1857.

Christensen, Olav. *Skiidrett før Sondre. Vinterveien til et nasjonalt selvbilde*. Oslo, 1993.

Clark, Grahame. *Prehistoric Europe: the economic basis*. Stanford, 1966: 282-315.
The Earlier Stone Age Settlement of Scandinavia. Cambridge, 1975.

Collinder, Erik. "Skidlöpning." In Viktor Balck's *Illustrerad idrottsbok*, Part 3. 1988.

Cooper, John M. "Aboriginal South American Snowshoes." *Primitive Man*. Washington, 1945, no. 3-4: 63-69.

Dahlbäck, Sigurd. "Skidorna och Torne-Kalix' folk." *På skidor* 1926: 19-32.

Dalen, Arnold. "Trøndersk terminologi." *På trønderski*. Ed. Alf Eggset and Jørn Sandnes, Trondheim 1988: 36-54.

"På ski og andor – om nordisk skiterminologi." Gunnerus-forelesing in *Det Kgl. Norske Videnskabers Selskabs Forhandlinger* Oslo, 1997.

"Les origines et la terminologie du ski en Scandinavie." *Proxima Thulé*, Vol. 3. Paris, 1998: 49-77.

"Scandinavian ski terminology." *History of Skiing Conference 16.-18.9.98*, Skiforeningen, Oslo 1998: 49-57.

"Scandinavian Ski Terminology and Its Dialectal Distribution." In: *Dialectologia et Geolinguistica* (Journal of the International Society for Dialectology and Geolinguistics). Alessandria, 7/1999: 9-26.

David, Richard. *Hakluyt's Voyages*. Boston, 1981.

Davidson, Daniel S. *Snowshoes*. Vol. VI of Memoirs of the American Philosophical Society. Philadelphia, 1937.

"The Snowshoe in Japan and Korea." *Ethnos* 18, 1953.

Davidson, H. R. Ellis. *Gods and Myths of Northern Europe*. Harmondsworth, 1964
Scandinavian Mythology. London, 1982.
Myths and Symbols in Pagan Europe: Early Scandinavian and Celtic Religions. Syracuse, 1988.

Dresbeck, LeRoy J. "The Ski: Its History and Historiography." *Technology and Culture* 8, October, 1967: 467-79.

Dronke, Ursula. *The Poetic Edda*. Oxford, 1969.

DuBois, Thomas A. *Nordic Religions in the Viking Age*. Philadelphia, 1999.

"Narrative Expectations and the Sampo Song." *Scandinavian Studies* 73 3, 2001: 457-74.

Dumézil, Georges. *Gods of the Ancient Northmen*. California, 1973.

Eichenberger, Lutz. "Fridtjof Nansen – the Originator of Skiing in Switzerland?" In Goksøyr 1994.

Egil's Saga. Tr. Gwyn Jones. Syracuse, 1960.

Egilsson, Sveinbjörn. *Lexicon Poeticum: Antiquæ Linguæ Septentrionalis. Ordbog over det norsk-islandske skjaldesprog*. 2. Udgave ved Finnur Jónsson. København, 1966.

Egnell, Sten. *Från spår och stigar*. Stockholm, 1979.

Farb, Peter. *Humankind*. Boston, 1978.

Firsoff, V. A. *Ski Track On the Battlefield*. New York, 1943.

Fisher, Margaret W. "The Mythology of the Northern and northeastern Algonkians in Reference to Algonkian Mythology As a Whole." *Man in Northeastern North America*. Ed. Frederick Johnson, Andover, Massachusetts 1946: 226-62.

Flateyjarbók: en samling af norske konge-sagaer. Christiania, 1860.

Fornaldarsögur Norðrlanda. Ed. Valdimar Ásmundarson. Reykjavík, 1889.

Gaski, Harald. *Sami Culture in a New Era: The Norwegian Sami Experience*, Davvi Girji OS, 1997a.
In the Shadow of the Midnight Sun: Contemporary Sami Prose and Poetry. Davvi Girji OS, 1997b.
"Introduction: Sami Culture in a new Era." In Gaski 1997a: 9-28.
"Introduction." In Gaski 1997b: 9-41.

Geete, Erik. "Holberg och skidlöpningen." *På skidor* 1936: 353-57.
"Gustaf Vasas flykt." *På skidor* 1948: 239-243.

Gelling, Peter and Hilda E. Davidson. *The Chariot of the Sun*. New York, 1969.

Gjessing, Gutorm. *Nordenfjelske ristninger og malinger*. Oslo, 1936.
Circumpolar Stone Age, vol. 2 of *Acta Arctica*. Copenhagen, 1944.

Goksøyr, Matti et al. *Winter Games, Warm Traditions* – Selected papers from the 2. international ISHPES seminar, Lillehammer 1994.

Gore, Rick. "Neandertals." *National Geographic*, January 1996: 2-35.

Granlund, John. "Svensk skidornamentik." *På skidor* 1941: 117-134.

Grettis Saga Ásmundarsonar. Ed. Guðni Jónsson. Reykjavík, 1936.

Griaznov, M. P. and Eugene A. Golomshtok. "The Pazirik Burial of Altai." *American Journal of Archaeology*. Concord, 1933.

Gripenberg, Bertel. *Afton i Tavastland*, 1911.

Gunda, Béla. "Snöskorna hos Karpaternas folk." *På skidor* 1940: 229-37.

Gusinde, Martin. *Die Feuerland-Indianer*. Wien, 1931.

Hallström, Gustaf. *Monumental Art of Northern Europe from the Stone Age*, I. Stockholm, 1938.

Hammarstedt, N. E. "Om skidor, snöskor och skarbågar och deras utvecklingsformer." *På skidor* 1929: 16-33.

Hansen, Lars Ivar og Bjørnar Olsen. *Samenes Historie fram til 1750*. Cappelen 3. opplag 2007.

Harva, Uno. *Die Religiösen Vorstellungen der Altaischen Völker*. FF Communications N:o 125. Helsinki, 1938.

Hatt, Gudmund. "Moccasins and Their Relation to Arctic Footwear." *Memoirs of the American Anthropological Association*, Vol. III. Lancaster, 1916: 149-250.

Helskog, Knut. *Helleristningene i Alta*. Alta, 1988.

Herberstein, Sigmund von. *Description of Moscow and Muscovy 1557*. New York, 1969.

History of Skiing Conference. Holmenkollen, Oslo Sept. 16 –18, 1998.

Holtsmark, Anne. *Norrøn mytologi: Tru og mytar i vikingtida*. Oslo, 1989.

Holmqvist, Wilhelm. "On the origin of the Lapp ribbon ornament." *Acta archaeologica* 5, 1934.

Hrafnkels Saga and Other Stories. Tr. Hermann Pálsson. Baltimore, 1971.

Hultkrantz, Åke. "Veralden olmai och världspålen." In Vorren 1994: 178-85.

Itkonen, T. I. "Finlands fornskidor." *På skidor* 1937: 71-89.

Jantz, Harold. "Schiller's Indian Threnody: A Problem in the Aesthetics of the Classical Age." In *Schiller 1759/1959*, vol. 46 of *Illinois Studies in Language and Literature*, 1959.

Jernsletten, Nils. "Sami Traditional Terminology: Professional Terms Concerning Salmon, Reindeer and Snow." In Gaski 1997a: 86-108.

Jirlow, R. "Gamla dagars vinteridrott i Transtrand." *På skidor* 1935: 27-46.

Kalevala: Epic of the Finnish People. Tr. Eino Friberg. Editing and Introduction by George C. Schoolfield. Illustrated by Björn Landström. Otava Publishing Co. Ltd. Helsinki, 1988.

Kalevala: The Land of the Heroes. Tr. W. F. Kirby. Introduced by M. A. Branch. Athlone. London, 1985. Translation first published in 1907.

Kalstad, Johan Klemet Hætta. "Aspects of managing Renewable Resources in Sami Areas in Norway." In Gaski 1997a: 109-26.

Kannisto, Artturi and Matti Liimola. *Wogulische Volksdichtung.* Helsinki, 1951.
Materialien zur Mythologie der Wogulen. Mèmoires de la Société Finno-Ougrienne 113. Helsinki, 1958.

Klepp, Asbjørn. *Ski og truger.* MA thesis in ethnology. Univ. of Oslo, 1976.
"Slutten for bygdeskimakingen og gamaldags skibruk." *På trønderski* 1988: 137-50.

Kock, Ernst A. *Den norsk-isländska skaldediktningen.* Lund, 1947.

Kristjánsson, Jónas. *Eddas and Sagas: Iceland's Medieval Literature.* Tr. Peter Foote. Reykjavík, 1988.

Krohn, Karle. *Skandinavisk mytologi.* Helsingfors, 1922.

Kuhn, Herbert. *Die Felsbilder Europas.* Stuttgart, 1971.

Kunicke, H. "Sibirische Märchen." *Märchen der Weltliteratur,* 1940.

Lahontan, Baron de. *New Voyages to North-America.* Chicago, 1905.

Laufer, Berthold. "The Reindeer and Its Domestication." In *Memoirs of the American Anthropological Association.* Lancaster, 1917.

Lehmann-Haupt, Christopher F. *Armenien Einst und Jetzt.* Berlin, 1910.

Liestøl, Knut and Moltke Moe. *Folkeviser I* (3rd ed., ed. Olav Bø and Svale Solheim), vol. 6 of *Folkedikting.* Oslo, 1967.

Lindgren, Erik. "Grims skidor." *På skidor* 1946: 278-80.

Linnæus, Carl. *Iter Lapponicum* 1732 (Lapplands resa). Stockholm 1957.

Lid, Nils. "Gamle norske skiformer." *Syn og Segn.* Oslo, 1934.
On the history of Norwegian Skis. Oslo, 1937.

Lindquist, Ivar. "Gudar på skidor." *På skidor* 1929: 8-15.

Lindkjølen, Hans. "Johannes Schefferus og bokverket 'Lapponia' utgitt 1673." In Vorren 1994: 23-35.

Loupedalen, Torjus. *Morgedal: skisportens vogge.* Oslo, 1947.

Lund, Bernt. *Trysil-Knud.* Illustrert av A. Bloch. Christiania, 1897.

Lunn, Arnold. *A History of Skiing.* London 1927.
The Story of Ski-ing. London 1952.

Luther, Carl J. "Geschichte des Schnee- und Eis-sports." in *Geschichte des Sports aller Völker und Zeiten* ed. G. A. E. Bogeng, 1926.
Das Bilderbuch der alten Schneeläufer. Erfurt, 1942.
"Von Holzpferden, Pferdefüsslern und Schneeschlangen." in *Olympisches Feuer,* Heft 1. Frankfurt, Januar 1962: 7-11.

Manker, Ernst. "Skogslapparnas skidor – anteckningar från Malå." *På skidor* 1938: 79-88.

"Trerännade lapska vargrännarskidor." *På skidor* 1940: 222-228.

"Lomsjökulleskidan." *På skidor* 1947: 167-173.

"Lapptrummornas skidlöparfigurer." *På skidor* 1952: 137-140.

"Zur Frage nach dem Alter der Renzucht: Einige Bemerkungen." *Zeitschrift für Ethnologie*, 78, 1953.

"Den bottniska skidtypen i nya myrfynd." *På skidor* 1957: 167-182.

"Fennoskandiens fornskidor." *Fornvännen* Vol. 2, 1971

Mark, Karin. "Zur Herkunft der Finnisch-Ugrischen Völker vom Standpunkt der Anthropologie." *Soviet Fenno-Ugric Studies VI*. Tallin, 1970: 211-20.

Mason, Otis T. *Primitive Travel and Transportation*. Report of United States National Museum. Washington, 1896.

Mechling, W. H. *Malecite Tales*. Ottawa, 1914.

Mehl, Erwin. "Altgermanischer Schneelauf." *Leibesübungen und Körperliche Erziehung*. Berlin, 1938. *Grundriss der Weltgeschichte des Schifahrens. I. Von der Steinzeit bis zum Beginn der schigeschichtlichen Neuzeit* (1860). *Beiträge zur Lehre und Forschung der Leibeserzeihung*. Stuttgart, 1964.

Meuli, Karl. *Scythica Vergiliana: Ethnographisches, Archäologisches und Mythologisches zu Vergils Georgica 3*, 367ff. in *Gesammelte Schriften*, Zweiter Band herausgegeben von Thomas Gelzer. Schwage & Co. Verlag (Basel/Stuttgart, 1975): 757-813.

Mierow, Charles C. *The Gothic History of Jordanes in English Version with an Introduction and a Commentary*. Cambridge, 1960.

Mo, Kristen. "The Development of Skiing as a Competitive Sport. Morgedal – the Cradle of Skiing: Fact or Fiction?" in Goksøyr 1994.

Müller, Peter Erasmus. *Sagabibliothek*. Vols. I-III. Kiøbenhavn, 1820.

Müller, Werner. *Die Religionen der Waldlandindianer Nordamerikas*. Berlin, 1956.

Nansen, Fridtjof. *Paa ski over Grønland. En skildring af den norske Grønlands-ekspedition 1888-89*. Kristiania, 1890.
The First Crossing of Greenland. Tr. Hubert M. Gepp. London, Longmans, Green, 1890.

Naskali, Eero. "Ski i lyset av gamle funn." In Vorren 1995:71-80.

Negelein, J. v. "Das Sternbild des 'Grossen Bären' in Sibirien und Indien." *Archiv für Religionswissenschaft* 27. Vaduz, 1929.

Nesheim, Asbjørn. *Introducing the Lapps*. Oslo, 1966.

Niemi, Einar. "Sami History and the Frontier Myth: A Perspective on the Northern Sami Spatial and Rights History." In Gaski 1997a: 62-85.

Nikkilä, Eino. *Suksen Tarina*. Porvoo 1966.

Nissing, Sven and Artur Zettersten. "Från hemslöjd till skidfabrik." *På skidor* 1943: 156-176.

Nordenskiöld, A. E. *The Voyage of the Vega Round Asia and Europe*. New York, 1882.

Olaus Magnus. *Carta Marina*. Venice, 1539.
Historia De Gentibus Septentrionalibus. Romae 1555. Introduction by John Granlund. Copenhagen, 1972.

Orel, Boris. "Ljudske smuči na bloški planoti, v Vidovskih hribih in v njih soseščini" (English Summary) *Slovenski Etnograf IX*. Ljubljana, 1956: 17-89.

Orkneyinga Saga. Ed. Finnbogi Guðmundsson. Reykjavík, 1965.

Ovsyannikov, O. V. "On old Russian skis." *Fennoscandia archaeologica* VI, 1989.

Paulus Diaconus. *History of the Langobards*. Tr. Foulke. Philadelphia, 1906/07.

Pindar. *The Odes of Pindar*. Tr. C. M. Bowra. Chicago, 1947.

Poems of the Elder Edda. Tr. Patricia Terry. Philadelphia, 1990.

Poetic Edda. Tr. Lee M. Hollander. Austin, 1988.

Prose Edda. Tr. Jean I. Young. Berkeley, 1954.

Procopius. *History of the Wars III, Book VI*. Tr. H. B. Dewing. London, 1919.

Quirk, R. *The Saga of Gunnlaug Serpent-Tongue*. Thomas Nelson & Sons Ld., 1957.

Radloff, Wilhelm. *Aus Sibirien*. Oosterhout, 1968.

Rask, Rasmus K. *Samlede tildels forhen utrykte afhandlinger*. Udgivne af H. K. Rask. København, 1834.

Raudonikas, W. J. *Les Gravures Rupestres des Bords du lac Onéga et de la mer Blanche*. Première Partie: Les Gravures Rupestres du Lac Onéga. *Les stations néolithiques du rivage oriental du lac Onéga*. Moscow, 1936.
Les Gravures Rupestres des Bords du lac Onéga et de la mer Blanche. Seconde Partie: *Les Gravures Rupestres de la mer Blanche*. Moscow, 1938.

Riedel, Herbert. "Leibesübungen und körperliche Erziehung in der osmanischen und kamalistischen Türkei." Würzburg 1942.

Rindisbacher, Peter. Prärie-Indianer mit Schneeschuhen auf der Büffeljagd. Aquarell from ca. 1825. Peabody Museum, Harvard University, Cambridge, MA. Catalogue Nr. 41-72/468.

Rosales, Diego de. *Historia general de el reino de Chile*. Originally published in 1674. Three volumes. Valparaiso, 1877-78.

Rosander, Göran. *Svenska Skidmuseet, Umeå: En vägledning*. Umeå, 1964.

Ryd, Yngve. "Traditionell tillverkning av björkskidor. Kluvet i norr och i söder." *Hemslöjden 1998/1*: 4-7.
"Tjurskidor på vårskaren. Sommarförvaring i myren." *Hemslöjden 1998/1*: 10-11.
Snö – en renskötare berättar. Stockholm: Ordfront, 2001.

Sakses Danesaga: fra Dan til Ingeld. Tr. Jørgen Olrik. København, 1911.

Sammallahti, Pekka. *The Saami Languages: An Introduction*. Davvi Girji, Karasjok, 1998.

Sarauw. Georg. "Das Rentier in Europa zu den Zeiten Alexanders und Cæsars." *Mindeskrift for Japetus Steenstrup*. København, 1913.

Savio, John Andreas. An Exhibition of His Selected Works in Texas, Washington and Alaska. Preface Rami Abiel. Savio Art Museum, Kirkenes, 1993.

Saxo Grammaticus. The History of the Danes, Books I-IX. Ed. Hilda Ellis Davidson. Tr. Peter Fisher.

Suffolk, 1999.

Schanche, Audhild. "Samiske urbegravelser." In Vorren 1994: 75-89.

Schefferus, Johannes. *Lapponia*. 1673.
　Lappland (*Lapponia* translated into Swedish). Uppsala, 1956.

Schiffner, Josef. "The Giant Mountain Range and Its Supposed Inhabitant Riebenzahl." Prague, 1805.

Schollmayer-Lichtenberg, E. H. Edlem von. *On Snowshoes*. Klagenfurt, 1893.

Schott, Wilhelm. *Über die ächten Kirgisen*, Abh. Berlin, 1865.

Scientific American. Supplement No. 1007. April 20, 1895.

Sejerstad, Francis. *Den vanskelige frihet 1814-1851*, vol. 10 of *Norges historie*, ed. Knut Mykland. Oslo, 1978.

Sellman, Yngve. "Den limmade skidan – framtidens skida." *På skidor* 1944: 142-51.

Semmingsen, Ingrid Gaustad. "Norwegian Emigration to America During the Nineteenth Century." *Norwegian-American Studies and Records*, Vol. 11. Northfield, Minnesota, 1940: 66-81.

Snorri Sturluson. *Heimskringla. History of the Kings of Norway*. Tr. Lee M. Hollander. Austin, 1977.

Speck, Frank G. "Penobscot Tales and Religious Beliefs." *The Journal of American Folk-Lore*, Vol. 48, Jan.-Mar., 1935, No. 187: 1-108.

Speculum Regale–Konungs Skuggsjá. Tr. Laurence Marcellus Larson. New York, 1972.

Stoltenberg, Einar. "Ski og skiløyping i Telemark i gamal tid." *Skien-Telemark Turistforenings Årbok* 1938-39: 1-23.

Strabo's *Geography*. Tr. Horace L. Jones. New York, 1928.

Ström, Folke. *Nordisk hedendom*. Göteborg, 1961.

Svidae Lexicon. Ed. Ada Daler. Stuttgart, 1967.

Sørensen, Steinar. "Skifunnet fra Steinhaugmo og de skinnkleddde skiene i Fennoskandias fortid." *Viking tidsskrift for norrøn arkeologi*, Bind LVI, 1993: 87-111.
　"Skihistorie i tusen år. Fortalt gjennom syv funn i Skimuseet." *Snø og ski*, 1995: 46-64, 102-03.
　"Daterte skifunn fra middelalderen: Et omriss av middelalderens skihistorie." (English Summary) *Collegium Medievale*, Vol. 9, 1996/1-2: 7-55.

Tacitus. *Germania*. Tr. M. Hutton. Cambridge, 1970.

Theophanes' *Chronicle*. An English translation of *anni mundi* (AD 602-813). Tr. Harry Turtledove. Philadelphia, 1982.

The Saami: People of the Sun and Wind. Ájtte svenskt fjäll och samemuseum. Jokkmokk, 1993.

Thompson, Stith. *Tales of the North American Indians*. Cambridge, 1929.

Tjerneld, Håkan. "Cervantes och skidlöpningen." *På skidor* 1943: 313-14.

Tomasson, Torkel. "Ur skidans historia." *Samefolkets Egen Tidning*, June, 1928a: 15-16.
　"Några tankar om skidrännans och de oliklånga skidornas uppkomst." *Samefolkets Egen Tidning*, September, 1928b: 21-24.

Ueberhorst, Horst. "Fridtjof Nansen and the Development of Skiing in Central Europe." In Goksøyr 1994.

Ulmrich, Ekkehart. "Facts and Fiction in the History of Skiing." In Goksøyr 1994.

Urbas, Tončica. "Krplje in smuči na pohorju." (German Summary) *Slovenski Etnograf IX*. Ljubljana, 1956: 90-116.

Utsi, Paulus. "As Long As We Have Waters." In Gaski 1997b: 109-17.

Vaage, Jacob. *Norske ski erobrer verden*. Oslo, 1952.
    (Hovedmedarbeider) *Norske skiløpere. Skihistorisk oppslagsverk i 5 bind*. Bind 6 Supplementsbind (Ungdomsbind). Oslo, 1969.
    Holmenkollen. Den norske bokklubben, Oslo, 1971.
    "Skimakerkunsten i det 19. århundre." *Norveg: Folkelivsgransking 15*, 1972.
    Skienes Verden. Oslo, 1979.
    "Våre eldste ski datert etter C^{14}-klokken." *Snø og Ski* Nr. 5. Oslo, 1981: 53-56.

Vajda, László. *Untersuchungen zur Geschichte der Hirtenkulturen*. Wiesbaden, 1968.

Valonen, Niilo. "Den finska folkkulturen i Nordskandinavien, särskilt skidans historia." In *Nord-Skandinaviens historia i tvärvetenskaplig belysning: Förhandlingar vid symposium anordnat av Humanistiska fakulteten vid Umeå universitet den 7-9 juni 1978*. Ed. Evert Baudou and Karl-Hampus Dahlstedt. *Umeå Studies in the Humanities* 24, 1980: 207-33.

Valvasor, Johann Weichard Freiherr. *The Honor of the Duchy of Krain*. Laibach, 1609.

Vergil. *Georgics*. Tr. Blackmore. London, 1931.

Vilkuna, Janne. "Kinnulan pienareunainen muinaissuksi." *Studia Historica Jyväskyläenna*. Jyväskylä 1990: 25-34.
    "Oldtidsski fra Kinnula sogn." In Vorren 1995: 64-70.
    "The binding of the prehistoric ski from Mänttä, Finland." In *History of Skiing Conference* 1998.

Vorren, Ørnulv and Ernst Manker. *Samekulturen: En historisk oversikt*. Oslo, 1988.

Vorren, Ørnulv. "Ski og skiløping hos samene." In *Norske Skiløpere*, vol. V, 1960: 159-65.
    "Lapp skis and skiing. I: Land transport in Europe." *Folkelivsstudier fra Nationalmuseet 4*, København 1973: 470-87.
    Festskrift til Ørnulv Vorren. Tromsø Museums Skrifter XXV. Tromsø, 1994.
    Samiske oldski. Funn i Nord-Norge fra 300 f.Kr. til 1500 e.Kr. Nordkalott, 1995.
    "Ancient Saami ski finds from the northern-most part of Northern Norway." In *History of Skiing Converence*, 1998: 16-20.

Weinstock, John. "Sondre Nordheim: Folk Hero to Immigrant." *Norwegian-American Studies*, Vol. 29. Northfield, Minnesota, 1983: 339-58.
    "The Role of Skis and Skiing in the Settlement of Early Scandinavia." *The Northern Review* #25/26 (Summer 2005): 172-196.
    "At the frontier: Sámi linguistics gets a boost from outside." *New Trends in Nordic and General Linguistics*. Edited by Martin Hilpert, Jan-Ola Östman, Christine Mertzlufft, Michael Rießler and Janet Duke. linguae & litterae Volume 42, de Gruyter, 2015.
    "Common Era Sápmi Language Replacement: Origin and Outcome." forthcoming.

Wergeland, Oscar. *Skiløbningen, dens Historie og Krigsanvendelse, nogle Bidrag dertil samt til Belysning af vore tidligere Værnepligtsforhold*. Christiania, 1865.

Werner, Helmut. "Klassische Sternbilder am Himmel der Tschuktschen." *Zeitschrift für Ethnologie*, 77. Braunschweig, 1952.

Wiklund, K. B. *De svenska nomadlapparnas flyttningar till Norge i äldre och nyare tid*. Uppsala, 1908.
"Några tankar om snöskors och skidors upprinnelse." *På skidor* 1926: 1-18.
"Ur skidans och snöskons historia." *På skidor* 1928: 5-56.
"Mera om skidans historia." *På skidor* 1929: 252-279.
"Den nordiska skidan, den södra och den arktiska." *På skidor* 1931: 5-50.
"Kalevalas trettonde runa och balladen om den gottländske köpmannens älgjakt." *På skidor* 1931: 59-69.
"Den södra skidtypens källa." *På skidor* 1933: 20-26.
"Untersuchungen über die älteste Geschichte der Lappen und die Entstehung der Renntiersucht." *Folk-Liv* Stockholm, 1937-38 (posthumous).
Lapparna. Nordisk kultur X. Stockholm, Oslo, København 1948.

Wilson, David M. *The Northern World*. New York, 1980.

Xenophon. *The Anabasis*. Tr. Henry G. Dakyns. Athens, 1969.

Zettersten, Artur. "Den södra skitypen." *På skidor* 1932: 7-27.
"Svenska skidtyper." *På skidor* 1934: 5-31.
"Den södra skidtypens urform." *På skidor* 1938: 375-377.
"Den södra skidtypens utbredning." *På skidor* 1939: 401-403.
"Om militär skidlöpning." *På skidor* 1940: 14-28.
"Den skandiska skidtypens ursprung." *På skidor* 1942: 13-22.
"När började man använda två skidstavar?" *På skidor* 1943: 19-24.
"Lapparnas pilbåge som skidstav." *På skidor* 1944: 83-88.
"Kunde Gustaf Vasa löpa skidor?" *På skidor* 1945: 284-85.

Åström, Kenneth and Ove Norberg. "Förhistoriska och medeltida skidor." *Västerbotten* 2 84. Umeå, 1984: 82-88.
"Skidan från Kalvträsk." *Västerbotten* 3 93. Umeå, 1993: 129-31.

Ski Book Index

A

Adam of Bremen 32
Alfred the Great 31
Arctander 202
Arctic Type 46-47, 49, 51-53
Arnljót Gellini 115-16
Asbjørnsen and Moe 116, 235-36

B

Berg 44-45, 47-49, 106
Berge, Rikard 211-212
Bergslien, Knut 188, 234, 235, Illus. 1, 19
Bindings 34, 50, 97-99, 195, 210, 221, 259-260, Illus. 10, 17
Birchlegs 187-188, Illus. 1
Birkely 22, 38-39, 41, 221
Bjørnson, Bjørnstjerne 238-39, 242
Bothnic Type 47-49, 51-53, 97
Brun, Johan Nordahl 210-211

C

Catlin Illus. 4
Central Nordic Type 51-53, 71, 95, 109, Illus. 3
Cervantes 191, 202
Children's Skis 108, Illus. 10
Chukchee 65, 76-77, 107, 288
Curved Front Ends 33, 100-01, 195, 199, 201, 207, 281

D

Daredevil 25, 213, 220, 223, 226, 241
Dass, Petter 205, 208

E

Egede 206
Egilssaga 111
Equal Length Skis 38, 41, 97-98, 103, 105-06, 191, 195, 222

F

Fennoscandia 24, 46, 49, 53, 56, 58, 60-62, 65, 108, 265, 274-75
Finno-Ugric 35, 56, 58, 60, 75, 77-78, 109
Flateyjarbók 91, 116-17
Frame type 288, 291, Illus. 25
Franks Casket 80, Illus. 8

G

Garborg, Arne 237, 250
Gaski Foreword,19, 64
Gaute Tinnske 214-15
Gjessing 40, 276
Gjest Baardsen 233
Gluskabe 25, 71-73, 75
Greek vase 75, Illus. 6, 7
Grettir the Strong 130-31
Grim's Skis 127-28
Gripenberg, Bertel 255
Gude, Hans 235, 242, Illus. 20
Gustaf Vasa 191-92, Illus. 12

H

Hallström 40
Hamsun, Knut 250-51
Han Dynasty 27
Hansen, Andreas M. 23, 59-60, 109, Illus. 5
Heming 115-27
Herberstein 34
Holberg 107, 206, 209
Huan-jù kî 30
Huseby 108, 254, 259-61, Illus. 21, 22

J

Jonge 209
Jordanes 29, 200

K

Kalevala 67-68, 73, 78, 106
Kalm 208
King's Mirror 113

L

Ladder type 23, 93, 285-86, 289, Illus. 25
Lake Baikal 23-24, 31, 59-60, 93, 108, 275, 290
Landström, Björn Back Cover, Illus. 16
Lascaux Illus. 27
Lassen 210
Legal Protection of Animals 130
Legends 71, 117, 119, 204, 212-13, 242
Lemminkäinen 25, 67-71, 73, 75, 106, Illus. 16
Lie, Jonas 234-35, Illus. 19
Loki 85, 87-89

M

Magnús Barelegs 116
Making Skis 96, 101, 104, 227
Manker 41, 45-46, 49
Meuli 306

Munthe, Gerhard 127, Illus. 16

N

Njálssaga 89, 90
Njord 85-86, 88, 251
Nordenskiöld 25, 35, 231-32
Norheim, Sondre 25, 99-100, 217, 220-30, 238, 240, 257, 259
Norske Selskab 211

O

Olaus Magnus 23, 192, 199-201, 297

P

Paulus Diaconus 29, 200
Pindar 74-75
Poetic Edda 80-82, 89
Pontoppidan 208
Procopius 28-29

R

Raschîd ud-dîn 33
Rask 34
Richard Hakluyt 33-34
Rindisbacher 24, Illus. 2
Rødøy 40, 41, 261

S

Sámi Foreword, 22-23, 25, 28-29, 32, 34, 39, 41, 48-49, 53-65, 67, 76, 95-97, 100, 102-06, 108, 110, 113, 115-17, 123, 192, 198, 200-01, 204, 208, 210, 212, 221, 231-32, 257, 276-77, 279, 281, 284-85
sana 60
Saxo Grammaticus 32-33, 63, 77, 82-83, 119, 126, 187
Scandic Type 49-50, 52-53, 95-97
Schefferus 56, 58-59, 64, 205, 221, Illus. 4
Scientific American 19, 261, Illus. 23
siida 63
Skaði 25, 81-89, Illus. 9
Ski Poles 38, 106-07
Ski Wax 107-08
solta 60
Southern Type 46-47, 49, 95, 105, Illlus. 3, 9
suks 59-60

T

Tacitus 27, 29, 86
T'ang Dynasty 31
Telemark 25, 47, 98-101, 105, 109, 116, 124, 195, 212-13, 215, 218, 220-23, 225-26, 229-30, 239, 243-44, 254, 257, 259-60, Illus. 17, 18, 21, 22
Terminology 108, 259
Trangen 197, Illus. 15
Trysil-Knud 213, 240-46, 248

Type A 45-46
Type B 46
Type C 47
Type C 1 b 47
Type C 2 a 49
Type C 2 b 50

U

Ull 25, 56, 81-86, 115
Unequal Length Skis 51-53, 68, 71, 96. 103-04, 106, 191, 201-02, 221-22, 240, 243

V

Valvasor 299, Illus. 26
Vinje, Aasmund Olavsson 219, 237, 250
Volund 25, 80-81

W

Wergeland, Henrik 233, 241, 244
Wergeland, Oscar 19, 188-91, 244
Withe Bindings 51, 97-99, 101, 107, 221-22, Illus. 9, 10, 17

Z

Zalavrouga 37-39
Zetlitz, Jens 209-11

www.ingramcontent.com/pod-product-compliance
Lightning Source LLC
Chambersburg PA
CBHW081217170426
43198CB00017B/2638